The
BOOK
GROUP
BOOK

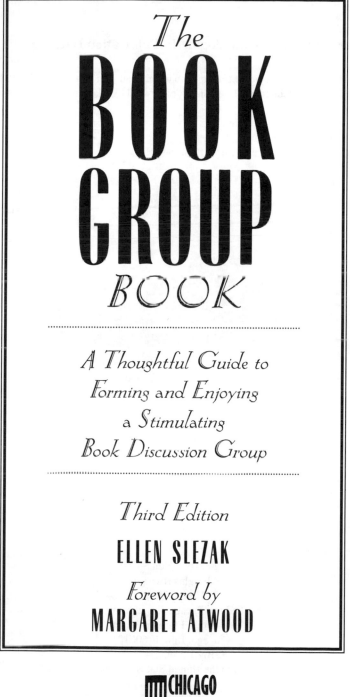

The
BOOK
GROUP
BOOK

A Thoughtful Guide to
Forming and Enjoying
a Stimulating
Book Discussion Group

Third Edition

ELLEN SLEZAK

Foreword by
MARGARET ATWOOD

CHICAGO
REVIEW
PRESS

Library of Congress Cataloging-in-Publication Data

The book group book: a thoughtful guide to forming and enjoying a stimulating book discussion group / [edited by] Ellen Slezak ; foreword by Margaret Atwood—3rd ed.
   p. cm.
   Includes bibliographical references.
   ISBN 1-55652-412-9
   1. Group reading—United States. I. Slezak, Ellen.

LC6651 .B66 2000
374'22—dc21

00-031531

To my mom, who rarely is without a book in hand

Contents

Foreword

SEVERAL YEARS AGO, when I was planning to visit my old roommate of 1961–62, in North Carolina—a private visit—she said a strange thing to me. She said, "I'll have to give a tea. If I don't my book group will kill me."

"What is a book group?" I asked.

Well, where had I been? She explained: a book group is the people who will kill you if you have an author in your clutches and don't have the book group to tea.

(They came.)

But then I read *The Book Group Book*, and learned more. Book groups, it seems, are the best little old word of mouth in town. Book groups—which have undergone a surprising growth in numbers and variety over the last ten years—are an encouragement to authors, who keep being told that the book will soon be dead as a doornail. Book groups are to early twenty-first century America what salons were to eighteenth-century Paris, and what improvement societies were to the Victorians.

Of course, not everyone in Paris belonged to a salon and not every Victorian craved improvement; similarly, not everyone belongs to a book group. In book groups, like-minded souls gather; what they have in common seems to be that a) they can read, b) they *like* to read, and c) they like to talk about what they have read. It's the liking to talk about it that divides the non-book group readers from the book group ones. Book groups are the graduate seminar, the encounter group, and the good old-fashioned village-pump gossip session, all rolled up into one.

What does this *talking about it* involve? When fiction is the subject, as it usually is, the talking about it usually consists of the group members trying to agree on what actually went on in the book, and whether they approve of what went on, and also whether they approve of the people who made it go on in this way, and what significance the author seems to have attached to what went on and also to the people who made it go on, and whether the significance provides a clue to our times, and whether they approve of *that*, and whether they enjoyed it, and whether they approve of one another's enjoyment. Literary criticism, in other words. Plot, character, and meaning, with maybe a few glances at structure and style.

Why this can take many pleasurable but sometimes contentious and nonunanimous hours has a great deal to do with the ambiguity and double-handedness of language itself, as pointed to by Mr. Dodgson when he claimed not to be able to interpret the Alice books: "Words mean more than we mean to express, when we use them, so a whole book ought to mean a great deal more than the writer meant." What V. S. Pritchett says at the beginning of his autobiography, *A Cab at the Door*, is true of most novelists: "I came from a set of story tellers and moralists. . . . The story tellers were forever changing the tale and the moralists tampering with it in order to put it in an edifying light." The changing tale, the edifying light: these too are the concerns of the book group.

The old truisms about art—that it should hold a mirror up to Nature (notwithstanding the fact that mirror images are backwards illusions), and that it should both please and instruct—are neglected by writers at their peril. The peril is that the book group will have nothing to do with them. If the book group members aren't convinced on at least one level of verisimilitude, it's thumbs down for the book. If a book is pedantic and sermonizing, off with its head. And if a book is written only to please, as most genre fiction is, the book group's members may read it as individuals, but they won't choose to discuss it, because there won't be much to say. It's possible to discuss a billboard, true, but not for very long.

I suppose you could say that the real, hidden subject of a book group discussion is the book group members themselves. I think they are quite brave. They are ready to reveal, in semipublic, their own reactions, their own biases and doubts and convictions, and above all their own tastes; not everyone dares. The beauty of a book group for the members is that you don't get passed or failed for your opinions;

whereas the beauty of it for an author is that it's a collective and very candid review that the author will never know anything about because it doesn't happen to appear in the newspapers.

Some book groups may dream of having their favorite author to tea, but they probably shouldn't bother. As (I think) *Elle* magazine put it, "Wanting to meet an author because you like his book is like wanting to meet a duck because you like paté." (The main event at the book group tea my old roommate threw was not anything I had to communicate, but the lemon squares, which were superb.) Most novelists lead outwardly dull lives and are apt to drone on about their rheumatism or the price of car insurance; anything to avoid discussion of their trade secrets and inner lives. In any case, to a true book lover the author is merely the empty, shriveling husk that's left when the book has been squeezed out of her. Trust the tale and not the teller, I say: the book group has already got hold of the important part, which is the book itself.

MARGARET ATWOOD

Introduction

MY MOM CALLED one afternoon a few months ago while I was working on this new edition of *The Book Group Book*. My mom lives 2,000 miles away. She's a voracious, solitary reader (no book group for her). She reads mysteries, mostly, with an occasional break for memoir or biography. She gets her books from the library, only. One of her favorite reading spots is the local Big Boy restaurant where she sits with a thermos of coffee and her book and leaves the waitress, Marlene, a big tip just for leaving her alone. My mom needs her daily books and reading time.

"Ell?"

"Yeah, mom?"

"I'm starting a book group."

Save your feathers, this announcement knocked me over just fine. It seems my mom, two of my aunts, and two of my cousins were enhancing their informal biweekly kaffeeklatsch to include a discussion of a book they'd all read. The first book up was a mystery-thriller (I sensed my mother's influence, though it turns out it was my cousin's suggestion) called the *Windswept House* by Malachi Martin. Good versus evil in the Vatican. One of my aunts, a member of this fledgling club, has been a nun for the past sixty-plus years; she even worked at the Vatican for a few years (this book would be a good choice everybody thought).

Flash forward one month. I am e-mailing back and forth with my cousin, a member of this ad hoc book group. She is frantic; the Vatican mystery book has sex and devil worship and what was she thinking, she's scheduled to pass it on to our aunt, the nun, the next day.

"Pass it on?" I ask.

She writes back and explains. My mom and aunts won't buy a copy of the book. They insist that it will be fine to take turns reading the one copy that my cousin owns. As my cousin noted, "It's about 800 pages, so it looks as if our first meeting will be in July of 2002."

I thought back to a conversation I'd had with my editor. She wanted this introduction to be "prescriptive," to give tips for what makes a successful book group. And prescriptive I will be. Rule number one: Unless your book group consists of a trio called "me, myself, and I," you're going to need more than one copy of the book.

For other rules and tips for a successful book group, you can go directly to the essays that make up this book. In this third edition, close to twenty contributors wrote new essays and another thirty-seven contributed lists. In addition to all this new work, you'll find the best work from earlier editions of the book. As always, I gathered essays and book lists from book group members across the country, with some help from Canada, too. Whatever your question about starting a book group, you're bound to find an answer here. But just so you don't miss any of the key tips to forming a new group or improving an old one, I'll list ten here, direct from the experts—*The Book Group Book* contributors.

1. Rotate leadership to keep anyone from dominating the group and to keep everyone vested in it. This from book group member Lee Voegtlen, in an essay about her group, which has lasted for more than thirty years. In doing research for this book, I visited Voegtlen's group on the day they discussed Bernhard Schlink's *The Reader*. The leader that day was Nancy1 (as distinguished from Nancy2 who joined the group later) and she was well-prepared with reviews and comments and questions. She'd gathered difficult-to-find biographical information about Schlink, and she even asked her German neighbor to translate the titles of some of Schlink's previous works that had only been published in German. She also kept a keen eye out for any member who needed help wedging her voice into the energetic discussion during the meeting.

2. Confront your divas. You know who they are. They monopolize the discussion. They insist the group read the book they suggested. They only want to meet when it's convenient for them. Slowly, the other, less diva-like members stop attending. Divas announce themselves loud and clear. Admit it, you know if you have one. Before your group becomes wan and pale, take a stand. Not convinced of the danger? Read Margo Nightingale's essay for details

on how a diva almost killed her group. Take it as a cautionary tale. Don't ignore the diva in your group.

3. Demand more of the discussion than sweeping praise or condemnation. Seasoned book group leader Diane Leslie tells a story about what to do should your discussion open with a tidal wave of disapproval. In short, the leader must be prepared to face down the naysayer and demand a more respectful look at the book.

4. Don't drink too much alcohol. Call it DUI (discussing under the influence), and book group member Darwin Steed, whose group meets at a bar, says it's not a good idea. But he does suggest that "a glass or two loosens the tongue and gets the gab flowing."

5. When in trouble, go back to your original purpose—"to focus on literature." That's advice from long-time book group member and essay contributor Lee Strickland. Her group took stock and rededicated itself to discussing the book, instead of their jobs, their kids, their dogs. One of the changes that helped them was as simple as switching from a buffet to a sit-down dinner so that they didn't cluster in small groups that strayed off topic.

6. Go to the library or your local bookstore for book recommendations or to find a group to join. You will find a number of essays in this edition that focus on leader-run groups, many of which take place in a library or a bookstore. (See essays by Hedy N. R. Hustedde, Laura Luteri and Judy Bennett, and Clare Peterson and Marie Dench, for instance.) Library-sponsored book groups are, by nature, open to anybody who shows up. It's part philosophy, part law. (Your tax dollars fuel the library; the doors must be open to you.) Bookstore-sponsored groups typically have the same philosophy, though in their case it's good business sense and not your tax dollars that props open the door. Both settings are great for book groups, especially for the person who wants to be in a group but doesn't know how to find one to join.

7. Choose your books carefully (especially when you are just beginning to meet). Too difficult may be as dangerous as too simple;

Christine Posinger and Martha Sloan are now skilled veterans at running book groups, but read their essay for this tip in regard to a group that was almost brand-new. As Posinger notes, "Only one person came to the discussion of *The Plague* by Albert Camus, and that one person had not even read the book."

8. If you prefer to wear your pajamas while you chat about books, check out the Internet. Do you want to talk about mysteries? Short stories? Oprah book choices? Pulitzer Prize–winning books? Biographies? If you, like essay contributor jade14book, desire "human contact minus human presence," get thee to the Internet. Many Internet servers or bookstores sponsor book groups on the Web. Read jade14book's essay for tips on what the Internet offers and how to get the most out of Internet book chat.

9. Be open to any given book's potential to change a life, but don't worry if your favorite doesn't do it for somebody else. Every book group member has experienced or witnessed that moment of epiphany where it's clear a book is much more than just a book. The intellectual part of reading can be exhilarating; the emotional response can be life-altering. But sometimes the books that are important to us just don't do it for others. And sometimes, others illuminate the importance of a book that we dismissed as not so special at all. Read Dave Narter's essay about how he "gives" literature to his high schoolers and how they respond to it. Remember, the beauty of book groups is that they come in all kinds of shapes, forms, and sizes.

10. Listen, especially to "the quiet voice." You love your book group. You've been meeting for years. You're lively. You're intelligent. Discussion flows, sometimes ricochets. You look forward to your meetings. Sounds like a successful group, right? Maybe. Read Susan Messer's essay for perhaps the most important tip of all: it might go even better if you quiet down and listen.

So now you have some ideas on how to make your good group better or to get your fledgling group flying high. Next step: what to read? Well, some book groups read what Oprah tells them to. And other groups admit they want to print T-shirts that say, "We read [title here] before Oprah did." But if you go to Part VI of this book, you'll find book group–tested reading lists from thirty-seven contributors. If your group wants nonfiction suggestions, you'll find them. Biographies? No problem. Memoirs? Check. Oprah's selections? All there. Classics? They're covered. Contemporary fiction? You've died and gone to heaven. In many cases, you'll find that an essay contributor also contributed his or her group's reading list. Put the two together and you'll have a more fully-developed picture of that group.

And if, after all this, you're still looking for reading suggestions, you'll find a number of newsletters, magazines, and associations that are devoted to book group members and that are ready to help you out

One of my favorite newsletters is *Select Fiction,* which bills itself as "a selective guide to well-received new fiction that did not hit *The New York Times* bestseller list and possibly passed out of view too quickly to catch the eye of readers looking for good new novels and short stories, serious and otherwise." This publication does your legwork for you, pointing out small press gems and big publisher midlist wonders alike. It recently changed ownership, but after reading the inaugural issue, I have faith in the new publisher's promise to continue in the same vein. *Select Fiction* is published five times a year and you can contact the publishers at P.O. Box 237208, Ansonia Station, One West 67th St., New York, NY 10023, (212) 496-1461, smwoofcttc@ wilkieltd.com or bruce@metawork.com.

BookLovers, a quarterly magazine, is another fine resource for readers and book group members. It has been published for close to ten years now. Each issue contains book group recommendations and reviews, author interviews, poetry reviews, and group profiles. You can reach BookLovers at P.O. Box 511396, Milwaukee, WI 53203, (414) 372-1410, booklove@execpc.com.

Essay contributor and book group leader Natalie Kemmitt is editor of a more recent publication, *Fiction & Friends.* It's published five times a year and it bills itself as "a book discussion on paper, [which] aims to satisfy a wish for a deeper, wider reading experience [that] will enhance reading in groups and reading for personal pleasure." For more information about *Fiction & Friends* write P.O. Box 5841, Lafayette, IN 47903.

The Association of Book Group Readers and Leaders (ABGRL) is still going strong. Membership brings a periodic newsletter and access to information about other book groups. You can contact ABGRL at P.O. Box 885, Highland Park, IL 60035, (847) 266-0431, rachelj@interaccess.com.

And, finally, here's a chance for you and your group to make a contribution to a different kind of book group: teen moms. Essay contributor and book group leader Karen Thomson's nonprofit organization, Literature for All of Us, provides books and book group leaders to run reading groups for teen moms. Thomson's essay gives more details about the work the organization does, or you can contact her at Literature for All of Us, 2010 Dewey Ave., Evanston, IL 60201, (847) 869-7323, lit4all@xsite.net.

Any of these could be good resources for you and your group; but remember, they're not the main event. The main event is the book and the discussion about it.

I wondered how my mom's main event went, so I called the other day to find out about it. Turns out her book group didn't go particularly well. By the time the last reader read *Windswept House*, the first one could barely remember what it was about. But on the plus side, my aunt the nun didn't perish from the mention of sex and devil worship. And my cousin found a bakery that made a crusty cheese bread and she served it with good strong coffee at the book group's morning meeting and everybody was really enthusiastic about that. They talked about what to read for the next meeting. My cousin suggested *Song of Solomon* or *Under the Tuscan Sun*, but my mom had another idea, and they all agreed to it. They'll read *Angela's Ashes* next.

My mom didn't ask for my opinion, but I'll give it anyway: Bravo, mom. That's a fine book. And, even better, I just happen to have two copies of it. I'll drop them in the mail for you.

PART I

See, It's More than Just a Book Group

People in book groups often tell me this. And the essays in this section show why, as they illustrate the bigger work that book groups and books do. Among other things, book groups connect people and show us we're not alone in the books we read, in the troubles we face. In this section, you'll see how a book group can help you read Proust or help you discover that you're a natural-born book group leader.

The Quiet Voice

Susan Messer   📖   Oak Park, Illinois

"If they only want to hear their *own* voice, they can stay home and do that."

I was quoting a member of my father's reading group, even imitating his Russian accent, as I tried to tell my own reading group of how I'd been feeling about our recent discussions. It was pin-drop quiet in the room (unusual for this rowdy bunch) as I continued with my small proposal—that our raucous, chaotic book discussions become more focused and, more, well, respectful. I wanted to hear each person's contribution, I said, not just those with the loudest voices. I didn't like having to elbow my way in to express a thought or raise a question. I inched my way further and further out on a social limb, peering intently at my thumb cuticles. Small beads of perspiration emerged from various skin pores.

Finally, another voice ventured forth.

"I think she has a point," Pat said.

I breathed. Relief. After all, my husband and I are among the newer ones in this group. Even though our years as members had somehow added themselves up to seven or eight, most of these folks gathered in my living room had been communing over books for close to twenty years. So I was in a sense the young upstart.

Don't get me wrong. I'd grown fond of these ruffians—Steve and Pat, Don and Nadine, Bob and Jody, Brad and Lee, Richard and Lillian. Respected the reading and the thinking that went on from living room to living room, month to month. Admired our work of trying to get at a book's meaning, its significance, its reason for being in the world. It's just that I wanted more of that work, and less of everything else: Clinton jokes, restaurant reviews, neighborhood gossip. I'd been losing patience with the culture: five splinter conversations going at once (some related to the book, some not), people shouting over one another, the quiet voices not heard, not responded to. What a roller derby. You needed shin guards.

In this group, we're all in our forties and fifties, and we all live within a few blocks of each other. The founding members tend to mythologize the group's past—including its lack of decorum: the time Don tried to have a group reading of *A Christmas Carol* (Charles Dickens), but everyone got smashed and the night ended in chaos. How everyone trashed *Small Is Beautiful* (E. F. Schumacher). I'll always remember our discussion of *Fima* (Amos Oz), when the group divided pretty much into the Jewish contingent (who could relate to Fima, the Israeli main character, as though he were a weird but unforgettable uncle) and the non-Jewish (who found him shiftless and odious). But Bob brought us all together by saying simply that he was "glad it wasn't a scratch-and-sniff book." (Read it and see if he isn't right.)

I'd been in two book groups before—one in Ann Arbor, which didn't seem to have any of these disciplinary problems, and one in Chicago, devoted solely to Proust's *Remembrance of Things Past* (or, in the newer translation, *In Search of Lost Time*). Compared to my current group, the Proust group had been reverential, monastic. We spent three years, a volume a year, about 100 pages a month, getting to the heart of the lyrical, obsessive Marcel. But when we finished with Proust, the group lost its purpose, and my husband and I proceeded sans group for several years. When Pat invited us to join her group, I was pleased, and flattered. I needed to be in a book group. Why? I'd come to depend on the community and communion of it, the varied viewpoints, the deeper understandings of two of my favorite pastimes—reading and conversation.

For our first meeting as part of the new group, we read *Yellow Raft in Blue Water* (Michael Dorris). I prepared in my usual manner—read carefully, made notes, marked important passages, reviewed the book on the day of the meeting so it would be fresh in my mind. But after experiencing the boisterous atmosphere of the first meeting, and re-experiencing it at the second (our house—Vargas Llosa, *The Storyteller*), I scaled back. I was barely able to speak a word. Then, as the years passed, and the number of less-satisfying discussions increased, I'd pondered occasionally with my husband whether to continue in the group, whether to find another one that might better meet my need to discuss, whether a quieter type like myself really had a place in such a noisy assembly.

My inspiration for finally speaking up came after I visited my father's book group, where the members were all in their seventies and eighties and had been meeting for close to thirty years. I'd flown in to visit my dad for Father's Day weekend. He'd been very sick (it turned out to be his final illness; he died a few months later), but somehow he pulled himself together enough to attend his book group meeting, and I went along. This group, much larger than mine back home (it probably had twenty-plus members), was almost parliamentary in approach—clearly a one-voice-at-a-time operation. An example: A woman named May had the floor, but another woman, Mary, wanted to interject. Did Mary shout out her comment? Grab the floor? Not in that living room. Instead, she must have sent out some subtle message to May, who noticed and gave Mary the go-ahead, on one condition: "I'll let Mary speak, but when she's done, I want my turn back." And that's how they did it. Astonishing.

At the end of their meeting, I complimented the group on how civilized they were. I told them how different they were from my group. And to illustrate, I described the muscling in, the shouting each other down, the anarchy. That's when the Russian fellow shrugged his shoulders, held out his hands, and gave me my opener: "If they only want to hear their *own* voice, they can stay home and do that."

The night I decided to speak to my group, we were at my house, discussing *Wuthering Heights* (Emily Brontë). I knew that folks would have a range of responses. A few, who had earlier confided their own dissatisfactions to me, would approve. Others would likely see me as a wet blanket. I could imagine all kinds of rejoinders and catcalls along these lines: "When it's at your house, do it however you want; when it's at mine, I do it my way." Steve, one of the founding members, simply said they'd been through this kind of thing before (not in the past six or seven years, though, I noted to myself). And that over the years, people either decided that they liked the group and its free-for-all culture or they didn't. My problem was that I felt both ways: I liked it. And I didn't.

Still, something changed on that wuthering night in my living room. Okay, I thought, maybe it did feel stiff at first; maybe some people did feel chastened, even angry. But my husband didn't think so. He thought they felt relief. First, each person, even the quiet ones, finally had a chance to speak. And maybe more important, to be listened to. Pat even managed to organize a round-robin (a first-ever for me in this group), each person naming a book that had been important to them in their teen or adolescent years. And so far (three or four meetings later), the more disciplined approach seems to be sticking. More or less. "One conversation at a time," someone will say when cacophony sets in, and I feel good about that. But frankly, I'm not even sure what I want in brass-tack terms.

I'm definitely not a parliamentary type. Can't stand raising my hand. Hate having to wait to be called on. Wouldn't like the artificiality of too much "going around the circle." In that mode, I fear that people are more concerned with preparing their own remarks than listening to the other speakers. And the circle might force someone to speak who really doesn't have anything to say at that moment. In the end then, it comes down to intangibles and unpredictables—the chemistry of personalities, the quality of the relationships, a critical mass of rowdiness, a particular book or snack or current event—that make the group more or less orderly, more or less comfortable for any particular member.

So why have I stayed for all these years? For one, in an odd way, I have come to feel connected with the people in my reading group. And I'm continuously fascinated by the range of responses a book can elicit. We've got a roomful of well-informed, sophisticated readers, and some think it's the best book they ever read ("biblical," "brilliant," "rich"), and some think it's the worst ("flat," "wooden," "superficial"). Or they conclude the same thing but to completely different ends:

Lee: (disparagingly) Another male sexual fantasy . . .

Brad: (approvingly) Another male sexual fantasy!

Also, in a group that has lasted over so many years, the characters in the books we read become, in a sense, members of the group, and the lives they lead weave together with ours into a common experience. We all know Heathcliff and Fima and the awful father in *Palace Walk* (Naguib Mahfouz), and we love them or hate them, gossip about them, compare their foibles one to the other, as if they lived and walked among us, all in the same world.

Finally, the group has piqued my interest in the idea of speaking up and made me notice how difficult it can be, how much courage it can take, even among friends, to stand alone with an opinion. Take, for example, our discussion of *The Reader* (Bernhard Schlink), one that occurred in our more parliamentary, one-voice-at-a-time mode. That evening, Jody, a softer-voiced member, kept telling us that Schlink was an apologist in his approach to the Holocaust. He tried, Jody told us, to paint over the Nazi evils with excuses about seduction (the Germans who did Hitler's worst work weren't children or adolescents, Jody pointed out quietly) and illiteracy (the Germans had one of the highest prewar European literacy rates, she continued). And even though she's the German scholar among us, and even though we refrained from shouting each other down, none of us accepted what she was saying. I know I didn't, as I was seduced by the beauty of Schlink's writing, and what I saw as the nobility of his inward search for understanding, his impossible task of relieving the collective guilt. That is, I didn't get it until later, when Jody sent me a review of Schlink's book from the *The New York Times*, which reiterated all she had been saying. Only then, in the quiet of my own living room, with all the voices hushed, did I start to see the book in a different light, and felt ashamed that I hadn't listened more closely to her at our meeting. Yet another lesson in how important it can be to listen to the quiet voice, and how even in a more orderly group, I still need to listen and be open to the possibility that I missed something big in any given book.

For this group's reading list, see page 328.

A Benign Dictatorship

KATHY EWING   📖   CLEVELAND HEIGHTS, OHIO

IT ALL BEGAN with *The Fever*, a novel by actor/playwright Wallace Shawn.

In seventy horror-filled pages, Shawn describes how we pampered Westerners profit from the suffering of Third World people. Near the end, Shawn recommends reading *The Fever* aloud at parties. Writing a review for a local alternative paper in 1991, I explained that, although I admired the book very much, I couldn't reconcile its vivid renderings of torture with social entertainment. But because the book had immense potential for discussion, my review closed with, "If I were leading a book group or a church study group, I'd assign it in a minute."

When my neighbor, Tricia, a Presbyterian minister and a money-where-your-mouth-is sort of person, read my review, she asked if I really wanted to lead a book discussion. Before I knew it, I had signed on. The logistics quickly fell into place. Sunday evenings were best for her and her church. I could choose books without regard to con-troversial sexual or religious themes, and the group would be open to the public as well as to church members.

So on a Sunday evening in September, almost ten years ago, we met to discuss *The Fever*, and nearly every month since, we have been meeting to discuss books at Noble Road Presbyterian Church in Cleveland Heights, Ohio. Among the other books that first year were

Road Song by Natalie Kucz, *Savage Inequalities* by Jonathan Kozol, and Adrienne Kennedy's *Funnyhouse of a Negro* and *The People Who Led to My Plays*. When I was ready to break for the summer, my group said, Let's keep going.

Through these years, we have read fiction and nonfiction, books by men and women of every ethnicity, old books and new books. What do they all have in common?

I picked them, or most of them.

This is a feature that appeals to our regular members. They like having no responsibility and enjoy reading things that someone else recommends, books that they otherwise may not have picked up. (A few of our one-time visitors, I suspect, would have liked a little more say.) My group tells me that they appreciate my benign dictatorship.

And it's gratifying for me. Whereas I usually am ignored when I tell friends and relatives what to read, now I'm guaranteed that at least a few people will read what I suggest and be willing to discuss it with me. I get all the perks of the English teacher—an enthusiastic, prepared "class"—and none of the heartaches—discipline problems and grading. Everybody in my group gets an "A" every month.

I have three criteria in choosing books. I must like—preferably love—the book. That's the only way I can do a good job leading a discussion. Then I require some intuition that my book group will also like the book. (So I've steered clear of my more idiosyncratic tastes—Nicholson Baker, James Herndon, Jim Grimsley.) And finally, there has to be something to say about the book. I have to be able to imagine a discussion about it.

Of course, not everyone enjoys every book we read. Some regular members, for instance, didn't show up for *The Drowned and the Saved* by Primo Levi, not wanting to face the horror of another Holocaust book. One member found Paul Monette (*Borrowed Time: An AIDS Memoir*) too self-involved. And don't even ask Roberta how much she hated Christina Stead's novel *The Man Who Loved Children*. My most recent flop was popular Joanna Trollope's *The Rector's Wife*, which I thought would be an enjoyable change of pace after a couple of months of intense memoirs (Kathryn Harrison's *The Kiss* and Mary

Karr's *The Liars' Club*). My high-toned group found Trollope a little pat and soap-operatic after all the great literature we've shared. You win some, you lose some.

Among our most popular reads have been Michael Cunningham's wonderful novel *A Home at the End of the World*; Ursula Hegi's sure-fire *Stones from the River*; and Don Snyder's troubling memoir *The Cliff Walk*. Toni Morrison and Anne Tyler are favorites, as is our South Euclid, Ohio, neighbor Mary Doria Russell (*The Sparrow* and *Children of God*). Sometimes, of course, the best discussions arise when everyone doesn't love the book. *Huckleberry Finn*, which brought up issues of racial stereotyping, inspired our most heated discussion, and Lars Eighner's quirky account of his three years of homelessness, *Travels with Lizbeth* (Lizbeth being his dog), provoked as much as it pleased.

Although we never intended to be a women-only group, we've had only three male visitors. A young man came with his mother to talk about *Huckleberry Finn*, and a member's husband came to discuss Margaret Walker's *Jubilee*. And Ed Reynolds came to talk about *On the Outside Looking In*, which concerns the alternative New York City high school where he's the principal. (His sister Mary is one of our regulars.) Though men rarely come, I hear now and then that husbands sometimes read our books when their wives recommend them.

Our members, ranging in age from their late thirties to sixties, have included working mothers, widows, single and divorced women, and stay-at-home moms. We always have a Presbyterian or two, but usually they're outnumbered by other-denominational women who live in the neighborhood or who have been brought by friends. By now there's a core of six or seven who almost never miss a meeting.

The miracle of our group is our compatibility and shared deep-down devotion to books. More miraculously, when new people wander in, they usually fit right in and start talking. I begin the discussion with a question or two about the characters or theme and have to do little else to keep it going. When we read Grace Butcher's *Child, House, World*, the local author visited us to read and discuss her poems. When we read Elizabeth Marshall Thomas's *The Hidden Life of Dogs*, we had plenty of our own dog anecdotes to fill the conversation. For *Another Marvelous*

Thing by Laurie Colwin, a member brought a plate of gingerbread made from Colwin's recipe in *Home Cooking*. For Isak Dinesen's *Babette's Feast*, we enjoyed a dessert feast at a member's home. Usually we just sit together, sans refreshments, talking and laughing.

For most of us, the group provides a night out with intelligent and funny women. For me, it's also an outlet for my evangelical teacher-self to share the books I love. For Tricia, it's an unusual opportunity to enjoy an activity at her church with no leadership responsibility. All of us, I suspect, would echo the answer Roberta gave when I asked her what book group meant to her.

"It's the only place I have in my life where I can talk about writing, not just plot and characters, but writing. We're not a bunch of dilettante suburban women making up pretty phrases, wearing our best outfits, and trying to outdo each other in insightful comments. No one's trying to accomplish anything. No one has an agenda. When I'm there, all that matters is the book and the group."

For this group's reading list, see page 254.

The Ann Arbor Society of the Written Word (A²SW²)

Paul D. Reingold   Ann Arbor, Michigan

THE A²SW² WAS founded in 1982, and it has met more or less continuously (nine or ten times a year) ever since. The book club began as most do: two coworkers found themselves talking about books, and lamenting how little time they had to read. Both of these readers had a common interest in Proust. One had read Proust to get through law school; he was trying to finish the last two volumes in his first year as a legal services lawyer. His colleague had recently read *Swan's Way*; she was looking for encouragement to keep going.

After a couple of dinners and too much wine, the A²SW² was born. Invitations went out to several kindred literary souls. The first book— *The Autobiography of Alice B. Toklas*, Gertrude Stein—was chosen for multimedia reasons, to draw a crowd. That month a well-reviewed, one-woman play, based on the life of Gertrude Stein, was showing in Ann Arbor. The founders correctly guessed that more people would respond to the invitation if it included a night on the town. The invitation was to read the book, see the play, eat dessert together afterward, and discuss what we had seen and read.

Quite quickly a group of six joined the book club. The first meetings set the tone for future meetings. The atmosphere was relaxed and casual, with a good dessert at the end of the evening. We often tried to match the book with an event. When the local art cinema showed Alec Guinness in Joyce Cary's *The Horse's Mouth*, we read the book. When Nadine Gordimer lectured at the university, we went, and we read Gordimer. We rotated the job of hosting the meeting, running through the membership in alphabetical order. Early on we established one strict rule: fiction only. And we decided upon Sunday night as the meeting night—a tradition that has been followed for most of the meetings since 1982.

Over the years the membership has fluctuated, from a low of four or five to a high of eight or nine. Six or seven seems about right, and those numbers have produced the best book club meetings. Often we meet less than on a monthly basis, giving ourselves a few extra weeks when the book is long, or when our schedules don't mesh. The first summer *War and Peace* crushed a third of our nascent membership, so we had to recruit hardier replacements in the fall. That meeting also gave us a funny moment when we discovered that the survivor who complained the most had (unwittingly) read an abridged edition.

The list of books has grown to the point where it is now an impressive document and a source of (mostly) fond memories. This statement about our book list captures the spirit of the book club:

> The Book Club chooses its next book(s) at the end of each meeting. We aim for variety, bouncing back and forth from the classics to popular fiction (to satisfy our curiosity). We keep an eye on award lists—the Pulitzer, the Booker, the National Book Award—and on the reviews. We prefer an international flavor. We avoid books that most of us have already read. This recipe has brought us a potpourri of very good reading (as well as the occasional trifle or dud that looks out of place on the list). The Book Club meets about every five or six weeks on average, for ninety minutes of low-brow discussion followed by a high-calorie dessert.

The best meetings tend to be of two types: the ones where people have strong opinions about what we have read and the ones where we have read several authors who complement each other. (I recall one memorable early meeting where we had read J. M. Coetzee, Nadine Gordimer, and Alan Paton.) Some of my favorite meetings are the ones where we have read an author who is new to me and whom I otherwise might never have found (James Salter, Pat Barker, and Rohinton Mistry), or where we have read an author who is well-known but whom I surely would not have read but for the book club (like Somerset Maugham, Virginia Woolf, and George Eliot). On a few occasions we have been so taken with an author that we decided to stay with that author for a second straight month, postponing what we had previously assigned. (Sometimes we will choose our books two or three months in advance, so that we keep a sort of running list.) Often we have revisited an author, for further reading, or to read a recently published book. My latest recommendation—an author I've been urging on the book club for several months, so far without success—is the Australian Patrick White, a Nobel Prize winner whose books are now mostly out of print in the United States.

In the 1980s one of the book club founders moved to Chicago, where she joined a Proust book group and finally got to finish what she had started years before. She wisely decided to make books her career—she now works as an editor and writer. It was she who suggested I write about the A^2SW^2 for *The Book Group Book*.

Only one original member of the book club remains, but the group is flourishing. It has nine fairly steady members, some of who have been regulars for years. It has a surfeit of lawyers. One lingering member comes only to the meetings at her house; she can't quite let go. Some people give us a try for a month or two and fall by the wayside. They either are not readers, or they are not interested in talking about the books they read. Occasionally we lose someone who is too academic, and who wants a more intellectual approach to the work. Our discussions can be of high quality and the group is quite bright, but we don't pretend to be literary scholars, and we don't approach the books from an academic perspective. For those of us who teach, the book club is a relief from our academic life, not an extension of it. Some of us keep up with the reading even when we are out of town for extended visits, or on sabbatical. And when one member of the A^2SW^2 went back to school to get a Ph.D. in literature, she used the book club as raw material for her dissertation on women readers, in part looking at differences between what men and women read, and how they read.

What most of us find is that the book club keeps us readers rather than makes us readers. We all lead busy professional and family lives, and without the book club, all of us would probably read less. The book club not only gets us in the habit of reading, but it feeds the habit, supplying us with an endless source of new books. Some of the books will become book club books. Most will not. But they will be added to the lists we all keep—lists of fiction and nonfiction, of American and foreign books, of new discoveries and old standbys. We will buy or borrow many of these books. We will take them home, or with us on vacation, and we will read them. Our night tables will pile up with books waiting to be read, and some of our homes will begin to look like libraries or bookstores.

In a town of transients like Ann Arbor, Michigan, periodically one of our ardent book club members must move away. The person leaving and the people staying are sad, but it is worse for the emigrant, who must not only make a new home, but must also find a new book group. A good book group is like a good mechanic: you leave either at your peril, as neither is easily replaced. Those of us left behind mourn for a while, but the departure is also an opportunity. There is an opening in the book club. We get to fill the slot with new blood. We can improve the gender balance. We can reduce the number of lawyers (at last). We add a person, or maybe two, and the group takes on a new character, begins a new history. The person who left, however, is bereft—once more a solitary reader. But sometimes, down the road, we hear that the departed member has started a new book club in his or her new town. We are not entrepreneurs or proselytizers, but we nevertheless feel a sympathetic thrill, as if our book club has been franchised, or its gospel spread.

In the end the book club is about a shared interest in reading and learning. For many people reading is intensely private and personal. But much of what we learn from books we cannot learn on our own. Even in the modest discussion of a mediocre book, the book club allows each of us to share what we saw in it, and in the sharing we learn things that we did not see ourselves. We might argue about what is there, or about the value of what is there, but we learn together, and our reading of the book is enhanced by the group's insights.

After eighteen years, the A^2SW^2 has become a routine pleasure in my life. I count on it every fifth or sixth Sunday night, year round, year after year. Friends and family will ask about the current book, or what's on deck (or on the long-term list). Diligent members of the book club will circulate some unsolicited research—a review, or excerpts of a biography of an author we are reading, or a list pirated from some other book group far away, with suggestions checked.

Although I live in a community of readers, I feel as if I have better access to good books than most people I know. And I am never at a loss for conversation; for members of a book club, it is not an idle question to ask, "Read any good books lately?"

For this group's reading list, see page 341.

The Book Club and My Grandmother's Crystal

KAREN ACKLAND   SANTA CRUZ, CALIFORNIA

BOOK CLUB STARTED when I and two other software company coworkers decided that we wanted more than marketing plans and C programming in our lives and invited several others to form a reading
group. We first met one Friday evening in spring 1988 to discuss Gabriel
García Márquez's *Love in the Time of Cholera*. In retrospect, the romantic drifting end of that book has set the tone for our meetings. We are
an unlikely group to have found each other and we are holding on.

There is a twenty-year spread between our ages. We grew up all
over the country—Maine, Iowa, Nevada, Illinois, and California. Our
college degrees range from mathematics, English literature, and sociol-
ogy to computer science. Our members include a gay man, a lesbian, a
married couple who originally met when she was his high-school English
teacher, and a single woman. If there is something that characterizes us,
it is an unexpected tendency toward silliness.

The silliness began when we switched from meeting for dessert on
Friday evenings to dinner on Saturdays and started matching the meals
to the books. We took these theme dinners very seriously at first, going
to the library to look up recipes in the Time/Life cookbooks behind the
reference section. We had *Pollo con Pina à la Antigua* with Oscar

17

Hijuelos's *The Mambo Kings Play Songs of Love* and Egyptian lamb stew, *yakhnit koosa*, with Naguib Mahfouz's *The Thief and the Dog*. We had tea in the park one Sunday afternoon and played croquet after reading *The Remains of the Day* by Kazuo Ishiguro. Barbara and Brian hosted the afternoon, bringing a table, linens, and complete tea service to the neighborhood park and showing up dressed in colonial whites. We even went camping in Big Sur, where we ate barbecued salmon, drank a half case of good chardonnay, and talked about Harry Crews's *Body* on and off over the course of the weekend. I suggested that book, and still defend it as fun, although it may not have warranted a weekend of discussion. As we sat around the campfire, Jim, who is often irritated by the irregular punctuation of contemporary authors, dramatized a story from John Muir's travels in Alaska as an example of a real story.

It didn't take long until we started to choose books by the type of food we wanted to eat. In a group of opinionated people and adventuresome eaters it was often easier to pitch a cuisine than an unknown book or author. "We haven't had Indian," Barbara might say and so we read *Jasmine* by Bharati Mukherjee. "My sister cooks good Mexican food," Cindy said, and we invited ourselves to her house and read a collection of stories about Latin American women subtitled *The Magic and the Real*. Cindy isn't a cook, but she is a networker, and realizing that the editor of the collection, Celia de Zapata, taught at San Jose State, she invited her to join us and lead the discussion.

Our evenings have a pattern. They progress from the initial checking of who liked the book as we gather with a glass of wine around the hors d'oeuvres to a meandering conversation during dinner, winding up with the conclusion and selection of the next book over dessert and coffee. We keep our books within reach to prove a point, but, despite occasional efforts to mark and bring in a favorite passage, we are not a literary group and at times our sloppiness has irritated those with more academic backgrounds.

No one leads the discussion and we jump from subject to subject. We do not talk about tone or place or voice. We also do not talk about politics, the environment, or people at work. We talk about the book and in talking about the book, we talk about ourselves. We know the discussion has ended when Greg asks, "Would you recommend this book to a friend?" We teased him about the question for a while, but now we wait for it, even asking it for him if he forgets, and go around the room with everyone answering individually.

There are other traditions. Greg calls to say thank-you the day after the meeting. Barbara always sends a note. We bring out the good glasses and company dishes and make an effort with the table arrangements. Somewhere along the way I realized that these Saturday evenings were only slightly different from the monthly bridge potluck group that my parents have been part of for more than thirty years. The irony of this is not lost on me.

One of the pleasures of our book group has been talking on and on about a book, narrowing in on a topic over a period of time that would not be possible in a more directed meeting or class. Several of us combined the book club meeting of Michael Ondaatje's *The English Patient* with a visit to San Francisco to see the Teotihuacán show at the DeYoung Museum. We talked about the book for the hour-and-a-half drive to San Francisco, over dinner for several hours, and during the drive home. Jim didn't like the punctuation in that one either, but I challenge anyone not to like the book. Cormac McCarthy's *Blood Meridian* also provoked prolonged discussion. We called a special, second meeting since we didn't understand it the first time, but even after this we were still puzzled, though we continued to be seduced by the beauty of the writing and appalled by the violence.

Some have said that they like the group because it means that they read at least one book a month, but that's not my reason. I have always read a lot. What matters most to me about the group is its continuity. When we first started meeting, I didn't think we would become much of a group—we were too different. But the silliness and the good food kept us together and somewhere along the line I realized that we were a group. These people are my friends. We have thirty-four books in common.

We had gone on so long that I thought we would go on forever. We had survived members moving away, getting married, having babies, earning graduate degrees, and changing jobs. Yet last winter we stopped meeting and we haven't met now for more than seven months. We've talked about starting again. We've talked about why we stopped. Mainly, we got tired of talking about what we were going to do about Dan.

Dan is the boyfriend of a friend and he didn't fit in. He would walk into a room where the host or hostess had gone to a lot of work getting ready—we all have full-time jobs—and say, "I only come to these things for the free food." The type of man who feels he is needed to keep conversation going, Dan once laughed at the idea of a women-only book club, wondering what they could talk about. He wears his former poverty like a badge on his sleeve and dares you to take a swing at him. It was painful to watch him regularly demean his girlfriend, who the rest of us like.

At first Dan didn't read the book, which didn't keep him from trying to dominate the conversation, but it made it easier to ignore him. Still it took energy to continue directing the conversation back to the book after Dan had gone off on a tangent about local politics or the inequities of being a white male these days. The book club stopped being fun. It was not clear whose responsibility it was to solve the problem. But we didn't handle it well. We just stopped meeting.

We spent so much time talking about Dan outside the book club, taking polls of who disliked him, that we finally exhausted our energy for the group. An old friend recently told me, "I think a relationship has a compromise quota, and you can use that up in the first six months arguing about which house to buy." I think the book club had a tolerance quota and we used it up talking about Dan.

Five of us from the original group have decided to meet again next Saturday to discuss E. Annie Proulx's *The Shipping News*, but this time we're talking about rules or a trial period. I'm uncomfortable with the idea of a secret ballot to exclude someone—after all, our group celebrates differences—but I also dislike the idea of the book club just disappearing. And, of course, we always did have rules. The rules were to read the book, set a pretty table, and to listen when someone else was speaking. The rules had to do with manners.

Years ago, when I was coming to terms with the apparent dichotomy between my sixties values and my determination to have a nice place to live even though I moved around more than was healthy for either me or my belongings, I realized the significance of nice things. I don't have crystal wine glasses because they are important—I have them because they were my grandmother's and she left them to me. But I use them because I like them. I came to see that not having things you can afford just because having them is nice shows a lack of attention to detail and a failure to make choices in your life. Flaunting bad manners because it makes others uncomfortable is only bad manners. I will accept the responsibility of excluding others from the book club because, like crystal wine glasses, the group is a choice for good friends, good books, and good manners, and I intend to go on making that choice.

Book Group Diva

MARGO NIGHTINGALE   📖   LOS ANGELES, CALIFORNIA

COLD MOUNTAIN, Speaking Truth to Power, Larry's Party, The Blue Flower, Mrs. Dalloway, To the Lighthouse, Shot in the Heart, Cider House Rules, Alias Grace, Cliff Walk, The House of Mirth, The Poisonwood Bible, Picture, Stealing Jesus . . .

It's really not a bad list when you look at it. In fact, it's a pretty spectacular list with wonderful gems of fiction and nonfiction. Then why did our book group, for all intents and purposes, ultimately fail on so many levels? The first word that comes to mind is *diva.*

Our group consisted of straight, gay, married, single, divorced, and diva. Our professions: attorney, playwright and temp, novelist and freelance writer, teacher, theater producer, sitcom writer, grief counselor, and wildly successful playwright and television and screenwriter. The latter, in case you couldn't guess, was our diva, whom I shall call Andrea.

Andrea started the group because she decided that Los Angeles was so terribly bereft of culture and intellectual curiosity that a book group was needed. Desperately. We agreed. She had rules for our group. By the end of the first year, we would all be writing novels. She also said no books were allowed that members had read before. No member could miss a discussion or they were kicked out. This was half in jest, half not. There were other rules too, but I forget them now.

Rules or not, we all approached the reading in our own way. One member read everything cover to cover and found something good to say about each book. Another member quit reading the second his attention wavered, and he found something critical to say about each book. (He was funny and self-effacing, so we forgave him.) Most of us fell somewhere between the two.

We loved *Cold Mountain*, though we were all so nervous—it was our first meeting, and we wanted this book group venture to be a success. We marched with Inman but were relieved to discover Ada carried her share of the chapters. Anita Hill's *Speaking Truth to Power* was tougher going, and some of the slouches among us cut to the chase and only read the second half of the book. When it came my turn to recommend a book, I chose *Larry's Party*, though I was lobbied by others to go with their choices instead—in this case, Hitler's biography (can you guess who wanted that?) and *Valley of the Dolls*. Reading at home later, I could sense a few chapters into *Larry's Party* that it wasn't going to be very popular.

As I suspected, everyone hated it, and jokes were batted back and forth around the brunch table—"Larry's nose hairs, Larry's ingrown toenail, Larry's boring." I had a hard time defending it, because I didn't like it nearly as much as *The Stone Diaries*.

We moved on to *The Blue Flower*, which only one member liked and the rest of us were too stupid to understand. Next, we decided on two Virginia Woolf books to coincide with the opening of the film *Mrs. Dalloway*. Nearly everyone enjoyed them, except for two who didn't read them. The teacher in the group (my husband) had no time, and the other flat-out refused but entertained us with Vanessa Redgrave impersonations of "Come to my paaaaaarrrrrty."

After Penelope Fitzgerald and Virginia Woolf, we decided we needed a good shot in the arm of nonfiction, so we read *Shot in the Heart*, the story of Gary Gilmore. *Cider House Rules* followed on its heels as there was a production based on the novel being mounted in Los Angeles.

It was during the discussion of *Cliff Walk*, one of our most beloved books, that things fell apart. Tensions had been brewing for months as life became more complicated and difficult for Andrea. She was tormented by the Hollywood industry, and, to a point, we were all empathetic. We cared about her. We really did. But I know for the writers among us, we'd have given anything to be able to bitch (even a fraction of the amount she bitched) about producers hounding us day and night, demanding rewrites, rewriting our scenes, sending us residual checks.

I'm not proud to admit this, but I thought if I was kind and compassionate enough to empathize with the horrors she faced (and there were plenty), in some weird karmic way, some of her success would rub off on me. Maybe I'd begin to eke out a small living as a writer instead of watching my first novel quietly go out of print.

Plus, Andrea could be very kind and generous. For her birthday, she treated everyone to dinner at a great restaurant. She was always generous with theater comps to various shows around town. And it was fun to have a drink with her, while she regaled us with hilarious and horrible tales of her life in Hollywood.

But I digress. The morning of *Cliff Walk*, we met at Jane's house. Jane was going through a painful separation and was dealing with a new full-time job and custody arrangements. There had been a flurry of e-mails about when and where to meet. I'd been at the center of the e-mails, and then feeling like a busybody, I bowed out, figuring Jane would finish up the last of the arrangements. But I didn't tell her this, so communications got screwed up, and, well, Andrea went to the wrong house for book group.

One way or another, the rest of us made it to Jane's. We waited for Andrea. Then we waited some more. Finally, the phone rang, and Jane disappeared to answer it. When she returned, her face was pale. She had just been royally bawled out by Andrea.

Everyone felt bad. I apologized for not e-mailing her one final time. It was a logistical error, a mistake. I was wrong. I was sorry. I had unintentionally inflicted a wound, but surely not a mortal one. Wrong again. Andrea was deeply offended, and not with me, but with Jane. She wasn't coming to book group that night.

I've gone over this morning a thousand tedious times in my head, and I've come to the conclusion that Jane's misstep was that instead of immediately gushing heartfelt, ass-kissing mea culpas to our wronged member, she laughed at the misunderstanding. Andrea shrieked, "I don't think it's funny!" and hung up.

I thought it would blow over, but Jane and Andrea refused to budge. Each felt the other owed an apology, which wasn't going to happen.

Andrea sent Jane a scolding e-mail about how she'd risen early to finish a screenplay just to be at the book group. Jane didn't answer and
instead chose to drop out of the group with the explanation: "I don't
have to answer to the teacher." Jane's thinking was that just because
Andrea was paid more than of any of us, it didn't mean her life was more
important or more harried than the rest of us. It had been a mistake.
Nothing more. I tried to make amends to the diva, explaining that I
was really to blame, but the diva didn't want to blame me. She wanted
to blame Jane. I tried to arrange a bury-the-hatchet lunch between them,
but Andrea refused to go, saying, "Great, now you're going to make me
act like a grown-up!"

The book group limped along. I can't remember *The Poisonwood
Bible*, because I was nursing a newborn in the middle of the night while
reading it, but it was a hit among some members. The next book, *House
of Mirth*, was also a favorite and led to discussions of being single and
married, having money, not having money, loneliness. After that, we
read *Picture*, as suggested by Andrea, who had missed the last three
meetings herself, because Hollywood was ripping her heart out. Still,
she wanted us to get a portrait of Hollywood in the 1950s. And in
Picture, Lillian Ross's take on the making of *The Red Badge of Courage*,
we did. It's a biting, funny book, and I looked forward to the discussion, especially since Andrea could offer her insider's view. But Andrea
didn't show up again due to another personal affront by some industry slimeball. She sent her husband and child as stand-ins. The icing on
the cake was when her husband read her list of recommendations for
our next meeting. Our diva might not be there, but we would feel her
presence.

Nobody was happy with book group. We were caught up in our
maelstrom of egos, swept up in her drama. Never mind that one of us
had just given birth. Never mind that another wrote screenplays that
weren't selling. Never mind that one was broke, that another's marriage
was splintering, that another ran a marathon. Nobody could compete
with the high stakes of Hollywood and evil producers and flaky actresses
and unethical screenwriters all too willing to stab you in the back. Our
problems and successes were peanuts compared to her life, which
oozed stars and money and pain and sorrow.

I lost any shred of patience I had left. It had all gradually become less about the books and more about empathizing with the diva. It wasn't all her fault. We had allowed the situation to fester. Many of us felt so devalued in our lesser lives that we kept our mouths shut, which even trickled into the way we discussed the books. We met less and less frequently. We were falling apart. Our diva grew sick of Los Angeles and all its shallow people and moved back to New York with her family. We didn't meet month after month. It seemed we had disbanded.

But then, a few months ago, one of our members called and wanted to know if we wanted to continue. I said OK. The thing is, I like the members of the group very much. I even liked Andrea when she wasn't behaving like a diva. We met sans diva—she lives in New York after all—to discuss getting back together. I suggested Lorrie Moore's *Birds of America*, and that's what we're reading next. A collection of stories. I figure if no one finishes all of them, at least we'll be able to discuss something. We've got a new member. She recently left her job to focus on writing a novel. She's smart and she's a good listener. Not a diva at all as far as I can tell. But Jane still has no interest in coming back.

Andrea called from New York recently to see how things were going. She said the people in the industry are still nuts, but New York is a great place to be. She says she's happy now. She's busy with two films, a television show, a new play, an old play, and she still wants to write a novel.

She said she was going to be in town for the next book group meeting. She said, "By the way, I hear we're reading *Birds of America*."

And so we are.

Communion

ROBIN M. NEIDORF   MINNEAPOLIS, MINNESOTA

BEFORE I KNEW what literature was, I knew book groups.

Throughout my childhood, my mother belonged to a book group, which met monthly at the house of one member or another. The book group intruded into the lives of my sister and me in small but memorable ways. At times Mom could not play with us or read to us because she had to finish her book for book group. At times our refrigerator was crowded with sliced fruit on trays and our pantry filled with cookies and pound cake that we could not touch; these were for book group.

We could have resented the book group, but the intrusions were relatively minor. My sister and I were generally content to play alone, and the group always left behind cake. If we thought about it at all, perhaps we dismissed the book group as unimportant adult stuff.

And then, on a lucky day in first grade when I happened to be home from school with some minor ailment, I witnessed the book group in our own living room.

I was not so sick that I couldn't get out of bed, and I was bored, so I crept down the stairs in my nightgown and hid behind the curve in the wall. From this vantage point, I could see that our living room was a circle of women on folding chairs, eating the forbidden goodies, drinking coffee out of Styrofoam cups (we were not yet saving the earth), and talking about books.

Did I hear which book they were discussing? I no longer remember. But the scene has stayed with me through the years in a way that few others from that period have. There was my mother, part of this group that was not my family. For the first time, to my childish eyes, she was more than my mother. She was one of these women who met solely for the purpose of discussing books, and even in first grade, that seemed to me a high-minded, intellectual, admirable thing to do.

I did not know then, as I do now, that literature is a point of convergence between different readers' lives. Discussions of literature are, of course, intellectual exercises, but they can also serve as a bridge between the disparate lives of readers and thinkers. We see ourselves reflected in the works we read, we read passages out loud and say, "I thought I was the only one who felt that way," and we hear others say the same. Our experiences suddenly become more than what they are. Yet at the same time, they are strangely diminished to mere biographical moments; as our perspective shifts from the individual moment to the universal experience, life falls into an accidental pattern of choices and fates that could so easily have been otherwise.

A book group, however, goes deeper than an impromptu discussion of literature. A book group is a steady, ongoing process, whether the group lasts a month, a year, or a decade. A book group is not a classroom; there are no prerequisites or requirements. A book group is not therapy; there are no "adult children" there. An ongoing group has a history, a context for discussion, and a variety of viewpoints, explicitly welcomed, that impromptu discussion, even between good friends, often lacks. A book group is a kind of communion.

I am now a member of a book group that has been meeting once a month for three years. While my mother's group, which met for several years and is now defunct, was made up of friends who together selected the themes and authors they wanted to cover, my group is made up of relative strangers (at least, we were three years ago) brought together by a common interest in the theme of the group.

The group is sponsored by the Bookshop of the Minnesota Women's Press in St. Paul, where the store motto is *Book Groups Are Our Business*. Groups are designed around a theme or an author, and up to twenty groups may be running simultaneously. Any given group may be composed primarily of people who already know each other from previous Bookshop groups, but each new group is a kind of chemistry experiment. Will it work this time or not? Will we find communion?

The name of my group is *Meet a Woman Every Month: Biography, Autobiography, and Memoir.* I chose it because, at the time, I was unhappy with the order and shape of my life. I had recently graduated from college. I felt like I had been fired from my lifelong job, and in a sense I had been. Suddenly, I could no longer define myself as "student." What was I? In my choice of book group, I sought out models of women's lives. I sought perspective on the process of composing a life.

What did I find? Simone de Beauvoir's intense intellectualism and equally intense devotion to Jean-Paul Sartre. Janet Frame's lyrical memoirs of growing up in New Zealand. Virginia Woolf's development as a writer, as well as her eventual breakdown and suicide. Jill Ker Conway's evocation of the droughts of her childhood in Australia.

As a group, we meet these women every month. We pick over the revelation of their lives. We argue over them, often running long past our scheduled hours.

With ten other women I would not otherwise have met, I have sat at a table too small for all of us, hungry because I've missed dinner, bladder painfully full because I cannot bear to miss a minute of the conversation, and completely engrossed in a debate about whether Anne Sexton was mentally ill, and what this issue does to our reading of her poetry and her life.

We have all come to book group from different places, with different priorities and distractions. Our discussions are not always firmly fixed on the book in question. Barb piques our envy with her stories of frequent trips to the Tetons and Lake Superior. Patty entertains us with tales of her teenage daughters. Our facilitator, Glenda, tells us about the difficulty of putting her mother's affairs in order after her mother's death, and also about the birth of her first grandchild who is, to the joy of the whole group, a girl. We all have pieces of our lives to share, discoveries we make, and questions we pose to ourselves between meetings, month to month.

I have found my role models, my sense of perspective, my options. They are not, however, between paperback covers. They are sitting around a too-small table, arguing with me.

In the course of researching literary markets a few years ago, a few jobs ago, I discovered that women are twice as likely as men to be readers of literature. My own anecdotal evidence from participating in book groups, witnessing book groups, and talking to people about them suggests that women are not only more likely to read literature, they are also more likely to seek out the ways and means to discuss it. "More likely" does not even do the numbers justice. Book groups, forgive the generalization, are made up of women.

When my mother met with her peers once a month throughout my childhood, they must have found the intellectual stimulation that eluded them in other aspects of their lives. When I joined the Biography, Autobiography, and Memoir group three years ago, I was doing the same thing. Is it coincidence that these groups, founded twenty years apart in different cities and by different people, are both all-female? Or is there something hidden in the structure of book groups that attracts women and not men?

I wish I could say I knew why book groups do not attract men. I can't even say I know why they do attract women. I only know why they attract me.

I see a world in which girls have few role models of women who regularly talk to each other and enjoy one another's ideas and insights. Discussions between women are too frequently dismissed as gossip, kaffeeklatsch, girl talk—essentially, unimportant chatter.

I know women who have been accused of being lesbians, as if that were a crime, simply because they take pleasure in the intellectual company of other women. I know women who preface all of their thoughtful remarks with the phrase, "I'm not a feminist, but . . ." I know women who are uncomfortable having an intelligent conversation with anyone at all. According to the constructs of gender that invade our upbringing, it is not "feminine" to think.

During high school, I had a friend who always made extremely insightful comments in our advanced placement English class. But she made them while scrunching her perm with manicured hands. It was a distracting gesture, affected just before we started our senior year, and one that contrasted with her knowledgeable statements about Sylvia Plath and Emily Dickinson. She would open her eyes wide, pout a little, scrunch her curls, and say exactly what was on her mind.

The gesture was ultimately very effective. I cannot bring to mind now a single intelligent thing she said about the literature we were reading and discussing in that class. But I remember the perm.

I think about my high school friend when I go to book group. A member of my group once remarked what a relief it is to come to the Bookshop, to enjoy stimulating discussion without concern for anyone's hidden agenda, to leave her defenses at the door. But we have to pick them up again on the way out, collecting them the same way we collect our scarves and hats in the winter, vulnerable if we accidentally leave them behind.

When the chemistry experiment is successful and communion is achieved, group members have no need to couch their comments with an affected scrunch of the perm. And for many of us who have decided that the competitive coed classrooms of formal education had their time and place, which is now over and done, book groups are primarily *fun*. How many places can women be themselves, stimulate their minds, and relax?

A few years ago, my life took an unexpected turn. I started an independent graduate program in writing, and I was laid off from my job in the editorial department of a literary publisher. The graduate program I had been planning for, the layoff I had not.

Given the circumstances, I decided to scale back on my entertainment budget. The budget was already lean, and sadly, I cut my book group.

It was the only decision that made sense, I told myself. I could use the enrollment fee for other things, like groceries and books for school. And I might not have time to read books for group, since I was working my way through a thirty-title semester book list for school.

The semester was a lonely one. I enjoyed my schoolwork and my writing, but I had no regular contact with anyone but my partner. No coworkers, no companions to speak of, no book group. When I wasn't reading or writing for school, I tended to have involved discussions with my cat. It was embarrassing.

One afternoon late in the semester, I stopped in the Bookshop. Glenda was working at the front desk, and she told me the book group had asked about me. On impulse, I bought the book they were reading for the next month and said that I would attend the meeting. I hadn't been to a group in four or five months.

On book group night, the first Tuesday of the month, I arrived and was welcomed by my old companions and a few new people who had joined since my leave of absence began. We settled down to discuss Judy Chicago's *Through the Flower*. It was a heated discussion; half the group had loved the book, and half had hated it. I, normally quite vocal about my opinions, sat in near silence.

"What do you think, Robin?" Glenda finally asked.

"I think I've forgotten how to talk to people," I said lamely. It was true. I was woefully out of practice.

Book group lasts two hours, however, and by the end, the old chemistry had taken over, fueled by equal parts laughter and thought exchange. By the end, it was as if I had never left. Driving home that night after leaving the Bookshop, I felt the buoyancy of connection, of counterpoint.

Of communion.

PART II

Good Groups,
Plain and Simple

S ome book groups have an agenda—an oft-repeated reason for being and a book list that focuses tightly on a specific area of interest to the group. But plenty of groups have no special handle. They don't have an official leader. They don't read only one particular thing. They'll try almost everything. They are as they appear to be—pretty special after all.

The Oldest Living Book Group?

LEE VOEGTLEN   📖   INGLEWOOD, CALIFORNIA

WHEN I WAS YOUNG, a drama professor friend took me to visit a Shakespeare book group he'd been invited to address. The ladies read and discussed Shakespeare's plays, in rotation, over and over, year after year. It looked to my thirty-something eyes as if they could have been doing this for about 100 years—they were all so *old*.

That is how my own book group must now look to our occasional young visitors. We've been going for almost thirty-two years. Not only do we have two of the original members, but most of those who have joined since are our contemporaries. Most of us are not on-line. We do not watch *Oprah*, though we cheer the fact that she is reaching so many with her love of books. Still, our junior visitors do not seem to consider us archaic or fossilized yet.

In the fall of 1967, a fellow member of the Inglewood-Hawthorne chapter of the League of Women Voters mentioned that she had a problem: she loved to read but never knew *what* to read. It was a short step from there to deciding to start a book discussion group. At first we were all Leaguers, which guaranteed a certain level of brains, diligence, and discussion skills. At our very first meeting, our leader chose a book she said she'd always wanted to read, Jack London's *The Iron*

Heel. I remember it vividly because we hated it. Thus was born our first rule: the person who chooses a book must have read it first. Later, delightful but not really discussible books such as Gerald Durrell's *My Family and Other Animals* prompted another rule: the book must lend itself to discussion.

Another rule was broken only once, with mixed consequences: if one member objects very strongly to a book, we'll consider that a veto and choose another. That momentous exception occurred when one member thought it would be fun to read *The Bridges of Madison County* and discuss why we thought it had become so wildly popular. That seemed like great sport to us all—except to our founding mother. We were so noisy in our acceptance of the idea that we never even heard her objections. The results: it was the liveliest, most hilarious meeting we've ever had. The leader brought *Doonesbury* cartoons on the subject and other funny news items. But founding mother promptly dropped out and has never returned, though each year we send her a reading list and beg her to reconsider.

From the first, we have rotated leadership, a different woman each month; and, we have succeeded in preventing anyone from dominating the group, though founding mother tried, and I have been accused. We now meet ten months a year, though in the early days we met through the summer, choosing lighter or unusual genres such as children's books or poetry. When a new member is suggested, we invite her to visit, then decide if we'd like her to join. In our thirty-two years there has been only one real problem: a woman who behaved so aggressively, and so devoted herself to putting down that month's leader, our oldest member, that we called a hasty meeting in the garden to agree that she would never be invited again.

Although we tend to specialize in fiction, our reading has ranged widely. Once our topic was the world at the time of the battle of Blenheim. We read an assortment of books about Richard III and discussed whether he was guilty of the crimes imputed to him by his victorious successors, the Tudors. We read classics: *The Brothers Karamazov, The Scarlet Letter, Walden, Faust* (both Goethe's and Marlowe's). We've read Shakespeare, Woolf, Austen, Moliere, Chaucer,

Aristophanes, Brecht, Twain, Hardy, Machiavelli, Balzac, Conrad. We also read many recent books, as soon as they make it to paperback: *Angela's Ashes*, *The God of Small Things*, *Cold Mountain*, *Stones from the River*, *Snow Falling on Cedars*. We've read quite a few biographies and other nonfiction such as Desmond Morris's *The Naked Ape*. We had a speaker, a member's brother, on witchcraft. Nothing narrow-minded about us!

Our routine for many years has been this: in September we have a potluck luncheon to plan our year's books. We've progressed from throwing titles into the ring and deciding who'll lead what, to each person coming with the book she wants to lead, to our current attempt to have each member present three books and let the members vote on which one they'd most like to read. Since our active membership hovers around ten, this neatly produces a leader for each month. Ever since the day when the leader-hostess (me) left the room to get more popovers and returned to find the group discussing not Richard III but Ibsen's *Ghosts* (a transition accomplished in one minute flat), we have not met in the leader's home. Another shift from early days is that we used to vie with each other to bake the most delicious goodies. Now there may be only an occasional dish from the deli or the bakery; a certain amount of energy does leach out in thirty-two years.

In earlier years, we also had social events: dinners with husbands, a play matinee, a tour of Olvera Street—the original center of Los Angeles, a visit to the Will Rogers museum, Christmas lunch in a fancy restaurant. No more. But we did have a luncheon to celebrate our thirtieth year, and many former members returned for that reunion.

I'd like to think that our group, which has never had a name fancier than "Book Group," might endure for at least another thirty years, though it's unlikely that I'll be around that long as its record-keeper and mother hen. Then again, though by now most of us are senior citizens, not one member has died during all our years. Clearly, books are good for one's health.

For this group's reading list, see page 381.

Literature by the Lake

KATHARINE W. RICE   📖   CHAPPAQUA, NEW YORK

IT'S 10:00 A.M. ON a warm Friday morning in June and seventeen members of the Fairview Lake Book Group, all women, are meeting at the home of one of our members on the shore of a small lake in Pennsylvania. Today Lois is our hostess, and after we have spent some time drinking tea or coffee and chatting casually with one another, we move to a large round table on her deck. Kay, the coleader of our group, rings her school-marm bell, which she brings to every meeting, and everyone quiets down.

Before we begin our discussion of Katharine Graham's *Personal History*, which all of us read over the winter months, we update each other on any news of interest to all of us. A new grandchild has been born; one of our members is going into the hospital for surgery; there is a local craft show or movie that some of us might want to attend. Every meeting is an informal information exchange center.

By 10:30 we are ready to begin our book discussion, which rapidly becomes lively and, yes, loud. Since all of us have known each other well for years, no one is shy about speaking up, and no one is afraid to disagree with the coleaders or the majority of other members. It seems as if everyone is talking at once so Kay rings her bell and restores some semblance of order.

The opening questions at this meeting, as is often the case at our meetings, is, "Why was this book chosen?" Kay explains that it covers so much in one woman's story: her transition from a pampered life into the hurly-burly of business, the workings of the newspaper publishing industry, her troubled marriage, and her husband's mental illness. Our discussion ranges over all these topics and even touches on the photograph of Mrs. Graham on the cover. "She looks like a frightened rabbit," says Kay, "yet I think she had guts." Jan says, "I wouldn't want to have lunch with her because I would only learn what she would *want* me to learn." All in all, we think it was a good book, but two or three of us do not think it deserved a Pulitzer Prize. Barbara volunteers to show us a tape at our next meeting of Charlie Rose interviewing Graham.

At around 11:45 discussion time is over, and Gail offers to read aloud a chapter from a book different from that under discussion, something we do at the end of the meeting. A few years ago, we read aloud from an earlier edition of *The Book Group Book*, so that we would know what other book groups were reading and how other groups came into being. More recently, we've been reading from *The Diving Bell and the Butterfly* by Jean-Dominique Bauby. It's a small volume exquisitely written by a man as he lay almost totally paralyzed in a rehabilitation hospital in France. By noon our meeting is over.

Selecting the dozen or so books to be read each summer is a difficult job. Each year our coleaders explain that they don't want to pick a work that everyone will love unconditionally because then there is no interesting discussion. Occasionally we read a best-seller, but it's not selected for that reason. We try to avoid titles that appear on *every* book group's lists. Jan and Kay want to stimulate and stretch minds and imaginations. They want to challenge us in some way, so they choose books that will lead to heated discussions or books that are beautifully written though the stories they tell may be difficult or painful to read. Occasionally they select lighter fare, as was the case with *Under the Tuscan Sun* by Frances Mayes.

Jan and Kay read voraciously year-round, and they exchange books with one another, always asking, "Would this be a good one for our group to read?" More than once the two leaders have disagreed on the

value of a book—Anne Tyler's *Ladder of Years* is one—but they offered
it to our group anyway. The women in the group enjoy the friendly
fireworks as Jan and Kay defend their points of view!

The Fairview Lake Book Group began six summers ago at the suggestion of Jan who felt that tennis, bridge, sailing races, and social
gatherings were not intellectually stimulating enough for the women
who summered around the lake each year. She took her idea of a reading group to Kay who welcomed it with joy. Kay was already a member of two other books groups that met in the winter. After a few phone
calls to friends and acquaintances, twelve women signed up. The group
has now grown to twenty-seven. We have several career women in our
group: a librarian, a professor of biology, a physician, a resource teacher,
a systems analyst, and a psychotherapist. Many women give hours of
volunteer work in their communities. No one is ever turned away and
members seldom drop out.

From the beginning, we have felt that our group is unique since we
meet once a *week* rather than once a month as most groups do. Also,
we meet in the summer, from mid-June to mid-September. Some find
it taxing to read a book a week, so the complete reading list is mailed
to members in November, and most of us get a lot of the reading done
before June comes around. We can also ask our family members to
give us some of the books for Christmas. However, as a concession to
those who do all the reading in summer, our leaders try to choose books
less than three hundred pages long, and all books must be available in
paperback. Kay scours garage sales, library discard sales, and even
recycling centers for copies of books we'll be reading. She also belongs
to a library that permits older books to be taken out all summer long
on "vacation loan." We borrow books from each other, and any extra
copies are set out on a table at each meeting. No one is ever chastised
because she hasn't read the selection for that week. Houseguests of
members are always welcome at our meetings even if they haven't
heard about the book under discussion. If any of our selections have
been adapted for film, we rent and watch the movie; this does *not* take
the place of a regular meeting. We watched two versions of *Anna
Karenina* this way. The film version of *The Scarlet Letter* was so dread-
ful that it led to hoots of laughter.

During the first two years that we met, each meeting centered on an author rather than on one particular book, and as a result, our discussions had no focus. Now we all read the same book with an occasional exception when it comes to books of poetry. Each year from our inception, we have studied a poet, and we expect to continue doing this. We began with Anne Sexton, who was unknown to some in the group. Her strong confessional poems generated an exciting discussion. We went on in subsequent years to study Sylvia Plath, Elizabeth Bishop, Nikki Giovanni, Mary Oliver, Emily Dickinson, and Billy Collins. For a complete change of style, we read *Beowulf*.

A longer book, sometimes a classic, is selected to be read over the winter, and the first two sessions in summer center on discussing it. In this way we've read *Anna Karenina* (Tolstoy), *Madame Bovary* (Flaubert), *Of Human Bondage* (Maugham), *Angela's Ashes* (McCourt), and *Personal History* (Graham). Subject matter covers a wide range: novels, biography and autobiography, travel, psychology, short stories, and even juvenile fiction. One summer we pursued a theme, that of the woman who deserts her husband and family. Four of our selections that year were *Madame Bovary*, *The Awakening*, *Ladder of Years*, and—our first venture into drama—*A Doll's House*. At two of our meetings, we invited a local author to speak to us about her career. We hope to attract other authors to do the same.

Every two or three years, we each put five dollars in the kitty to cover postage and book purchases. However, we don't have an official treasurer. Our secretarial duties are performed by Kay's husband or by Gail. And Gail, an aficionado of the Internet, brings us interesting background on books and authors. Each letter or list that goes out to members includes an intriguing quotation on books or reading. For example, "A book is like a garden carried in the pocket" (a Chinese proverb) and "Anyone who can read can learn how to read deeply and thus live life more fully" (Norman Cousins).

Once every summer, members are asked to write down the titles of books they have read on their own that they feel should be considered for the following summer. Kay and Jan review these lists carefully, and then for the most part blithely ignore them! So far this has not resulted in any hurt feelings. Rather, the books chosen often earn the highest compliment, "I *never* would have read these on my own; thank you for deciding we should read them." Though some members approached a book on gender change (*Conundrum* by Jan Morris) with distaste, they later felt it opened their eyes and changed their attitudes. This inspired our leaders to continue to seek out books on controversial subject matter.

As for members themselves, we are in many ways a homogenous group. We're all between sixty and eighty years of age, college educated, married (two widows and one divorcée), almost all with children and grandchildren, all homeowners living less than two miles from each other in the summer, and all but a few have known each other for many years before the book group began. Yet at meetings, our opinions on books and authors are as varied as they could be, and discussions can be intense and sometimes hilariously funny as a result. No hard feelings have developed among us; on the contrary, the bonding among us seems stronger than ever.

Not everyone can make every meeting, but everyone who shows up makes every meeting worthwhile. Because our group has grown so large, outsiders sometimes suggest that we divide into two smaller groups; this idea always meets with vehement protests. The dynamics of our group work so well and the interaction between Jan and Kay—one cynical, outspoken, sometimes profane and the other gentler, more romantic—balances so perfectly that no one wants to change it.

We met during the summer of 2000, confident that our Fairview Lake Book Group will remain strong and very, very special far into the twenty-first century.

For this group's reading list, see page 349.

Too Busy to Read, or Why You Won't Find Any White Whales Around Here

RODD ZOLKOS   CHICAGO, ILLINOIS

OK, IN FAIRNESS to our book group, I begin this essay with a confession. The title is a lie. Oh, it was true once, some months ago when those words first took shape in that portion of my brain controlling the smart-aleck functions. They emerged as I considered our group for this essay, time and again returning to what frequently seemed our mantra—keep it short.

Back then the white whale seemed an impossible quest. To be sure, from time to time he'd venture near, coming almost within reach before sounding beneath the waves of fellow book group members' unenthusiastic responses and disappearing once again. How could they allow the leviathan to slip away, I wondered? Didn't they recognize how absolutely essential it was to overcome the monster and, in so doing, triumph over our own nature (if that's the interpretation you prefer). Cursed whale! Wouldst thou never taste the barbed steel of our group's keen insights?

"Hah!" you say. If my passion for the whale truly ran so hot, why not challenge him alone?

43

"Hound!" says I. "Would Ahab set out in a dinghy?" I think not. This manner of obsession demands company. Besides, the challenge fit well with our group's effort to diversify its readings—a look at our list showed a woeful lack of nineteenth-century American whaling novels.

No, to my mind, the white whale was a challenge best met as a group, and the only possible reason for our quaking at the sight of the great beast was the fear of its impressive bulk. And not simply a bulk measured by the number of pages, but the real heft given each page by a language thick with everything from pidgin English to the arcane lexicon of the American whaleman.

"It's too much," said some. "We have lives."

"But isn't book group a chance to improve those lives by allowing our minds to visit fantastic places and share all manner of magnificent experiences?" I asked. And what could possibly be more fantastic than cramming our minds together on the decks of a tiny, stinking, sailing craft bound on a three-year voyage with a crew whose goal was to wreak mayhem on the sea-going mammalian population only to become bit players in a ritual dance between a crazed captain bent on an unholy vengeance and the homicidal cetacean who'd prove his match?

Clearly, someday we must confront the whale together.

Lo, perhaps our hearty book group crew finally caught the fever of my obsession. Without so much as a single doubloon nailed to a mast— or our group's latter day equivalent, the promise of free beer to any who made the journey—the group agreed to take on Melville's *Moby Dick*.

Actually, I think the reason we finally took action lies in large part in a step our group made about a year ago. It followed an evaluation of where we were as a group and where we wanted to go, with much soul-searching over our future direction. And, indeed, whether there should even be a future.

Things had been getting a little ragged around the edges with our group. Meetings would change, months would slip by in which we wouldn't meet at all, and attendance was threatening to achieve that critical phone booth level. In assessing our status, some members wanted more structure, others more challenge. Ultimately, both were achieved, though the structure, I think, was key.

On a chart of organization types, our group would probably rank just a little north of anarchy. But over the years we've all kind of preferred it that way, picking one book and one meeting place at a time, with no leaders and no real rules (although reading the book is highly encouraged). And for a long time it worked, though as lives became busier and distractions became greater, it had grown obvious that a little bit of (trust me, I'm shuddering as I write this, just ask my loving spouse) "planning" was necessary.

Not too much, mind you. I think we stayed true to our scruffy minimalist roots even as we made two key planning decisions that seem to work well for us. First, we picked a regular evening each month that, with only the most extreme exceptions, is book group night—no questions, no arguments, no changes. Second, and probably more significantly, we took the radical step (for us) of choosing books and sites two months in advance.

Obviously, many book groups succeed quite nicely by planning their reading list a year at a time, and that's all well and good—for them. For whatever reason, I don't think anyone in our group would dare suggest we embrace planning in quite such extreme fashion. But, even at our group's most vibrant periods in the old, disorganized days, most everyone possessed of a life argued they didn't have time to read "long" books.

Now as I've alluded, my loving spouse, Kathy, herself a founding member of our group, has been known on rare occasions to take issue with what she considers my reluctance to "plan" more details of my life away from the workplace. The exception, she would allow in an irritated tone, being the odd tee time. Typically, I plead no contest, with but a plea for leniency based on days spent working in a highly structured, deadline-driven environment that prompts me to eschew planning to the extent possible in my social life.

That excuse doesn't cut it? You're right, your honor, and in fact I'll go so far as to allow that this little bit of extra planning by our book group is what made it possible for us to achieve something we couldn't in the past. Two months to read gave members the time to tackle something like *Moby Dick* and tend to their lives as well. Just as the *Pequod* would never set sail without its masters planning for the voyage by stocking it with casks of fresh water, barrels of salt pork, and plenty of extra canvas, so I can see where our chances of successfully navigating our group through more challenging books have been advanced by extending our planning an extra month down the road.

"Ah," you say, ready to guide sharpened steel to my analogy's hump, "planning ahead didn't save the *Pequod* or her crew when it took up with the white whale." Hey, I read to the end. I know what happened. And, while our group had a far better time of it with the whale than did the crew of that ill-fated Nantucket whaler, our encounter wasn't completely successful either. Not everyone showed up for *Moby Dick*, though I think planning a decade ahead wouldn't have been enough to prompt the no-shows to sign on to this particular voyage of obsession.

And, I think none the less of them for it. After all, more than one recent conversation with some of my most well-read coworkers went something like this:

Well-read coworker: Read anything good lately?

Me: Moby Dick.

Well-read coworker: The whole thing?

But at least with the advantage of the extra month, those who didn't make the journey were able to choose to miss the boat rather than have circumstance make the choice for them. And for the rest of us, it meant we could spend what all agreed was some quality time with old Moby, Ahab, Ishmael, and the rest of that wacky gang aboard the *Pequod*. And while nobody jumped up when the *Moby Dick* discussion ended on the suggestion to read *Ulysses* for the meeting two months hence, I believe our new format will lead us to tackle some works we might previously have dismissed as too challenging for busy sorts like us.

For those of us who made the trip, it was truly a voyage of discovery. Those who hadn't read *Moby Dick* before learned what all the fuss is about. We also learned a thing or two about whales. Most of all, though, we learned that massive works needn't be out of bounds for our group.

As for me, well, let's just say that if Kathy's eyeing the horizon for signs of my embracing planning, I'll spout this once. Planning works for our book group. It delivered us the White Whale.

Literary Lunch Bunch

BETTY KUHL   BAKER CITY, OREGON

OUR TOWN, Baker City, Oregon, population 9,500, is in the eastern part of the state. We are 300 miles from Portland and 120 miles from Boise, Idaho, so, except that we are on I-84, we are somewhat isolated. We make our livings ranching, lumbering, and working in federal offices, mostly the United States Forest Service and the Bureau of Land Management. Tourism is becoming more important with the renovation of our town's historic buildings and the sesquicentennial celebration of the Oregon Trail, which runs through our county.

Twenty years ago the American Association of University Women (AAUW) sponsored two book groups in our area. One group for working women who preferred contemporary fiction met evenings. After a few years this group disbanded. Our group, the second group, met with sack lunches at noon at the home of a special AAUW member, Leona Fleetwood. She had been a full-scholarship student at Washington University in St. Louis and had come west to teach school at some of the early gold-mining towns in our area. She later served as Baker City librarian for many years. She was confined to her home, and we were all happy to meet there because she was a fountain of knowledge about many things, especially literature. She had even introduced children's literature to many of our offspring through the puppet shows she professionally produced at the library each Saturday morning.

47

Our group chose an author each month and we would each try to read at least one book—but usually two or three—by him or her. We borrowed most books from the library, as there was no bookstore in the county at that time. Later, Leona and I and two other women opened a bookstore that still flourishes. Our library is wonderful though, and for years we had the honor of having the largest circulation of books per capita in the state. Some reasoned this was because of our long, cold winters; there was nothing to do but read.

We eventually opened the book group to others who weren't AAUW members, but we kept the membership at around eight. Only fourteen different women have belonged to the group, and we are now fairly constant with five old faithfuls, all in our early seventies. Others left town, Leona died, two lost their hearing, and three lost interest as we advanced toward more heavy reading.

After Leona died, we met in the library meeting room for several years. Interest waned and attendance was sporadic because we lacked the stimulus of Leona's leadership. Consequently, we started meeting in each other's homes. The hostess calls a few days in advance to remind us. It is unusual that anyone is missing, and we are always on time. Sometimes I feel we should take in a few more members, but right now we are such a congenial group, I hesitate to rock the boat. We certainly serve as a support group to one another, and we adjust our meeting dates to accommodate vacations, doctor appointments, and acts of God.

The hostess prepares coffee, tea, and a sweet treat, but we each bring a sack lunch. When I owned the bookstore and had to return to work at one, we usually all disbanded together at that time. Now that my daughter and her husband own the store, we often linger until two and find that the extra time provides more in-depth discussions and still allows lots of time to catch up on families, trips, and local current events.

Although we are compatible and good friends, chances are we will not see one another until our next meeting. We have a special intimate bond through our love of books and seem to prefer this exclusive association rather than expanding our relationship to other areas.

Contrary to one Baker City newcomer's statement that she was sure one could not find a single copy of *The New Yorker* in Baker

County, three of our book group members subscribe to it and often bring something from the current issue into the discussion.

One of our most remembered books was *The Aquarian Conspiracy* by Marilyn Ferguson. It was an inspiration to us all. Only half jokingly, we all expressed the belief that we had been living according to these theories and that is how and why we had come together in a book group. We have all been active in our community, supporting worthwhile endeavors and serving on numerous boards and committees. We have each lived here at least twenty years.

We have read a good share of the prominent women authors, both contemporary and classic. We have covered most of the western writers, especially admiring of Wallace Stegner and Vardis Fisher. We read poetry at least once a year; that is my favorite meeting. Because of all the material we receive at the bookstore, we are able to enjoy the *Bloomsbury Review* each quarter plus publishers' advance reviews.

We have expanded our horizons in our reading and have found new dimensions of exploring great works of literature. I am sure all of us would give up other pleasures long before we would abandon the Literary Lunch Bunch.

Thirty-Five Years of Treasures: Books and Friends

CAROLYN SOSNOSKI   📖   OLD LYME, CONNECTICUT

ON A SUMMER EVENING in the seventies, I took my two young daughters and a friend of theirs to book group at fellow member Sandy's home. The children played upstairs in the "mother-in-law" quarters that were unoccupied at the time. Downstairs we began our discussion of *One Flew over the Cuckoo's Nest* by Ken Kesey.

During the discussion one of our members excused herself to use the ladies' room. Suddenly, we heard shrieks of laughter. The woman emerged from the bathroom, in hysterics, and Sandy began to laugh, too. Then the three girls came pounding down the stairs, clamoring to know what was happening.

Sandy led them to the bathroom and showed them a hand mirror on the counter, with a note taped to it that read "Use it if you dare." She explained to the girls how Big Nurse in *One Flew over the Cuckoo's Nest* had used a hand mirror to check how well the patients had cleaned the toilet bowls. The note Sandy had taped to the underside of the rim of the bowl read, "I never thought you'd stoop so low" (in reverse printing, of course, so it came out right in the mirror).

Our book group has been going strong for almost thirty-five years. Paula, our acknowledged leader, and I met in fall 1964 through Paula's husband, John, when I had been a member of a great books discussion group at a nearby high school and John had taught that September in the adult education program. Paula and I were each expecting first babies, who turned out to be daughters born within a couple of weeks of each other in November.

During the early months of 1965, Paula and I visited each other for lunch or coffee. We compared notes on the babies, and also on what we had been reading. In June 1965, we each cornered a friend or two and gathered at Paula's home one evening to discuss two short stories, Faulkner's "That Evening Sun," and Jackson's "The Lottery." Much of our early reading was classical or "semiclassical." We read works by Shakespeare, Shaw, Ibsen, Flaubert, Dostoyevsky, Hemingway, Stendhal, and Camus. We were so excited about the book group in those early days that we wanted to meet every two weeks, but we soon realized that wasn't possible. We settled on once a month.

We each take a turn hosting the group in our home. A couple of members live quite a distance, and since it is not practical to travel to their homes, they bring refreshments to our Christmas meeting.

We generally have planning sessions about every six months. We are fairly informal about the process of choosing books. The person who suggests a book, which must be agreed upon by all members, becomes the leader of the discussion of that book.

The leader finds background material on the author and guides the group in analyzing the theme, style, and characters. She usually tries to find literary reviews to share with the group. Our oldest member, who is in her eighties, just loves reviews.

Sometimes our reading revolves around a theme. Many years ago, we used a newspaper column by Ellen Goodman as a guide for our summer reading. We read Mary Gordon's *The Other Side*, Sue Miller's *Family Pictures*, and Wallace Stegner's *Crossing to Safety*. Occasionally, our local libraries offer a series of discussions based on a theme such as family relationships. Some of us have participated in these discussions and have brought ideas back to our own book group.

For many years the August meeting of the book group was special. Paula's sister Joan, a professor of French and dean of freshman students at a local, private, liberal arts college, would lead the discussion. She'd suggest something ahead of time, often a play, and tell us which translation to get. Sometimes we were able to find the selection in our libraries, or she would put a number of copies on hold at the college bookstore.

When Joan was our leader, the discussion was more like a class. She had so many details and anecdotes to share. She had been to France many times and had seen performances of most of the plays done there in French. She had also taught the plays and stories to her college students, so she could anticipate the questions that we asked about the themes, characters, playwrights, and settings.

Joan died seven years ago. Her funeral at the college chapel was a celebration of her life. She had touched the lives of many. In our book group, we miss her immensely.

The December meeting is typically held at Sandy's; she has usually decorated for the holidays, and the refreshments are appropriate for a holiday gathering. We read poetry at this meeting. For a number of years, Sandy chose the poems and copied and distributed them to everyone ahead of time. Recently, group members have picked a favorite poem or two and have brought copies for everyone else. December meetings are always a festive and enjoyable time.

Mary is known as the member who calls the author to ask for an interpretation of the ending of the book. Many years ago we read a book called *Holdfast Gaines* by a local author. The conclusion was ambiguous, so Mary called the author. Ever since, when we can't agree on the meaning of something we are discussing, we suggest that Mary call the author.

When we read Rosalyn Carter's *Lady from Plains*, Mary wrote to Mrs. Carter and told her of our group's interest in her book, inviting her to our meeting. Mrs. Carter graciously declined, but wished us well, in a letter that we read at the meeting. Mary also is famous for dressing up as the gangster character Abbadabba Berman from E. L. Doctorow's novel *Billy Bathgate* when we discussed that book.

Our most recent meeting was held at the church that one of our members attends. Ann, a social worker, presented a video program on dealing with stress. It was a relaxing and helpful evening. We learned to see the absurdity in a difficult situation, to take ourselves more lightly, and to find some action to take. The video was based on a book by C. W. Metcalf and Roma Felible titled *Lighten Up: Survival Skills for People under Pressure*.

We have had three or four new members come into our group recently, bringing our numbers to twelve. Though it took the group a while to assimilate these new members, they added new ideas and dimensions to our discussions.

I've asked several group members why they think our group has managed to exist for so many years. No one is sure, but there are a few theories. Our original members were all at home with young children. And though we enjoyed the privilege of being full-time mothers and homemakers, we also enjoyed reading and craved more intellectual stimulation. Also, many of us were transplanted from our home cities or states. We were looking for new acquaintances and friends with the common interest of reading.

No doubt another reason for our longevity is that Paula is a strong but diplomatic leader who is liked and respected by all members of the group. She was an English major in college and has always been a voracious reader and is articulate in expressing her ideas. She also encourages others to express their opinions and makes sure everyone has a chance to speak. She has been a good role model for all of us and has encouraged us when we take our turn leading the discussion.

During the early years of the group, there were members who were looking for a purely social outlet. They lost the books, often didn't read them, or didn't do their "homework." They soon realized that this was not the group for them and dropped out of their own accord.

We have been supportive of each other in happy and sad events in our lives. We attended one member's retirement dinner a few years ago. Many of us attended the funeral for another member's husband a few months ago. We try to show that we care about each other, especially when we are experiencing illness or other trouble in our lives. Humor is undoubtedly another factor in our longevity. We laugh a lot and try not to take ourselves too seriously.

We have taken time to celebrate our years together. On our tenth anniversary, we had a special cake, and we have a photo of ourselves looking thin and tan and young. On our twenty-fifth anniversary, we had a potluck dinner at one of our member's homes. We invited past members to join us at that time, and many of them came and celebrated with us. I'll have to tell you about the thirty-fifth-anniversary celebration in another edition.

The Chapter Four Society

CINDY THELEN AND
DAVID VICK

WESTERN SPRINGS,
ILLINOIS

IT'S INTERESTING TO sense people's reactions when you mention that you belong to a book club. By their tone of voice or expressions, you know they are imagining a stuffy group of pseudo intellectuals discussing a dry piece of classic literature. Or they're flashing back to their English lit class in high school and wondering why any sane person would willingly re-create that experience as an adult.

Well, anyone attending one of our group meetings would very quickly have all of those stereotypes and images shattered. Our meetings are characterized by lively conversations (sometimes two or three going on simultaneously and almost always quite loud), food and drink (the more, the better), and laughter (lots and lots of it).

We started with a small group of friends gathered around a kitchen table four years ago. Our goals were simple—to read all of those books that, due to our busy schedules, we never seem to get around to; and, what's more, to discuss them with others who were reading them at the same time. Today the group has grown to twelve members (off and on) and still includes the original founding members. Most of the group lives in the Chicago area, but we communicate via mail, telephone, and taped messages with a member who has relocated to Colorado.

We began the group with one premise—the only rule would be that we all read whatever book was chosen, whether or not it's a book we think we're going to like. This premise still serves as our guiding foundation. It broadens our reading horizons and helps us to discover new authors, genres, and subject matters that we may not have considered in the past. As we have discovered along the way, some of these choices (though certainly not all) turn out to be treasures.

This rule also helped us choose our name. In the first year, one of our selections was Stephen Hawking's *A Brief History of Time*. (Yes, we were *really* looking to expand our horizons with that choice.) Since this book covers subjects ranging from black holes in the universe to quantum physics, it can become complex, especially for nonscientists. Each member, charged with the responsibility of completing the book, diligently attempted to grasp the concepts described by the author. We read and reread chapters, trying to understand. The shortest chapter in the book—chapter four—was the most confusing to us. To some, this was the point at which they gave up their quest for an in-depth understanding of physics. When we conceded that chapter four had beat our book group, we rewarded the victory by taking its name.

The strength of the Chapter Four Society lies in the diversity of its members. The society is made up of women (two-thirds) and men (one-third), single and married, with children and without, with differing levels of formal education, and of various occupations and religious and political views. Most of the members originate from the Chicago area, but several have been transplanted from other locations, including three who were born abroad.

The relationships among the members vary; the founding members have been good friends for a number of years. New members are recruited from coworkers, friends, acquaintances, and relatives. We have tried to limit the number of active members to about a dozen, so that we have a manageable number for a meaningful discussion. Some particularly enthusiastic members started by reading the books before they were officially invited to join the group.

The requirements for joining the Chapter Four Society are few but important. You have to be able to follow (and participate in) at least two or three conversations at once, you have to laugh, and you have to respect the book selections of other members.

The logistics of our group are fairly straightforward. We rotate the honor of selecting the book each month. Originally, this rotation schedule was based on when a member joined, with new members moving to the end of the list. Currently, we set a selection schedule for the year at the January meeting. This way we know when each member will choose for that year, but each book is not announced until the end of the previous month's meeting. January's book is usually decided by a group vote (or *voot grope*, as it has come to be known after a meeting at which a particularly potent sangria was served). We never limit ourselves to a certain type of book—anything goes. We simply have decided to respect the decision and recommendation of the person making the selection.

Our meetings are held on the third or fourth Friday evening of each month, eleven times a year (we usually skip the end of December due to the holiday). The member selecting the book hosts the party. This changing location eliminates the possibility of the group being a burden for anyone and adds a bit of fun. The host decides the evening's fare, which can range from chips and pretzels to a full meal. Theme food, such as carrot cake for *Watership Down* or Milky Ways and Starbursts for *A Brief History of Time*, is sometimes served. Typically, we have several appetizers, drinks, more drinks, dessert, and coffee. Most hosts have gotten the message that good food and, more important, a variety of beverages are the key. Our group has even become beer connoisseurs, with stern glances given to the host serving only domestic lite.

The evening begins with social time—somewhat unnecessary as this group is characterized by being social at all hours. When we get around to discussing the book (and so far we always do . . . eventually), we begin with a prediscussion rating where each member assigns the book a rating of one to four. Loosely defined, one is poor, two is fair, three is good, and four is excellent. We've had numerous conversations about the rating system—how each person interprets it, whether it has any value, whether we need both pre- and postdiscussion ratings, whether we can give fractional or zero ratings. In any case, it works for us as a good starting place for discussion.

The format and structure of the discussion are up to the hosting member. Some hosts choose to provide biographical information about the author or historical information about the time period; others describe the reason for their selection or provide current media information on the subject. Sometimes we just launch right into the discussion. The Society is flexible and creative as to the style of the discussion. There is a conscious attempt to allow each member to express his or her opinion. But sometimes emotions reach a fever pitch, with side discussions and shouts erupting from all points in the room. Our out-of-town member is then left with a tape recording that could be mistaken for the trading floor at the Chicago Board of Trade.

The topics discussed are as varied as the subject matters of the books and the members themselves. For some people, the characterization in books is very important. Could they identify with any of the characters? Did they care about what happened to them? For others, the setting may be important. Did the author paint a picture of the locations? Were physical scenes described so that you felt like you were there? Others focus on how the book made them feel. Did it have an impact on their lives? Did it make them think or feel differently about anything? Could they identify with a particular moral/ethical dilemma? Sometimes, our discussions have zeroed in on the author's style, including everything from point of view to word choice. Some members prepare discussion materials prior to their arrival. We've seen everything from pop quizzes to genetic charts of the characters. We've even had discussions about the artwork on the cover and the size and format of the book. (Did you know that *Einstein's Dreams* fits perfectly into an overcoat pocket and even has a built-in bookmark?)

After it appears that all opinions have been exhausted (anywhere from thirty minutes to three hours later), each member gives a post-discussion rating. We record these ratings in the Society's archives as a history of the group's opinion of the book. This is definitely not an exact science (how does one compare Sidney Sheldon with Shakespeare?), but it does preserve the group members' feelings at the time the book was read and discussed. The idea of the pre- and postratings is to measure how a member has gained (or lost) appreciation for a book after discussing it with others. Recently, along with the postdiscussion rating, we also have begun to ask each member to assign a word or phrase that best describes his or her feelings about the book.

After our discussion, we usually continue to socialize as we eat more dessert. Sometimes, we veer off into other activities (depending upon how tired and/or silly we are). One night we decided to write a novel (we have written the first few paragraphs and have outlined more); another night one of our members gave us an art lesson; on another occasion we watched the video of the movie version of our current book. Sometimes the host just can't get rid of us!

At each meeting, everyone contributes two dollars to the Society's treasury. These payments accumulate and at the end of the year we vote on a charitable organization to which we'll donate the money. Past recipients have included a local hospital, which purchased books for its children's ward, and an inner-city music school, which purchased music books. Our goal is to share our love of reading with those who may not be able to afford it.

As with most groups, the Society has suffered its share of growing pains. We have gone through periods when attendance has been low and too few members have completed the book to have a meaningful discussion. For us, the keys to surviving these troubled times have been persistence and a spark. A spark can be the introduction of new members to replace those who, due to busy schedules and flagging interest, can no longer make a commitment to the group. New members add a whole new dimension to the group dynamics, and often offer opinions that may not have been previously expressed. Also, current members feel a renewed sense of dedication when it's the first discussion for a new member.

Another area that the group is constantly working through is the members' differing needs for structure and control. We have had many debates about the structure of the group itself, including, but not limited to, topics such as discussion guidelines, agendas, rating systems, what should be included in our archives, who keeps the archives, whether we need archives, how books are chosen, when books are chosen, how new members are chosen, do we need a set of bylaws, who prepares the next newsletter, and do we need a newsletter.

Often, we have basically agreed to disagree. That is, we are all aware that each person has different needs in these areas. Some members would prefer to operate completely informally, with absolutely no structure; others like the idea of having bylaws, agendas, minutes, officers, and specific discussion outlines. Since this is an example of the very diversity we claim to value, we have agreed to leave it up to each member to do whatever he or she wants when hosting the meeting. This way, each member can have his or her needs fulfilled at some point during the year, and we can all look forward to variety in the format, as well as the content of each discussion.

Our list of books is, well, eclectic. It includes classics, modern fiction, and some nonfiction. We have experimented with different genres, such as short stories and plays. Some of the best discussions have been on books that have engendered widely differing opinions, such as *The Painted Bird* (ratings ranged the full gamut, from zero to four, on this one) and *Frankenstein* (pro creature vs. pro doctor). The topics suggested by some of the books discussed have included good versus evil, the nature/existence of a supreme being, equal rights, sex, power, domination, survival, racism, stereotypes, alcoholism, addiction, metaphysics, and the meaning of life. I guess it's easy to see why some discussions get a little heated!

Our advice to those of you looking to start or join a book club is simple. You need to keep only three things in mind: respect, diversity, and laughter. If the members truly respect one another, they will listen with an open mind to divergent opinions and read new and different books; it will be a true learning experience for everyone. If members are diverse—whether in gender, age, occupation, religion, ethnic background, life experiences—you will all benefit. And laughter is definitely the key.

Belonging to a book club can be one of life's most enjoyable experiences. Our members truly care about one another and have a good time because they feel free to be themselves. I'm sure these are the reasons our group has thrived for so long.

The Chapter Four Society is approaching its tenth anniversary. As we continue to grow and learn, we know that our diversity and commitment will take us through our first decade and into the next century.

For this group's reading list, see page 367.

Double Dipping

BARBARA BERNSTEIN   BOWIE, MARYLAND

IT WAS NOT predictable from my earlier years that I would become a book club member. A slow reader, I shied away from courses requiring a lot of reading. I was always more comfortable with calculus and statistics than with metaphors and imagery. However, I do love the power of words, so when a friend who lives thirty minutes away told me she was forming a book club, I asked if I could join. It opened up a new world to me. In fact, I enjoyed the book club so much that I told my local friends about it and many of them wanted to join too. When schedules conflicted, my neighborhood friends and I formed a separate book club. As you can see, then, I'm a double dipper.

It's interesting to compare my two book clubs. The group that I originally joined generally meets in Takoma Park, Maryland, where most of the members live. It's a liberal-oriented group of about ten women, all of whom have families and most of whom work part or full time. We read mainly good-quality modern fiction but also some nonfiction. We meet in peoples' homes over drinks and light refreshments. Most everybody reads the book and we stay on topic and discuss it for a good portion of each meeting.

My neighborhood book group is centered in Bowie, Maryland. We meet at a restaurant and have dinner while we chat. There are only about seven of us, but our tastes are more diverse, so we read a wider range of books. If we can't agree on a book, we sometimes read whatever we want and then have show-and-tell at the next meeting. This way introduces us to a lot of new possibilities for reading. Once we all saw a movie and discussed it rather than reading a book. Most of us have families with kids still in school and most of us are or have been educators (I was formerly a math teacher), so we talk a lot about local education issues. Often, at least one of us hasn't read the book, and once or twice we talked so long about other things that we didn't get around to the book at all. Nonetheless, restaurant book club discussions have certainly been fun. For example, sometimes everybody in group hasn't read the book, but the waitress has. As a matter of fact, we've gotten some pretty good book suggestions from waiters and waitresses.

An important decision in any book club is the method of book selection. At times this is a difficult matter, fraught with the necessity of compromise and cooperation. Both of my book clubs tend to select books by consensus. But people sometimes have different ideas on how a consensus should be achieved. For example, should one individual have veto power if she really dislikes a book that is suggested? Somehow, both groups reach a decision in a friendly way without formal rules.

Once books are chosen, read, and discussed, someone has to keep a list of books read. I keep ours. It started out as a simple reading list, but it eventually turned into a scrapbook that includes pictures of meetings or events that we celebrated together (birthdays, baby showers). This has proven to be a great way to jog our memories on what we've read and what we've done.

A book club is a special kind of group, composed of people who need to be great listeners. It's essential to respect different points of view in a book discussion and in my groups, we often agree to disagree. We reveal a lot about ourselves through the book discussion and sometimes it's surprising what we learn. For example, we discussed *Before and After* by Rosellen Brown, a novel in which a teenage boy is suspected of murder. The book presents an illuminating look at the very different reactions of the boy's mother and father. In essence, the mother hides nothing and seeks the truth, while the father wants to protect his son at the possible expense of truth and justice. As our discussion began, we went around the circle and talked about how we thought we'd react in the same situation. I thought most of the members would put family loyalty and protection over truth and justice. To my surprise, we were pretty evenly split.

I have found that books that are best for discussion are not necessarily the best books. That is, a book that everyone reacts to the same way, even if we all loved it, doesn't always stimulate a dynamic discussion. Good discussions tend to arise either when there is a difference in our perceptions of the book and the characters or when the book touches on topics related to our own lives. Reading is enriching precisely because it enables us to experience a different life, and yet also allows us to recognize what that life has in common with our own.

Some books have prompted particularly interesting discussions. *City of Joy,* by Dominique LaPierre, looks at the poorest of the poor in Calcutta, India, where such people live in slums, in the direst of circumstances, experiencing constant hunger, and often dying from exposure to all kinds of diseases including leprosy and tuberculosis.

Another fascinating book was *Home Fires* by Donald Katz. This is a sort of literary equivalent to the TV show *An American Family*, which aired twenty years ago and looked at the daily life of the Loud family. In *Home Fires*, Katz interviewed family members and friends to provide a detailed, nonfiction account of the Gordon family, where the children came of age in the sixties. Since most of our book club members also grew up in the sixties, we could relate to many of the themes and events in the book and we had a lively discussion.

A novel that prompted a good discussion and opened our eyes to something we hadn't thought much about was Joanne Greenberg's *Of Such Small Differences*. This profoundly sensitive story deals with people who are deaf, blind, and unable to speak.

We also read Walker Percy's *The Thanatos Syndrome*, which is about a psychiatrist who notices changes in the behavior and demeanor of nearly everyone in town. Ultimately, he uncovers a criminal plot involving psychoactive drugs that were put in the town's water supply. This story provoked considerable discussion because the changes in the behavior and mood that the doctor observed were in many ways for the better. We talked about the risks and the benefits of the increasingly common use of antidepressants. We even kicked around the questions of whether drugging a city's water supply might cut down on crime. Could this be justified ethically if done with full disclosure?

Another book that made for good discussion was *When Nietzsche Wept* by Irvin Yalom. It is a purely fictional account of how psychotherapy might have developed if Friedrich Nietzsche had met Sigmund Freud and his associate Joseph Breuer in the late 1800s. This book powerfully conveys what the interpersonal emotional process of psychotherapy feels like. It is especially interesting because of the real historical figures and events involved and because many book club members are in the helping professions (social worker, nurse, psychotherapist).

I could go on. After all, between my two book clubs, we've read and discussed a large number of books—too many to mention here. But be assured, all of the books on my book clubs' reading lists have enriched my life twice over—once in the reading and then again in the rehashing. There I go, double dipping again.

For this group's reading list, see page 239.

Four Women Reading

EDIE JAYE COHEN, SHELLEY ROSE, RITA WUEBBELER, AND LANE RAPPAPORT

ATLANTA, GEORGIA

OUR READING GROUP, which is small, is, as Lane Rappaport describes below, like a "well-made patchwork quilt." Like panels in a quilt, each of the four women in our group seems similar on the surface. However, a closer look shows our subtleties; each woman is unique, her voice strong and distinct. The following essays represent four voices; each reveal how snugly the years have stitched us together.

Edie Jaye Cohen: The book group is the longest committed relationship I have been in as an adult. Four women comprise our group: two straight, two lesbians. Two of us are Jewish. Two of us are native southerners, and one is German. All of us are well traveled. Our age difference spans a mere decade, with three of us clustered in our midthirties. We are all feminists, and our desire to read books by or about women brought us together.

What has happened over the years, however, is that while the books remain our reason for meeting, we have become the story. Over simple meals or elaborate hors d'oeuvres, in one living room or another, through every season, ours are the stories we tell first, and I believe ours are the stories we come to hear. During a conversation one day, Rita commented that we had all been witnesses to a lot in each other's lives, and I was struck by that truth.

Over the years, the book group has alternately been for me a source of joy and ambivalence, and at times I have wanted to withdraw, not always finding there the sustenance I sought. I never have withdrawn or spoken of it, and now as I think of Rita's words and the three women with whom I share this experience, I know why: from one book group meeting to the next, we have chronicled our journey together from youth into maturity.

At some point years ago, we began bringing each other a bookmark from our travels. Before beginning any new book, I sort through my bookmarks and pick the one I believe will complement the story I am about to read. The connection is unclear, yet a relationship develops. The relationship consists of a story, a listener, and a means of marking place. The relationship I have to these three women is much the same. We are the story, and like a bookmark in a book, the book group marks our place in the passage of our lives together.

Shelley Rose: Our book group first got together in January 1988. I had just read Sonia Johnson's book *Going out of Our Minds*, and I was so moved, confused, inspired, and activated that I needed to talk to others about the book. I invited (nagged) three friends to read the book and invited them over to discuss it.

We sat in front of a fire on the living-room floor with munchies and wine and had a wonderful, several-hours-long discussion. Topics from the book led us in numerous directions and our conversation branched off onto one road after another.

We all left that evening feeling so warm, close, and stimulated. We knew before the evening ended that we had to do it again. We set the next date and decided that each of us would bring prose or poetry to read aloud and share with the group.

More than a decade later, we are still at it. Meeting every four to six weeks, we easily reach consensus on a book to read. Book group feels as much like a support group as a reading group now. It is special time set aside to be with this group of women. Occasionally someone may not finish a book; sometimes we barely discuss the book. But, I always look forward to the time set aside for book group. If nothing else, it provides me with the reason I need to ensure that I read at least one book a month.

Rita Wuebbeler: Having left my native country of Germany eight years ago to live and work in the United States, I often long for the feeling of having a family. The book group is part of my new American family that gives me support and nurturing. This occurs not only in the mental sense but in the physical one as well, since one of our book group rituals is sharing a small meal together at the beginning of each meeting.

More important than the physical nurturing is the mental support and inspiration we give to each other. During the course of our existence, two of us have opened our own businesses (one selling bookmarks), one has found an editing job that she enjoys, and the fourth one is directing a regional arts advocacy organization that all of us support. One of us has bought a house, one has sold one, and two have moved to new apartments and/or houses. We have taken trips together and held book group meetings at the beach and in the mountains. We have shared friends in far away countries ("Why don't you stay with my old friend in England on your next trip?") and have been witnesses to each other's breakups and new loves.

The book group has made us a deeply bonded quartet that loves to read and share books, ideas, stories, and bookmarks, which we bring to each other from our journeys. And each bookmark represents a piece of the colorful tapestry of our lives woven into each other.

Lane Rappaport: Our small reading group can be described as a well-made patchwork quilt. We represent a hodgepodge of backgrounds and patterns that bring a richness to our discussions. Incorporating a true sharing of information, ideas, activities, and valued friendship, our group is unique. We are an interesting, supportive, energetic, cerebral, vibrant, vocal, and individualistic group of women, and we enjoy our time together very much.

Because of our stability, a definite community spirit exists. We perform various activities to enhance that community spirit and select books that help us understand more about the world and its people. For example, we made a weekend vacation from the idea of meeting in another city. We packed our bags and traveled to Florida. Besides enjoying the sunshine, the sea, and the beach, we thrived on the camaraderie of sisterhood.

Our book choice that month was *West with the Night* by Beryl Markham. Markham wrote autobiographically about her experiences in Africa and her solo flight across the Atlantic Ocean, from east to west (the first completed flight). It was an inspiring book filled with adventure and suspense. In a way, her book was symbolic for our reading group since we made an adventure that weekend. Perhaps soon we will truly make a patchwork quilt including squares of our book list titles.

For this group's reading list, see page 391.

The Carlton Book Club

DARWIN STEED   TORONTO, ONTARIO, CANADA

THE CARLTON BOOK CLUB got its start, quite by accident, in a bar *on a dark and stormy night*. A discussion of Irish writing had been engendered by the consumption of three pints of Guinness each and by Eugene Beggs, who carried a copy of *Finnegans Wake* in his briefcase, and who pulled it forth to demonstrate that the book had to be read aloud to make sense.

He was right. *Listening* to Joyce's writing we understood much more of what he was trying to communicate. We had so much fun taking turns reading that we decided to meet some weeks later and read more of the book. By the third meeting, one of our members (there were five of us to begin with, which soon grew to nine—all men) suggested we investigate another author. We settled on Jonathan Swift and took turns reading our favorite sections aloud. Soon we had covered *Gulliver's Travels*, and, by the fifth and sixth meetings, *The Horse's Mouth* by Joyce Cary and *The Third Policeman* by Flann O'Brien.

Toward the end of the first year a woman asked to join and almost all the men showed enthusiasm for taking the group out of its male-only confines. Soon a few other women indicated a willingness to be part of the group and the membership grew rapidly to what is now seventeen in total—ten men and seven women. Our occupational makeup is interesting. We've got an accountant, an animator, an architect, a TV writer (children's programming), a copywriter, an environmental geologist, a renovator, a lawyer (it's surprising to me that we have only one lawyer in the group), two doctors (one a dermatologist, one a general practitioner), a computer technologist, a homemaker, a hotel interior designer, a bartender (from the bar where we started), a hairdresser, and a teacher. We're now nearing the end of our second year and the club still meets in bars, but only those where we can commandeer a semiprivate room. Some of the group (the women) have pushed us (the men) into exploring the work of women authors and after reading *Mansfield Park* by Jane Austen, we tried some contemporary (and to be patriotic) Canadian authors. We settled on *Teaching Pigs to Sing* by Cordelia Strube and liked it so much that we went to her next book, *Dr. Kalbfleisch and the Chicken Restaurant*. We tried, and liked, *All the Anxious Girls of the Earth* by Zsuzsi Gartner, but the opinions were mixed on *The Love of a Good Woman* by Alice Munro.

Our attendance averages only about sixty percent, though our members are genuinely enthusiastic and the group is united by its common dislike of television (some don't even own one). Most of us work with computers in our professional lives and are reluctant to spend yet more time staring at the Internet even in search of new reading material. This begs the question: where then do we find our books?

Not from Oprah, whose choices some of our members have sampled and found rather simple minded. And not from bestseller lists, which include too many books that we haven't found challenging enough. Instead, new book possibilities are found by our members perusing reviews in book periodicals (the *Times Literary Supplement*, for example) to which some of them subscribe, and from word of mouth. Don, the hotel interior decorator, travels a fair bit and is in the habit of asking people what their favorite novel is. This is how we discovered *The Horse's Mouth* by Joyce Cary and *Nostromo* by Joseph Conrad, which we are now reading.

To anyone wishing to start a book club, I can easily recommend doing so in a bar. As the Irish discovered early on, a glass or two loosens the tongue and gets the gab flowing. But members should be flexible and prepared for change. Our club has gone from being a men's group to being one that embraces both sexes and is much more focused on finding and sharing good writing and less on getting pissed. Though we still meet in bars, the consumption of alcoholic beverages has declined significantly. (Two of the original members have dropped out, however, citing a "loss of focus.") I, for one, welcome these changes. The truth is, rather too much beer was consumed during those early *Finnegan* weeks.

PART III

Groups with a Twist

Some book groups are unabashedly special interest. They may read only nonfiction, or only fiction by gay men, or they may restrict membership to feminist women. Some have less formal agendas and probably wouldn't identify themselves as special in any way. But when you read about and visit as many book groups as I have, you begin to see that some groups really have stretched in an attempt to meet members' needs. These special-interest groups are flexible, not restrictive. You want to read only one book? Step right up, we have a book group and author for you. You want to inoculate yourself against the Gantt Charts, cubicles, and bottom lines of your corporate life? Read on for instruction on how to start a subversive book group.

And Then I Read . . .

JADE14BOOK AS TOLD TO F.R. LEWIS   ALBANY, NEW YORK

MY SCREEN NAME is jade14book and I am a bookaholic.

Recently, an on-line book group read *The Bachelor Brothers Bed and Breakfast*, written by Canadian humorist Bill Richardson, and narrated alternately by a pair of bachelor brothers. It included notes from satisfied customers, the "gentle and bookish, and ever so slightly confused" who shared a bit of their lives, reading and real. After the initial flurry expressing love or boredom, group members found not too much to say, and chat drifted to books they were reading, stuff their kids were getting into, what the job was like, places they wanted to visit. Not convinced it was imaginary, some planned to track down and visit the bed and breakfast.

Pleasant little thing, this book—jolly, all agreed, but not the best choice for chat: there was simply nothing much to talk about. This was true enough, though the reason had less to do with the book than with the nature of the group attempting discussion. Viewed from the proper angle, the ardent readers gathered in squares of white space on computer screens all over the U.S. of A. could easily be sheltered guests of the bachelor brothers.

Flash back to late fall, 1997: newly on-line, in my clumsy, uncybernated way, I happened upon a site called Book Central and discovered I had landed in the Eden of book chat. (A more appropriate comparison than I realized at the time.) I meandered Book Group Message Boards A–B, C–G, H–L, M–R, S–Z. I scrolled past too-cute names nested among the *B*s; a group called Contemporary Fiction, with its suggestion of too much currentness to accommodate my usual reading habit (two to three years behind); most of the genre and single author groups (no predicting what this might do to one's own writing); and the self-help and religious. I landed eventually in my cup of broth: Literary Fiction.

When I arrived on the scene, the group was voting its winter schedule. Could I resist a title like *American Tabloid*, even though it was written by an author whose name was unfamiliar to me? Did I not want to read the most recent Anne Tyler, which by happy coincidence I had purchased the previous winter at a used bookstore in Florida?

Such are the pleasures—two of them at any rate—of on-line book chatting and commentary: keeping up with old favorites and tasting the new and often delicious. And, for she who has the disposition of an ingrown toenail, there is the added pleasure of human contact minus human presence, an experience that bears vague resemblance to having characters who come alive in your head take over the story.

Curiosity got the better of me and, after setting myself up with Literary Fiction (which later joined forces with Contemporary Fiction to become Currents and Classics), I rambled the index. A group called Oprah and More (OAM) read the Oprah picks and general fiction. When I came upon it, the group was engaged in marathon conversations on Toni Morrison's then-new novel, *Paradise*, with a group called Book Bunch. Each group hosted two chats, each pair chats on half the book. Hotly contested were the roles of writer and reader. While publicizing the novel, Morrison took the position that writers write and readers read, making the search for meaning collaborative. Several folks objected vehemently and often to the author's refusal to interpret the book for her audience.

Hotly contested topics can bring out the best or the worst, depending on the skills and intentions of the leader. While one leader may bristle at the mere suggestion of agreement with Jill Ker Conway's view that memoirs are the fiction of the 1990s, another—expert, as she or he is expected by the community coordinator to be, at "smiling from the wrists down"—will see that no one's contribution is belittled. That is, the range of person-to-person contact begins to look a lot like life.

As one leader explains, "Basically I just try to be welcoming and make everyone feel like they matter to the group. I hated it in other groups when I would post and no one would respond. Made me feel like an outsider. I wanted OAM to be a fun cyber-escape." A good on-line leader, she says, is like any good leader: "fair, organized, kind, and with a personality that is strong but not overbearing."

In general, readers meet every two weeks to chat about a book. The best chats usually include about ten or twelve readers. As the leader of New England Reads (NER) points out, a handful of eager "voices" communicating their excitement for and joy in reading can make an hour hum; but more than twenty-five can buckle the walls.

Too many is not usually a problem, however. Typically, groups nominate and vote on titles to be discussed over a three-month period. But, asks the NER leader, "who can guarantee the book a member nominates in October will be the book a member will want to read or talk about in December?"

To lure readers to chats—and to keep nonchatters connected— most leaders send reminders and produce monthly newsletters. Sometimes newsletters cross-pollinate. The Pulitzer Prize–group newsletter always includes a listing of other groups reading PP-winning books and authors. Reflecting her passion for discovery and her delight in sharing, the Literary Adventures leader produces a veritable news- paper, complete with photographs, and brimming with historical, biog- raphical, and literary information, as well as Web links.

Message boards can also be the major group venue for sharing books and lives. In fact, conversations are a minute-by-minute occur- rence on some message boards. The tendency seems to be to read and write quickly, and that haste sometimes raises hackles. Anyone who par- ticipates needs not only to maintain a sense of humor but also to be somewhat circumspect about exercising it. As is true with the reading experience in general, we do not all bring the same experience nor read from the same point of view.

The Red Dog Salon was a hangout for the intelligentsia: they read poetry, French novels (in translation), and eschewed chats. Except for the occasional author visit, that is. This short story writer was captivated by Jim Shepard during a talk about process and story. Shepard wrote the novel *Nosferatu* and the short story collection *Batting Against Castro*.

Over my not-quite two years on-line, I have become a surfer of sorts. I convinced myself that this practice would encourage me to read my Alp-sized to-be-read pile of books down to manageable proportion. (Right. Sure. Uh-huh.) Although in 1998 I devoured more than two hundred volumes and reread a bunch more, I've been buying faster than I've been reading and I'm reading as fast as I can. Now, if I eliminated those trips to the public library. . . No! Never!

In June of 1999, Book Central ceased to exist on AOL. But such was the original sponsor's devotion to reading and readers that the site did not come down until Eden had moved west, adopted by Oprah. If you happen to be in the neighborhood, be sure to stop in at the Short Story Group. Despite my usual reluctance to engage in any activity that requires ongoing cheerfulness, there I will be: jade14book, committed co-leader.

For this cyber-reading list, see page 287.

Throw the Book at Them

JEAN R. TROUNSTINE   TEWKSBURY, MASSACHUSETTS

THERESA CAME UP to me after the first class and took off her baseball cap. "Thanks," she said, somewhat sheepishly, digging her foot into the floor, her eyes fleeing my face. "I liked the stories." We were an odd couple: me, a college professor carrying briefcase and books, and she, unemployed, a former addict and alcoholic, recently sentenced to literature and probation instead of prison. We stood together for that moment, not in a courtroom, but in the president's office at a community college where I taught. Theresa had just completed her first seminar in Changing Lives Through Literature, but she wasn't ready to go.

"What did you like about the stories?" I asked her, equally unsure of my footing, trying to read her desire to lag behind the others who had already left the classroom.

Snapping her hat back on her head, she looked up and smiled. "Those women. I'm surprised that I liked them because they're like me."

I continued to think long and hard about Theresa's comment as I drove home that evening, considering the six women I had just met. One lived nearby, but five had come twenty miles by van from a neighboring city in Massachusetts to Middlesex Community College in Lowell. Women without much formal education, without transportation or support, they had been arrested over and over, been in and out of jail. They came armed only with hope. They had a desire to try once

79

and for all to find a way out of crime through a deceptively simple program that I had the nerve to think might actually do what it advertised:
change their lives.

I was no stranger to this population. I had worked in Massachusetts
prisons for the past seven years, creating a drama program that had
taught me the power of the arts and humanities to transform lives. I had
seen women, illiterate and insecure, become alive on stage. One key
had been to help them create characters that used parts of themselves.
Another was providing challenging literature that they felt was beyond
their grasp. To make what was impossible, possible—that was my goal.

But here I was, trying another program, one I was beginning, in
many ways like Theresa, for the first time. I had seen up close how
our prisons are burdened by expense and repeat offenders. I had seen
how many criminals are warehoused rather than trained or educated,
how good programs are few and far between. I yearned to find out if
I could make a difference with these women on probation. I had been
impressed with the success rate of the men's program, started a year
before. I wanted to create a program for women, to try to affect their
lives before they got to prison.

As I drove home that first night, I thought about the women (whose
names have been changed here to protect their privacy). Besides Theresa,
there was Addie, a waitress who had dropped out of school in ninth
grade and had no support from the father of her child. Devora, a woman
with AIDS, whose police record spanned several pages, had earned her
GED behind bars. Jesse was twenty, a young mother with three children,
unemployed, and living in a local shelter. Nina, a Latina woman with
nine brothers and eight sisters, had never held a job or completed high
school. Bonnie was a forty-three-year-old single mother and former
prostitute with a history of childhood sexual abuse. Two of the women
had bounced back to the streets before the first session ever began.

They all had done some prison time and had knocked around the
criminal justice system, having served sentences for crimes such as
possession of drugs, prostitution, assault and battery, shoplifting, and
theft. But these women were different from their male counterparts.
They had no support from worried wives and no encouragement to

find jobs. Their drinking and drugging had often brought them abusive boyfriends who threatened their lives and parents who kicked them out of the house. Most had managed their pregnancies and young children alone. They all had lives of failed commitments, longings, and unfulfilled dreams. They all had ceased to believe in themselves.

They were just like the mother in Tillie Olsen's short story, "I Stand Here Ironing," I thought, a bit smugly and proud of my choice, as I rounded the corner onto my tree-lined street. We had begun the seminar with this story because I knew the offenders would identify with both the mother and daughter characters. Most of women's literature does not take us into struggles on the high seas or paint pictures of fighting the elements but rather shows us life in a smaller sphere where women triumph or at least survive against all odds.

The women had listened intently to find out about the characters while I read aloud. Afterward, we talked about who they sympathized with. Like these offenders, Tillie Olsen's narrator struggles to make ends meet. She is deserted by her husband and has to make choices that are heartbreaking: putting her child, Emily, in an institution; going to work and leaving Emily with the lady in the downstairs apartment; bringing Emily home sick to a house full of other children. The daughter eventually finds fulfillment on stage but does poorly in school. Theresa had said, "The mother tries so hard to understand where she went wrong. But it's too late for Emily." I had assured her it was not.

Two weeks later, we all returned to the oblong table in the president's office, an academic environment that challenged them and a room that encouraged the women to feel special. They had been told to read Anne Tyler's *Dinner at the Homesick Restaurant*, to take notes and to think about the characters. They were not to be tested or quizzed; they would not have writing exercises.

What they brought to the table was their ability to understand, "to pick out what was most important," as Addie said, and to be able to listen to the insights of others. This time, Judge Joseph Dever, the judge who had sentenced most of them, and Val Harris, their probation officer, sat with them, as equals, ready to participate in the discussion. I chose Tyler's book because it emphasizes relationships and because I hoped it would enable the women to see that all families have problems.

Bonnie arrived late, as her son had been in an accident. She talked about how hard it was to read the book while working two jobs, going to school, and raising her children. Not surprisingly, she had mixed reactions about the mother, Pearl Tull, a cold but feisty lady who raises three kids in an unsympathetic world.

"That's my family," exclaimed Jesse, who looked to be a typical college student and, in spite of her homeless status, loved to read. She had dropped out of school in the eleventh grade after having a baby, and saw this program as a lifeline. "I understand my mother more after reading this book. Just like Pearl, you couldn't love her but you couldn't hate her. Every so often, she'd yell and scream, but you couldn't blame her, raising three kids all by herself." Somehow we all knew she was talking about her own strength, as well as her mother's. She had seen herself by understanding Pearl.

Nina, dark-haired with solemn eyes, sat quietly, looking furtively around the room. She shrugged her shoulders when she finally admitted that she did not read the whole book. She "couldn't get into it," she confessed. "I had too many problems this week." I knew that Nina was in therapy and dealing with an abusive uncle who had terrorized her from childhood. Nina was confused, and reading about this family had frightened her. I asked her to write a book report to clarify her thinking after she finished it, but when we filed out of the room that evening, she quickly ran to the elevator, clutching her cigarettes.

I drove home that night, anxious and alone. Teaching this course was different from my regular college classes. I saw the women every two weeks. And in between they had to live their lives without drugs and alcohol, attend other programs required of their probation, and deal with more stress, it seemed to me, than the average student. I wanted the books to touch them, teach them, and give them courage. I wanted them to feel the power of language and find that literature offers redemption, a way out; but, their lives were dark. I feared that twelve weeks might leave them, like Nina, running for the elevator.

"Where is the hope in this book?" I asked the evening we were discussing Toni Morrison's *The Bluest Eye*. Nina, who had not turned in her book report, sat twirling her dark hair around a pencil. She looked up, "There is no hope. It's awful what happens to Pecola." Pecola, the sad African American girl who wants desperately to have blue eyes so she will fit into the white world, is raped by her father.

Bonnie agreed, saying she hated reading the book. Her repeated battles with alcoholism and drugs had landed her in prison. "A better place than home," she cringed, where she, like Pecola, had dealt with incest. But Theresa, an African American, heatedly began to argue with them, pointing out how Claudia, the narrator, survives to tell the story of her growing up, with wisdom and insight into her community. She pointed out how Pecola is lost but not all children are. Bonnie then admitted she had hated reading the book because it hurt. All of a sudden Nina looked up and smiled at Bonnie, and in that brief exchange, they both realized that they were not alone. I wondered if that exchange was as important as the lessons they learned from the characters.

"I think Claudia is the hope," said Theresa, defending a book she had read twice because she understood the world Morrison describes. We then discussed how we could all identify with Claudia, the survivor, the one who lives to tell the story. Nina, still struggling with her own memories of being abused, seemed unsure. I left the class, afraid we would lose her.

But it is not just the texts that are empowering for these women. A healing happens in the discussions, as they seek to understand together how characters get through their struggles. The class allows them to hear each other's perspectives, to share their ideas, and to see that their opinions are valued. Thus, by class three, the women had formed a bond, nodding at each other's comments, taking cigarette breaks together, laughing, and telling stories.

And so, Nina came back, to delight in Sandra Cisneros's *House on Mango Street*, the poetic tale of a Mexican American girl who grows up in a poor Chicano neighborhood in Chicago and dreams about having a home. Nina saw herself in Esperanza, whose name means hope in Spanish. She talked about her favorite part, the time when Louie stole a yellow Cadillac and flew down the street, followed by cops, with Esperanza waving at him. She talked animatedly about Esperanza's ability to survive with so little. Addie, divorced and wanting to get out of her waitress job, saw courage in Esperanza, who wants to move out of the ghetto. Nina proudly announced that Esperanza realized she must come back and help her people.

By this time, the probation officer told me she looked at the seminar as her bimonthly reading group. The class held an unexpected intimacy for all of us, including Judge Dever, a gentle man, who countered many of the women's negative experiences with men. We had originally imagined a female judge, thinking that some subjects would be better discussed with only women present. From the beginning, it was clear that we were primarily a group of women interested in women's issues. Men could participate in, but could not dominate, the discussion.

Judge Dever became a role model in the class, not an authority figure: he listened, paid attention to what the women said, vigorously shared his ideas, and validated their insights. He felt our discussions were as interesting as those he had been in with other judges. I too was feeling free of constraints: no papers to correct, no tests, no grades. I had the luxury of listening and of enjoying many different perspectives. Changing Lives was changing me as well.

The women were growing in ways I hadn't anticipated. Theresa said she felt proud of her heritage after reading Toni Morrison and wanted to read all the rest of her books; she also enrolled in a local community college for the next semester. Jesse too decided on college, aiming to be a nurse. The other women reported feeling better about themselves; they were staying out of trouble and completing something they never imagined they could. The impossible was becoming possible.

With Barbara Kingsolver's *Animal Dreams*, the women almost fell into the room and began discussing the book as if it revealed the lives of their favorite friends. Jesse and Devora loved dissecting the male-female relationships as shown through the main character, Codi, and her Native American lover, Loyd. "I wish I had a man like Loyd," said Devora, whose boyfriend beat her, "but Loyd with one *l*, is he for real?"

The women laughed a lot that evening because the book allowed them to fantasize and act like kids sharing secrets. They talked about

Loyd's strength and sensitivity. Nina decided he was a "wimp," but Devora kept wondering if she could ever find someone as kind as he. Jesse, facing the cold and winter at the shelter, wanted to focus on Codi, "a privileged woman," she said, "because she has a home." We all saw the character in a new way after that.

Jesse went on to compare Codi with Esther, the main character in Sylvia Plath's *The Bell Jar*, which we had read two weeks before, who also seemed to Jesse to have so much. "I never understood why she went crazy," she said of Esther, who is a promising young journalist but who has not faced her father's death. The women started talking about the characters they had met, almost as if they were in the room. I didn't want our discussions to stop and wished sometimes that I could hop in the van and ride back with them to their homes.

Twelve weeks after we began, I entered a packed courtroom. Judge Dever, now in his robes, was in the lead. It was a regular district court day for the hundred or so people who milled around the first session, but for us, it was graduation day for Changing Lives Through Literature.

The graduates sat in the front row with their families and friends. They were dressed up and ready to receive a positive judgment in a room where they had once been tried for their crimes. "All rise," the courtroom hushed and we walked up to the judge's bench.

Judge Dever began by saluting the women's achievements in the name of the law. I followed, telling the interested onlookers about the difficulty of the books we had read and about the nature of the course. Then, Val Harris gave the onlookers an overview of the women's plans for their futures. Judge Dever led us down into the courtroom, where one by one, we presented the women with framed certificates and roses. After the ceremony, Jesse asked the judge to pose for pictures with her and her three daughters.

Changing Lives Through Literature may not be for everyone. This program must be voluntary. In fact, some men and women have chosen to go to prison rather than be "sentenced to literature," as I often tell my community college students. Some offenders, perhaps as many as sixty-five percent, are illiterate, and these people can't be candidates for the program.

However, more than 100 men and 21 women with a combined record of more than 750 convictions have completed the course. "Only six have been convicted of new crimes and nine face pending charges," the *Boston Globe* reported of eighty men in August 1993, citing that men convicted of similar crimes had a far greater recidivist rate. Although the women's program is still too new for any statistics to be meaningful, we have had only a few rearrests and are encouraged that the program seems to be keeping people out of prison. Costing less than $500 per student, the program is far more cost-effective than prison at $30,000 a year per bed.

The women who choose this program are not necessarily avid readers nor are they aware of the power of literature. They are, however, willing to look at their lives through the characters they meet. In discovering very dark places, they also find joy, new choices, new thoughts, and hope.

"This is just the beginning for me," said Theresa the day of graduation. And, as we walked out of the courtroom, I noticed she was carrying her books.

A Journey Down the River

ROBERT WAXLER   📖   NORTH DARTMOUTH, MASSACHUSETTS

ON THAT FIRST night, Jeff came with his father, a man in his early fifties, I guessed, short and stocky, with a permanent limp and a cane. His stepmother stayed out in the parking lot, seated for over two hours in the front of the paneled truck, smoking, waiting for the two men to return from the humanities building with the news.

Much later, I would be told that Jeff's old man had spent several years in Walpole, the toughest prison in the state. He had come up to the university that night to make sure that his son made it into the classroom, an uncertain place, known to them only as a vague location on a college campus where a judge had sent eight criminal offenders to participate with me, an English professor, in discussions about literature. For these eight male offenders with 148 convictions among them, this kind of seminar, I assumed, beat going to jail.

Jeff quit school after eighth grade. He became a drug dealer, making, according to his own reports, more money than most college graduates. Now, twenty-two years old, with a young daughter and a dedicated girlfriend, he wanted a change, not only a change from the revolving door of drugs and violence, but a fundamental change of life, a change from the dead beat of late twentieth-century culture. Jeff would tell me later that I looked anxious that first night, a little frightened. I told him that he was wrong about that; he was the one with the

87

sweaty palms. He was Pygmalion, and I was the professor. Or was it really the other way around?

I had always believed that good literature had healing power. It could change lives. At its best, it made people self-reflective, thoughtful. And, yes, during the twelve weeks that these men gathered together to talk about stories concerned with male identity, violence, and confronting authority, reading literature did prove that it could make a difference. The initial anxiety that we all felt that first night gave way to a kind of magic. We found ourselves sitting around a table, listening to each other, amazed by the variety of perspectives. "How do I stack up against your college students?" Jeff wanted to know. In truth, they were all teaching me more than I could tell them.

One night we were discussing *Deliverance*, a novel by James Dickey about four suburban men who decide to take a white-water canoe trip through the backwoods of rural Georgia. These men on the water get much more than they bargained for. The journey down the raging river draws these middle-aged suburbanites into a confrontation with their own primal selves, finally killing one of them and permanently changing all of them.

In the novel, Lewis is the macho man in the group, the apparent leader, filled with confidence and possessing a hard and well-disciplined body. As we talk about Lewis that night though, we begin to see flaws in the man. His bravado inspires action, yet he seems overconfident. He strikes out without thinking and in doing so never learns from his mistakes. His friends depend on him because they cannot depend on themselves. If they have become too comfortable and soft through suburban living, Lewis has become too egotistical and self-centered. In the end, it is not Lewis, but his buddy Ed who demonstrates genuine courage by delivering the men from the primal rage of the river.

"As I was reading the novel," said John, one of the offenders around the table that night, "I was trying to picture myself in the characters' places." John had finally identified not with Lewis but with Ed. Ed tended to lay back and wasn't the leader type, John claimed. "But when he had to, he took over. That's how I am. I procrastinate, but I can do what has to be done."

In a sense, both John and Ed must have recognized themselves through their experience, through that journey down the river. They became empowered, found their strength, understood they could make choices. And as I look back now on that first series of literary seminars for male offenders conducted nearly three years ago on the campus at the University of Massachusetts, I imagine that we all went through similar experiences in those twelve weeks in that seminar room. We were drawn together through language, articulating the shape of our selves through the limitations of characters discovered in stories. Around that long wooden table, we were all somehow set free.

I will be starting the ninth series of discussions soon, but the first one is the one I'll never forget. I compare the others with that one when I can, but often in memory the others simply blur into the original. I know though that all these men love adventure stories, plots with action that hold their interest. But once we get into the rhythm of discussion, it is not the plot but the characters that possess us. It is as if each character mirrors an aspect of our own lives.

Sea Wolf by Jack London remains one of our favorites. It tells the story of a rugged sea captain, Wolf Larsen, a great American hero, once met never to be forgotten. Larsen is a man of gigantic passion and rage, a monomaniac committed to the belief that might makes right. He is convinced that power defines all relationships. In the story, Larsen is contrasted with Humphrey Van Weeden, a wealthy young man who at first cannot stand on his own two legs and who, unlike Larsen, believes in immortality and the value of the human spirit.

Van Weeden is a literary critic who remains passive and incapable of taking care of himself until he is thrown into a life-threatening confrontation with Larsen. Then, like Ed in *Deliverance*, he seems to gain the energy and aggressive power of self that allows him to emerge finally as a more complete man than his rival Larsen. In the story, Larsen dies; Van Weeden is delivered. "I used to be like Wolf Larsen," one of the men in the group claimed one time. "I thought I could manipulate everyone. I was stupid then."

These men are often filled with rage and over the years they have externalized that rage, often turning it against others. For them, the passive and dependent Van Weeden is a wimp who must remind them of some of the school teachers who taught them literature and language in the classrooms that helped mark their failures.

I like to believe that in the seminar room that this image associated with language and literature changes for them just as Van Weeden changes and gains his manhood as *Sea Wolf* moves forward to its completion. The rage of these male offenders is shaped into the energy of words and that shaping power becomes its own ritual, a ritual validated for them by the other male participants around that long wooden table. We are all initiated during those moments into a new world defined by language and literature.

If literature helps change their lives by making these men comfortable with language and themselves, the judge in this program also makes a difference. These criminal offenders have for too long felt isolated, as if they were caught in an enormous present moment, unable to extricate themselves from it. They have been marginalized and pushed aside by the mainstream. In essence, they have been silenced. Language becomes a social force in these discussions, an enabling power that binds them together and allows them to recognize that they are capable of humanizing the world that surrounds them. They learn that they can create a future for themselves.

But these men have also felt the dull round of the criminal justice system, the punishing authority of a judge in dark robes. If literature is to change them by allowing them to connect with its magic, then the criminal justice system must also change in their eyes. Literature helps these men to see that there are many perspectives on an event, many interpretations of a story. It allows them to understand that as men they can legitimately pursue the meaning and complexity of literature and language. So too, through the rituals of this program they learn that judges can be more than the dark robes of authority.

It was after a tennis match that I first suggested to my friend Bob Kane, a district court judge, that we try this literature program. I had always believed that literature should play a central role in public policy issues and so I challenged Bob with the idea. "Take eight tough guys coming before your bench who you are ready to send to jail and send them instead up to the university for a series of discussions about literature," I suggested. "If you're willing to do that, I'm willing to design the seminar and lead the discussions."

And so it began. No doubt it took considerable courage on the part of the judge, a feared prosecutor in an earlier phase of his life, to agree to such an apparently soft idea, but once we got going we realized that the judge himself was not only an important administrator in the process, but a central participant in the drama of changing the lives of all those seated around that seminar table. He too claims that it's been one of the best experiences of his life.

As a professor of literature, I could engage in discussions with these men as part of my expected role, but this judge, Bob Kane, proved unusual in this context. For the criminal offenders, a judge tradition-ally represented the enemy, a symbol of the criminal justice system that punished them. Ordinarily, the image of the judge confirmed their alienation from the mainstream of society. He was an authority figure who menaced them and who refused to validate their humanity. He was the dark robe that simply passed judgment on their criminal behav-ior, often with only a few perfunctory words.

Judge Kane rewrote that story for these men. Not only did he give them another chance by recognizing their promise, but he often sat at the table with us, contributing his insights and interpretations of the lit-erature. He became a voice equal to the other voices around that sem-inar room. For the criminal offenders, the judge became a man among other men, still a representative of the authority of the criminal justice system, but now also a representative with a human heart ready to cer-tify and validate these other men as part of a group that included him. In open court, as part of a final graduation ceremony, these men received praise and certification of their work from the judge. As a result, the story of the relationship between these men and the criminal justice system changed.

The men in this program are smart. They have often survived bru-tal family histories, drug and alcohol addiction, and their own pent-up rage. They range in age from nineteen to forty-five. Some are married; some are not. Some have children of their own—a future that they want to contact, even help to nurture. Language and literature can help deter violence and crime and at the same time add important dimensions to a sense of manhood. These men know that now.

As Jeff once put it, the challenge of walking into a college classroom where his opinions are valued by a college professor and a judge was a challenge superior to the one he found on the streets. I am convinced that through their reading and discussion of literature, these men are all bringing hope away from that long wooden table in our seminar room.

Serious Reading

DAVID WELLENBROCK 📖 STOCKTON, CALIFORNIA

A MAJOR PLEASURE of reading serious nonfiction books is discussing the ideas in those books. In college, this discussion is not limited to the classroom. Instead, a common fund of knowledge is built and the sources of this knowledge often find their way into conversation and discussion all over campus. But after college and outside a university setting, this common fund tends to dissipate and seems sometimes not to exist at all. The result is that many of us read fewer and fewer serious nonfiction books. About fifteen years ago, I found a few people who agreed with me that the added fillip and pleasure derived from the fairly hard work of reading such books was missing from our lives.

Initially, we tried to remedy this with a reading group consisting of three and then four couples. That group originally intended to read about half fiction and half nonfiction. But the mix of personalities was unsuccessful and the group imploded after two years.

Almost immediately, in October 1982, we set up another reading group. This group had some different guidelines and a new composition. The group is faithful to those guidelines and is thriving, after twelve years and more than eighty books later. Thinking about it, we see four main reasons for our success: quality membership, a challenging reading list, stable organization, and a regular order of proceeding.

What We Look for in Members

Membership is critical. Diversity of perspective is necessary, but it cannot be so great that every discussion reduces itself to first principles. There is also a need to maintain a reasonable size—a sufficient number so that various viewpoints are expressed, but not so many that the participants have little opportunity to talk. We started with six members and immediately increased to eight. For a number of years we worked very hard to make sure every member could make every meeting. We now have eleven members and assume that two to four members will miss each meeting. This leaves us in fine shape, as we have found that eight participants is a very good number for a discussion.

We were fortunate at the time of formation to have four of us who had known each other for about twenty years (three classmates and a professor). This started us off with a large common fund of knowledge and a core membership of very compatible people.

We've had some turnover through the years, but we've been careful about making additions. We try to keep professions and perspectives in balance. Specifically, we are careful not to invite too many lawyers or people associated with Raymond College, University of the Pacific. Members have included lawyers, college professors, bureaucrats, students, business people, a farmer, a journalist, a doctor, a dentist, and a state legislator. The group has a social aspect also, and we try to nurture it by selecting compatible, nice people.

We have, on occasion, invited people for a specific meeting. For example, we were joined by an eastern European immigrant for a discussion of Václav Havel. For the discussion of *The Enigma of Japanese Power*, we invited a college professor who had taught history in Japan for a number of years during the postwar period and who was returning for the pending school year. Group membership was not offered to these guests, but everyone seemed to enjoy and benefit from the variation.

When selecting members, particularly if the nominee is known to only one person, we generally invite the person for a single session and, if the group reaction is favorable, suggest full membership a few days later. We have had a number of one-meeting members. But we keep the situation from being uncomfortable by extending invitations only for one session.

Losing members is a more serious problem. When members move out of the area, there is no issue. Even a member who rarely shows up isn't much of a problem. In such a case, we keep the person informed of the next meetings for a while, but if they miss several meetings in a row, we ask if they want to continue. If they do, we let them know that if they miss two successive meetings, they will be dropped. In such a case, we simply don't inform them of the next session. A bigger problem occurs when a member is not working out or becomes disruptive. In this case, the group must do something.

The major sources of disruption are a lack of intellectual honesty, continual negativity in discussion, and failure to maintain the scope and course of the discussion. Presumably, a member or two must talk to the disruptive force, explain the problem, and agree on a course of action. The person may have to be dropped from the group.

This summary of what's disruptive in turn gives some insight into what we're looking for in potential members. The primary qualities are that members be nice, well informed, intellectually honest, and self-confident. Niceness is undervalued in America at this time, but there's a lot to be said for civility, manners, and consideration; the group is an important social, as well as intellectual, element in our lives. We value people who are sufficiently informed and bright so that they can make positive contributions to the meetings and discussions. We also want people who will follow the evidence and logic. And it is important that members don't take the discussions personally—to attack a strongly held idea is not the same as attacking the person who holds it, but by the same token, in attacking an idea or intellectual position, members must be sure not to attack the person holding that idea or position.

Reading Challenging Nonfiction

Our reading list, while selected by consensus, consists of nonfiction. (We have not been absolutists and have actually selected a couple of novels. However, the primary motivation for one selection was that one member denied having read a novel for about forty years. It seems unlikely that another novel will be selected in the near term, unless it is virtually speculative thinking, such as Carl Sagan's *Contact*.) As evidenced by our reading list, social sciences, public policy, and philosophy have formed the core of our readings. Occasionally we have selected a topic rather than a particular work.

Members make recommendations in various manners. Among these have been: bringing in a book and letting everyone take a look at it; bringing in a book review; nominating and describing the book verbally. Fortunately, our members don't have agendas and the selection process has not posed any significant problems. The number of recommendations waxes and wanes and we try to keep a bit of a backlog for lean times. (Often the backlog serves as a springboard for other nominations.)

Often a very new book is nominated. We generally try to wait at least six months before having a go at such a book. On a practical level, the book will probably be out in paperback and more readily available at the library. What's more, the media hype will be off the book.

In selecting a book, it is not necessary that everyone falls in love with it. Indeed, some of our best discussions have been about books with which everyone, or nearly everyone, had serious disagreements. For example, *Anarchy, State, and Utopia* by Robert Nozick came under heavy criticism, but on the way home one member commented that the discussion was so good, it should have been tape recorded.

Our reading has not been subject specific, but we do tend to return to themes. These themes are long-term interests of the membership, even though we have never attempted to delineate what they are. They have evolved as the membership has changed, as the temper of the times and intellectual thought has changed, and as we have increased our common fund of knowledge.

Part of the value of a reading group is the element of randomness and breadth it gives to its members' own reading. It provides sufficient impetus to read books one might otherwise slough off. It provides reading suggestions that one simply would not come across, if left to one's own resources. Other people's preferences push us out of our intellectual nests. Our method of book selection has served us well; it is a benefit that is appreciated more and more as time goes on.

Stability, Without Ironclad Organizing Principles

Our group has little organization. A self-appointed secretary has maintained records of what was read and where we have met and when. In the early years, that person was responsible for any rescheduling that was required, but that role has been eliminated. Now if anyone wants to reschedule, that person has to do the arranging. Rescheduling has almost been eliminated because, as mentioned above, we have increased our membership and accepted the fact that people will occasionally be absent.

The group has been very careful about making changes. The formula we have developed has been successful over many years. Undoubtedly, much of the success has to do with the membership. But it is believed that our conservative approach to changing the group has been important. When changes are made, it is generally by consensus and they are made over the course of a few meetings, rather than at a single setting. For example, we have never added more than two members in any one year so that the group culture could be maintained. When we did add two members at the same time, they were couples.

We do not appoint a discussion leader for any meeting. Typically, the discussion begins spontaneously. Many of our members have taught so someone is always ready to fill the initial void with a question, often directed at the book's nominator. Discussions have no format and they are generally wide ranging. The less interesting the book, the wider the field of discussion seems.

A Regular Order of Proceeding

While we don't have ironclad rules for discussion, an order of proceeding has evolved and is now well established. We meet at 7:30 P.M. and as soon as most of the expected members arrive, we address the housekeeping issues.

The first question is when will we next meet. We generally try to meet every six or eight weeks. If we meet more frequently, the reading becomes a chore rather than a pleasure. In addition, this permits enough time to obtain the book, which has been a problem at times. If we meet less frequently, interest fades. Obviously, there are deviations, particularly around Christmas.

The next question is where will we next meet. Meetings are rotated from home to home, though not in any strict order. We go to Eric's only once each year as he lives in San Francisco, and that is generally on a Friday evening. The host provides coffee and pastries.

The most intriguing question is what will we next read. This can take some time to answer, but the process is interesting in itself. Some books have been nominated intermittently before finally being accepted or dropped. The most successful nominations are when the book is brought in rather than merely described or presented through a review.

Generally, by this time, everyone has arrived and the discussion begins. The meetings run between two and three hours. There is no preset termination time.

For this group's reading list, see page 386.

Writer's Group 101: The Evolution of a Book Group

JOHN M. RODERICK   WEST HARTFORD, CONNECTICUT

THIS STORY STARTS out as small as small-world stories get. I was brows-ing the book displays at the annual convention of the American Society of Journalists and Authors in New York City when a remotely famil-iar voice asked, "Is that really you?" I looked up and there was the bright, smiling face of Patricia, one of my star older students in a fea-ture writing course I had taught some ten years ago. We laughed at our simultaneous "What-are-you-doing-heres?" and joined each other for the conference lunch.

I learned that Patricia had continued with her avid interest in writ-ing and had developed that talent into a successful one-woman com-pany that produced scripts, brochures, and a host of related writing projects for clients in industry and the business world. She learned that I still had a penchant for the more creative side and had just completed my first novel and was wondering what to do with it now. Patricia gasped in amazement. "I did, too!"

At the ASJA convention luncheon, then Mayor of New York Edward Koch was presenting a keynote speech on his recent bestseller to a massive crowd filling the banquet hall of the Hyatt Regency. Koch was explaining how he always wanted to write and why he chose to write about his experiences as mayor. As he absorbed the communal admiration from this group of fellow writers, Patricia and I exchanged glances and said almost simultaneously, "We could be up there."

There was no boasting in it, just the realization that successful writing starts with the desire to write; develops with the discipline to write; improves with the willingness to revise; evolves with the courage to send work to editors; and succeeds when all of the above combine in some kind of serendipity and a publisher says yes. From that moment on, I think both Patricia and I had resolved that our closet novel writing efforts were going to become more public.

Our public sharing would begin in a modest way: we agreed to send each other a draft of our completed novels. A month later we met again over lunch and talked nonstop for three hours about the strengths and weaknesses we saw in each other's work. We moved to discussing other writer's books. She said it reminded her of when she was in my class ten years before. It reminded me of the same thing only this time I was learning as much about my own efforts in this writing pursuit as Patricia was about hers. Our mutual excitement about how our scratchings on paper moved another person to laughter or tears fueled the same fire that must be smoldering to spend so much time at this activity we call writing in the first place.

We decided then and there that this experience of sharing words in such critical detail was too valuable to lapse into a typical it-was-nice-bumping-into-you departure. Patricia knew two other writers, one a publisher of a small weekly newspaper and another a budding psychologist with a penchant for capturing the unusual in the ordinary events of our lives. Thrown together by the energy and enthusiasm of Patricia, our writer's group of four evolved.

We began meeting once a month at Patricia's house. We had agreed that each of us would bring whatever we were working on and share it with the group by reading it aloud. I'm not sure why, but we never reached a consensus that an added element would be gained if we also brought copies for the others to read. We agreed that hearing the writer read his or her own work gave a dimension that might otherwise be lost in our interpretation of their words. I suspect, however, that, in my case anyway, the pressure of the deadline of these monthly meetings had just as much to do with my resistance to making copies for everyone ahead of time. There was no "ahead of time." Often it was just knowing that I would be meeting with these three other writers and that they would be bringing something to the table that motivated me to produce.

In fact, this was the first benefit of the group that manifested. It made us all imminently aware that our writing was not for ourselves only; it was for an audience and we owed that audience something. Knowing that the reader over my shoulder (or in this case, the listener) was there changed the process of my writing or, at least, part of the intent. I had always wanted to be true to the vision I was trying to capture in words, but now I became vividly aware that I wanted others to like that vision also.

Soon we discovered that many of the problems that we were encountering as writers had a common ring to them. What does point of view really mean? How is it established? Does it matter if it shifts? We wondered how other writers solved these problems. Before long we were bringing other peoples' work to our gatherings—published works of those who had found a solution.

We began reading each other's discoveries. Sometimes they were successful novels whose practitioners discovered techniques that worked (Elmore Leonard's practice of getting inside the head of a multiplicity of players or Judy Blume's immediacy of first person). Sometimes they were articles, like those in *The Writer* or *Writer's Digest*, that explored technique. Nonfiction as well as fiction found in magazines helped us formulate our ideas and served as models to emulate in our own writing. Our fledgling writer's group was becoming a book group without us ever intending it to happen.

The personal effort that I brought to the proceedings was a thorough revision of that novel I had shared with Patricia, chapter by chapter, month after month. There was enough continuity of the story and story line for my audience's insights to grow more and more valuable as we all got deeper into the tale. We took notes throughout our readings. Each, in turn, talked to the writer about what he or she specifically liked or did not like. The critiques were offered in a manner of mutual respect and kindness, even when our evaluations were harsh. We grew to trust this harshness, and the revisions that resulted were always improvements, sometimes dramatic ones. We embellished with examples we discovered elsewhere ("Remember when Joyce Carol Oates wrote . . ." or "Imagine if John Irving were writing that scene: how would it change?").

We often found things to laugh about during our exchanges—an essential ingredient to balance the sometimes negative reactions. We usually started each session by filling each other in about the rest of our lives during the month since our last get-together. A lot can happen in a month. Patricia was in a serious boating accident in one interim. Judy's divorce became final. The other Judy's newspaper folded. I was hospitalized. But whatever events shook our lives, we continued to write and to read and to share these efforts with each other.

Support groups have grown important in our society where a hectic pace often mitigates making real connections. And support for writing, with its whimsical nature and sometimes resistant spirit, is no exception. We each grew as writers from the experience. Contributing significantly to that growth were the examples we drew from other writers who became a part of our discussion and our mutual reading background.

Under the guidance of this writer's-reader's group, I completed that first novel and have begun the pursuit for an agent. Patricia is well on her way toward finishing her novel. Judy the editor came up with numerous editorials that found their way to her readership. And Judy the psychologist discovered the voice that allowed her to share her ideas with a larger reading audience.

We all benefited through sharing what we were reading and the books and articles that said something to us. Our writing improved, to be sure. We gained insight into the process and how we related to that process. Through the immediate reaction of this audience that we had grown to trust so fervently, we came to appreciate the potential power of our own words as well. We became motivated to continue with an activity that, at times, repays us with little more than frustration and rejection. But we persist. We know that if we can move this small group with our words, we can move the world as well. What's more, it goes without saying, we became friends.

Woven between the dozens of stories and scripts and chapters shared were the events of our lives that made us more than just writers and readers; we were people who wrote and read. That recognition of what we had in common helped us to appreciate our individual uniqueness as well. Writer's Group 101: it became as vital as the words we wanted to share.

Wake Watchers

MURRAY J. GROSS   📖   NEW YORK, NEW YORK

WE ARE LITERALLY a "book" group. Singular. We read one book: *Finnegans Wake*.

This last and most inaccessible of the works of James Joyce is why book groups were invented. The author created his own language with original words and endowed ordinary words with novel meanings; most people are not able to read the *Wake* alone—unless truly heroic or from a different planet. After two or three pages either your eyes will glaze over or you will demand your money back from the bookstore complaining that they sold you the foreign language edition. Sure, there are those solitary souls who undertake the *Wake* with a critic in one hand and the *Wake* in the other, but it is tough going and just not as much fun.

That is not to say that one should ignore the Joyce industry. Most critics who have written on the *Wake* have thought long and hard and we take full advantage of their labors. We do not worry that we will be corrupted; we invariably disagree with everyone, but, at least, we have interpretations to stimulate our own—a starting point.

What is obvious (the only obvious thing about the work) is that reading the *Wake* is both a visual and an auditory experience. It must be read aloud. Replete with puns, the sense of the language and fun of the *Wake* is in the sound. You can read it aloud to yourself or listen to recordings, but the best way to do it is to join a reading group.

Our Finnegans Wake Society meets once a month at the famous
Gotham Book Mart on West 47th Street in New York City; we read
short portions of the text and then discuss them. The advantage of a
group is more than just reading aloud, it is also the input from other
members. Our group consists of a few academics, lawyers, computer
analysts, doctors, a sailor, artists, a chauffeur, scientists, teachers, actors,
poets, and ladies and gentlemen of leisure. (Who else would have the
time to really tackle this tome?) We have French, German, and Italian
speakers; we could use an Irish speaker—the only one we had went
home. We have a Latinist (there's a lot of *culpa* in the *Wake* as well as
puns in forty languages, including Esperanto and Volapuk) together
with Christians, Moslems, Jews, mystics, and even a UFO spotter. We
never know when an otherwise unknown allusion will spark a member's memory and the mixture charges up the atmosphere.

Is it a novel? The critics can't agree. It doesn't matter. It is a treasury of poetry, comic skits, puzzles, nursery rhymes, war stories, children's games, proverbs, fables, myths, ballads, and bawdy language.
All of this is jumbled together in fragments linked by words that Joyce
created and that mean different things to different people. It is not a work
to admire from afar; it is an adventure to experience. No experience is
necessary, but immersion in *Finnegans Wake* usually stimulates interest in other works.

This is how our group works. Among the themes in the *Wake* are
the Crimean War, the Book of Kells, Napoleon, Tristan and Isolde,
incest, the fall in the Garden of Eden, Egyptian mythology, and many
others. The drive to understand and fathom Joyce's allusions sends
members on their own reading military history, biographies of Napoleon,
Celtic mythology, the Koran, Richard Wagner, the Bible, the Egyptian
book of the dead, Freud, *Ulysses*, and Joyce's other earlier works, letters, notebooks, and much, much more. Flushed with discoveries, they
bring explanations, pictures, excerpts, and sometimes more questions
back to the group. To read this one book, we read many books.

A basic feature of the *Wake*—either because of some fundamental
property of its complexity, or, perhaps, its underlying virtuosity—is
that you can find parts that support any theory you may choose. There
are those Joyceans who not only search for a single key to *Finnegans*

Wake but also think they have found it: one is sure the *Wake* is about William Stead, a Victorian publisher and reformer who went down with the Titanic; another is convinced that it is biblical, but not simply based on the Bible, nor even the Book of Genesis, but specifically chapter three of the Book of Genesis. A man I know who writes for *Field and Stream* proclaims that fly-fishing constitutes the major theme of the *Wake*. Most of us are persuaded that its intricacy transforms the *Wake* simultaneously into a history book, dream book, bible book, media book, music book (we all know the ballad *Finnegan's Wake*), and even a prophecy book. As with our sensory nervous system when it is bombarded with masses of information, the main job is to block and screen out extraneous noise. So it is with the *Wake*, which also seems overloaded with noise that is actually multiple meanings striking us simultaneously. The first task is to focus on a specific level.

Unlike music, where the mind can experience simultaneously disparate voices, we can hold ideas in focus only one at a time. It is like the Necker cube that alternates between views as you look at it, but both views never appear at the same time. The ideas is to focus.

The manner in which our group proceeds is a slow reading of small parts of the *Wake* in which we attempt to focus just on one level. To experience the result of such a slow reading of a passage, read aloud the following text from *Finnegans Wake*:

> I've a hopesome's choice if I chouse of all the sinkts in the colander. From the common for ignitious Purpalume to the proper of Francisco Ultramare, last of scorchers, third of snows, in terrorgammons howdydos. (432.35–433.02)

The passage occurs about two-thirds of the way through the book and introduces a mock sermon to a group of young women. Given time, even on this first reading, you, the common reader, could offer some interpretations of this passage. With help from some other Wakeans, I will give my own brief rundown of some meanings on one level.

To start, one gets a general feeling of the religious nature of the passage. Bearing in mind the coming sermon, the words "sinkts in the colander" certainly evoke "Saints in the calendar"; thus, "ignitious" evokes St. Ignatius of Loyola. With this baseline, we can then search for corroborating evidence. The feast day of Loyola is July 31, the last day of a hot months, perhaps "last of the scorchers"—less persuasive would be his birth place of Pampeluna and his wounding at Pamplona being indicated by "Purpalume." A close follower of Loyola, St. Francis Xavier, seems to be indicated by Francisco Ultramare—Francisco being the name Xavier was born with. His feast day is December 3, which certainly could be the "third of snows," the third day of a snowy month, December. This, coupled with his mission being overseas—Ultramare— in India and Japan. In addition, Loyola and Xavier were both Basques and by separating the syllables in colander we discover that they were "co-landers."

The "sinkts in the colander" (with hesitation I repeat one critic's suggestion that both kitchen colanders and saints share a "common" trait: both are holy) or saints in the calendar brings us not only to the sin in "sinkts"—a concern of saints—but also to the words themselves: "common" and "proper" are liturgical terms relating to the prayers of saints. This ties together sin and the Litany of the Saints, a prayer that has the line "we sinners beseech thee, hear us." In Latin this is "te rogamus, audi nos," which Joyce twists into "terrorgammons howdy-dos." Clearly, he expected us to hear the *Wake* as well as to read it!

Back to the beginning of the passage: "I've a hopesome's choice" suggests Hobson's choice, which is a choice between taking the one offered or none at all, in effect, no choice at all. Joyce is indicating that man has some sort of choice but that it is severely limited. Either take the way of the saints, that is, goodness, and we have "hopesome" or reversed, "somehope"; or, instead, "chouse" (which means to swindle and is derived from the Sultan's "chaush," an official interpreter who swindled certain Turkish merchants in London) and with the sin of "sinkts" we sink into the abyss of damnation and suffer the fires and freezing of hell in the terror of death. At the same time, Joyce could be indicating a Calvinistic approach, that is, that there really is no choice for salvation; we have only a Hobson's choice.

There you have it. Just one analysis of part of one level in a two-sentence passage. As to whether this is a correct or proper interpretation (or, indeed, what constitutes the correct or real analysis of a *Wake* passage), that is subject to discussion. With repeated slow reading, however, the meaning of a passage often emerges. The payoff is that tremendous thrill that comes with discovery.

And that is what keeps us *Wake* Watchers reading and rereading and discussing this one wonderful book.

For this group's reading list, see page 258.

Let Your Goals Determine Your Guidelines

JOHN W. HASBROUCK　　　　　　　CHICAGO, ILLINOIS

I'VE HEARD IT said that reading alone is like drinking alone, but for some reason I just couldn't bring myself to agree. I've always loved to read alone. How could it be a vice? Then I began to understand. It's not that one shouldn't read alone, but that reading and discussing a book with others is simply better. Being in book discussion groups has made me a better reader, speaker, and listener.

In early 1993, I formed two book discussion groups in Chicago. One was a great books discussion group concerned with liberal education for adults, formed through the Great Books Foundation. The other was a special-interest group concerned with exploring a specific genre of imaginative literature. This group was formed through an independent library and archival institution.

The distinct goals of the two groups make for an interesting study in contrast. The different formats appropriate to them as determined by their respective goals tended to illuminate one another. While I had my hands full leading two groups, I found that my experience in each helped me view the other with a fresh perspective.

I became interested in great books through the work of philosopher and educator Mortimer J. Adler. Dr. Adler cofounded the Great Books

109

Foundation in 1947, and he has championed great books discussion since the twenties. Great books discussion exists for adults who want to improve their understanding of fundamental ideas and their skills in the liberal arts of reading, speaking, and listening.

An important moment leading to the formation of the group occurred when I discovered Dr. Adler's unpublished manuscript, "Manual for Discussion Leaders: Preliminary Draft for Use in Great Books Community Groups." From it I learned the nuts and bolts of great books discussion. Of course, I could learn only so much without actually leading a group, but I did learn a basic concept of liberal education: people should learn to think and to think well for themselves.

I also learned to distinguish three levels of questioning: analytic, or what does the author say; interpretive, or what does the author mean; and, evaluative, or what of it. Analytical questions are matters of fact and have a single right answer; interpretive questions can have several right, though contradictory, answers; and evaluative questions are answered by judgments formed by opinion. It so happens that opinions are not all created equal but are more or less well founded. It's through discussion that differences of opinion are resolved.

Reading about how to lead a group was one thing; actually forming a group and putting these ideas into practice was another story. I approached various friends, neighbors, and coworkers I thought might be interested in joining. In my enthusiasm, I even confronted strangers in used bookstores and on public transportation who were reading great books, inviting them to join the group. Soon we had enough people to get started.

Our first discussion on the *Declaration of Independence* took place in the Wicker Park Fieldhouse, a city-owned building. Nearly everyone was late, and I thought maybe the group wasn't going to get off the ground. But soon people began wandering in and the Wicker Park Great Books Group was launched. The stark, empty room featuring pale yellow brick walls, linoleum floors, and metal folding chairs actually helped discussion—there were no distractions. But eventually, the group's craving for cappuccino prompted a move to a neighborhood café, which has since become our stomping ground.

The *Declaration of Independence* was ideal for a first discussion, since its fundamental tenets are open to wide interpretation. Phrases like "self-evident truths," "unalienable rights," and "all men are created equal," with which we had all been familiar since childhood, suddenly struck us with their full weight. Dissecting these concepts, we began to read this document as we never had before.

The foundation provided interpretive and evaluative questions and discussion guidelines. At the end of the meeting, many questions were left unanswered, but everybody was excited. I'd heard that it would be a good idea to end the first meeting when discussion was at a high point and tell everybody that this was only a taste of what's to come. The ploy worked.

One advantage to starting a group through the Great Books Foundation is that it provides several series of readings collected in inexpensive paperbacks along with prepared questions. This eliminates the need to spend time creating a reading list. The foundation puts a lot of thought into the choice of readings, the order of their presentation, and the questions. As I will explain later, my other group had to devise its own system to choose books for discussion.

Another plus is that the readings are generally short and people are able to read them carefully without feeling overloaded. Many readings are self-contained excerpts from larger works. The foundation recommends that participants read selections at least twice, but I've met people who read them four or five times before coming in. These people can really contribute to discussion.

Most people feel that the recommended guidelines help discussion, but rules do get broken, and sometimes the meeting becomes a free-for-all (which can be great). The key isn't so much to follow the rules to the letter but simply to keep the guidelines in mind and refer to them when needed.

One rule in great books discussion is that comments should be supported by the text. This means everybody has to be alert while reading and commenting. It's an exercise in thinking. We avoid outside sources like biography, historical material, and literary criticism. This material can be fascinating, but the goal here is not to learn about an author or culture. Ideas are what's important. The goal is to communicate well and better understand fundamental ideas. Historical facts and the opinions of others don't change the meaning or soundness of ideas expressed in the text. It's up to participants to find these ideas and deal with them. In great books discussion, bringing in outside sources is letting someone else do the thinking for you.

One of the first lessons I learned was when apparent disagreement arose concerning a question about the selection. I say "apparent" because, quite often, it was just that. Participants may have actually agreed but had expressed their positions from different viewpoints, resulting in a misunderstanding. Other times, participants had not clearly established the issue at hand, and were in fact dealing with different issues altogether. In these situations, real disagreement (or agreement, for that matter) is impossible. This was a lesson in communication: speaking and listening—skills we had come together to improve.

The issue of partial agreement is related to this. Sometimes participants insist that others either totally agree with them or be told that their views are completely wrong. Partial agreement is when people make a sincere effort to discover common ground. It may have to start on the most basic level. Had they read the same book? Yes. So at once, there is some agreement, however small. Are they dealing with the same question? Yes. Progress is made slowly. Eventually, it can be determined precisely where their views diverge. Then real discussion takes place—rhetoric happens. People are more or less persuaded that a given interpretation or evaluation is valid.

Even in works of nonfiction, ideas may not always be explicitly stated. It becomes the group's job to discover and evaluate the author's positions. In imaginative works, ideas will often be implicit and open to differing interpretations. Again, it's up to participants to analyze the work to find out what is being said and interpret it so as to determine what it means and, ultimately, to evaluate its relative worth.

Dealing with short excerpts from philosophical writers can require a lot of patience. The text may seem obscure. These discussions may never get past the analytical stage. Still, however far we do get, there is always that sense of having made progress, having somehow deepened our understanding. For example, only four or five people came to the discussion of Karl Marx's *Alienated Labor*, and none of us felt we had a grasp on the reading. It seemed to be over everybody's head. We decided to focus on two paragraphs to see if we could figure things out. This turned out to be one of the best discussions ever. By the end, we had learned more about Marx's ideas and his method than any of us had learned by reading alone. To me, this was proof positive of the value of close reading in a group.

I've found my experience in a great books discussion group to be rewarding socially as well as intellectually. Sitting down with a group of adults who have come together with a genuine desire to learn and immediately entering into friendly meaningful conversation about important issues and ideas, sometimes with people I've only just met, is a great thing to do.

My other book group, the Gerber-Hart Gay Men's Fiction Discussion Group, was formed through the Gerber-Hart Gay and Lesbian Library and Archives, located on Chicago's North Side. The group is devoted to advancing gay cultural literacy through the exchange of ideas surrounding important books with gay themes. Like other areas of special interest, it's at once narrow and broad—narrow in that it's more or less distinct from other areas of inquiry and broad in the diversity of subject matter available.

When I approached Gerber-Hart's board of directors with the idea of starting a men's discussion group, they were enthusiastic. A women's discussion group had been meeting for several years and the board was immediately interested in having someone coordinate a men's group. We decided that the group would meet monthly and a notice was placed in several local gay newspapers. All that was left to do was to create a reading list.

Selecting books for discussion was something I didn't have to worry about in the Wicker Park group. The Great Books Foundation creates its reading lists from the three-thousand-year tradition of the West, a tradition that has been called "the civilization of the dialogue." These books, being centuries old, can be judged with an objectivity unavailable to groups reading contemporary works. Nonetheless, an appropriate reading list can be created in a special-interest group if the group's goals are well defined.

I created the group's initial reading list after searching out the canon-ical works within the field. After reading through several historical works and the recommended reading lists of some well-known authors, I arrived at a list of acknowledged classics for the first six meetings.

The group, though small in the beginning, was a success from the start. We first discussed *The City and the Pillar* by Gore Vidal. People were very opinionated about the book's value, because Vidal wrote it when he was twenty-one. An interesting aspect of this selection was that Vidal actually rewrote the book with a different ending fifteen years after it appeared, and republished it with an afterword detailing his thoughts surrounding it.

The goal of any group determines the format of the meetings. Since the purpose of this group is not to improve skills in the liberal arts but rather to become a more informed person with a better understanding of a particular culture, the guidelines for discussion are different from those of the great books group.

For example, while the book remains the focus, outside sources such as biography, history, and criticism are welcomed and even encour-aged. Any material that sheds light on the book or its author can increase one's understanding of the book's meaning and place within the cul-ture. Gore Vidal's afterword to the rewrite of *The City and the Pillar* is a perfect example of this.

Aesthetic judgments play a large part in Gerber-Hart discussions. Interestingly, while discussing books considered to be classics, our group found that a classic may not necessarily be a great work of art. This insight, however, was rarely disappointing or surprising. That a not-so-great book produced by someone from a particular cultural milieu has become a classic can be attributed to many factors. What's impor-tant is that even if a book didn't provide a great literary experience, its discussion can provide a better understanding of the culture from which the book came. Naturally, the reverse can also be true. A great novel may be all but unknown to the audience who could most appreciate it.

As the group became more established, we decided that the selec-tion process should be democratic. We came up with an easy, fair, effective system to accomplish this. At the last meeting of every six-month period, members suggest books they'd like to discuss. Members are asked to consider their suggestions from several angles. Does the book have historical value? Does it deal with a range of ideas that will stimulate discussion? Is it long? Controversial? Brand-new? Popular? Difficult? Available? Boring?

We create comprehensive list of suggestions and distribute copies. Everybody then marks six books he's interested in discussing. The discussion leader then determines the six books that received the most votes and asking for a show of hands in the case of a tie. The group then quickly and somewhat arbitrarily decides in what order the books will be discussed. The process generally takes about thirty minutes and is quite reliable in helping select good books that people want to read.

The Gerber-Hart group established itself quickly and within six months a core group of members attended and still attend nearly every discussion. For some reason, this was quite different from the Wicker Park group, which took much longer to establish. Just before I started the Wicker Park group, an experienced great books discussion leader told me the group should be pretty much established "in about three years." I thought he was joking. Now I know better. Things came together sooner than my friend predicted, but it still took longer than I originally thought it would. While it didn't happen overnight, it was worth the effort.

A special-interest group such as the Gerber-Hart Gay Men's Fiction Discussion Group is a great opportunity to bring together people with common interests who come from varied backgrounds. New friendships occur naturally. Outings, dinners, and other diversions are easy to plan with a roomful of acquaintances. In 1994, several members of the Gerber-Hart group went to see the Chicago production of *Angels in America*, Tony Kushner's Pulitzer Prize–winning play, which the group had discussed. Of course, we discussed the play after the performance and compared the experience of reading it with seeing it performed.

Whether you're in a great books group with people who have nothing in common but a desire to learn, or a group where people share a common interest, book discussion groups are at once fun, interesting, exasperating, and entertaining. They won't replace solitary reading, but they will expand your world.

A Chorus for Four Voices

BECKY HEMPERLY, SANDRA DEDEN,
GLORIA LaBRECQUE, AND
ERIKA ABRAHAMSSON

MEDFORD,
MASSACHUSETTS

BOOK GROUPS COME in many forms, from large, theme-oriented ones to less formal, meet-and-eat varieties. Our book group is a chorus composed of four distinct voices that create harmonies and counterpoints for each other. Each member has her time as a soloist. Everyone gets a chance to sing melody. The group began as a duet, grew to a trio, then to a quartet. The piece goes like this.

Becky: I started a book group to avoid arrest. I needed to keep myself from clutching a half-groggy subway commuter by the lapels and demanding his views on skewed marriage surveys and the she-devil image of women in the movies. I had to prevent myself from calling up every talk radio show in town. I wanted to avoid pummeling my friends and coworkers with a database full of facts and figures about the repression of women in American society (those enraging, engaging facts you always wished you had on hand).

I was reading Susan Faludi's *Backlash: The Undeclared War Against American Women.* This book should come with a warning label: Do Not Read This Alone! This book must be discussed, harped on, disputed, embraced. It proves that you don't need a CD-ROM drive to experience interactive media. One of my problems was that no one else I knew had read *Backlash*. And to make things worse, I was facing the first September in twenty-four years during which I was not in school. Gone were the built-in, book-chewing, idea-thrashing sessions that had become as comfortable as my old college sweatshirt.

So I did the only natural thing—I called Sandy, a graduate school friend, grabbed her by the lapels, and began flogging her with details from Faludi's book. After thirty minutes, she consented and a book group was born.

Initially, Sandy and I were a bit reluctant to call ourselves a book group, but all the components were there: we met regularly, usually for two hours every two weeks. We enjoyed reading, discussing, and handling books. We had intelligent, meaningful conversations about writing style, the role of editing, character development, the use of writing devices, and more. We learned more about each other and our views of the world. And of course, we ate.

In our book group, consensus was easy to come by, and we quickly decided to focus on reading creative nonfiction. Why? First, we were both former English majors who felt that the curricula we'd been weaned on was high fat and fiction heavy. Second, as nonfiction writers ourselves, we hoped that studying various types of creative nonfiction would provide insights for our own works. We took turns choosing which books to read, a practice we still follow.

Sandy: Becky and I were sitting in a café drinking coffee, having an intense conversation about *Backlash*. This conversation intertwined with our mutual complaint that there should be a group around for us to join as readers and writers of literary nonfiction. At some point, our "should" became "why not?" and we had our book group.

This spontaneity isn't to say that the idea came out of nowhere. The idea of belonging to a group had been with me since I decided to become a writer. I was jealous of famous groups of writers such as Gertrude Stein's gang in Paris in the twenties and the Boston-area poets in the fifties, including Robert Lowell, Elizabeth Bishop, Sylvia Plath, Maxine Kumin, and Anne Sexton. I wanted to be part of such a group the way the scarecrow from *The Wizard of Oz* wanted a brain. If I only had a writers' group, then I'd be a real writer.

I met a poet, who recommended that I join a group led by her friend. I was ecstatic: I was on my way to the emerald city. My euphoria soon shriveled when I called the group leader and discovered the session would cost three hundred dollars for ten weeks. I was pretty sure that Hemingway didn't pay Gertrude Stein to sit in her living room.

Instead, I decided to enter a graduate writing program and take a class called Writing the Nonfiction Book. In the class, I met Becky and discovered that genre of writing called creative nonfiction, originally dubbed the "New Journalism" in the fifties.

My longing to connect to reading and writing nonfiction was fulfilled when Becky and I began discussing *Backlash*. For me, the book group has become a special time when modern life—the television, radio, telephone—cannot intrude. In our living rooms, backyards, and neighborhood cafés, I can spend time simply and richly, enjoying conversations about the books at hand. And like the scarecrow who realizes that he had a brain all along, I have come to realize I am a writer. And that to gather with people who are intelligent and care deeply about words and writing is all I ever needed to support my habit.

Another more practical benefit of the group has been to slow down my reading speed. I have a tendency to devour books whole, reading them quickly to find out what happens next, only to forget most of what I've read as soon as I finish. The group helps me to slow down, savor, and delight in the words, phrases, and subtleties. Discussing important points with others also cements the book in my mind and leads to discoveries I would have missed at my usual breakneck pace.

Becky: Although we did make an effort to savor each book, Sandy and I still managed to read a fair number of works. After beginning with *Backlash*, we moved to *The Soul of a New Machine* by Tracy Kidder. We had both heard so much about this book from friends and professors, we felt we had to give it a try. While not a flint to spark debate, *Soul* showed how a book can go from being a groundbreaking exposé to a history book and still maintain its initial integrity and hold its readers.

We followed by reading *Wouldn't Take Nothing for My Journey Now* by Maya Angelou, which I couldn't help thinking of as Wouldn't Pay Nothing for This Book Again. Given how much Sandy and I had enjoyed Angelou's previous works, we could only explain this padded yet slim and thinly written volume as the publisher's attempt to capitalize on the author's increased name recognition following President Clinton's inauguration. Nevertheless, the book provoked animated discussions about the importance of editors, both the writer's internal editor and the editors of large publishing houses.

After our experience with the Angelou book, we decided to choose a book that we knew a bit more about. *New York in the Fifties* by Dan Wakefield filled that criterion. Both Sandy and I had worked with Wakefield as a teacher and advisor during our graduate school years. In this case, the book took on added interest because we knew the author and yet glimpsed other aspects of our mentor that we hadn't seen before.

Sandy: Dan described his own literary scene in Greenwich Village in the fifties, when he and his peers actually used novels to help them understand their lives. They would quote these books to each other and could even recall passages today.

Becky: And while my living room was far from the White Horse Tavern, we like to think that the flavor of the discussions were much the same.

Sandy: Soon after finishing Dan's book, our fledgling book group began to grow. We don't actively recruit members, but we don't discourage people who inquire about the group. For many people, the focus on nonfiction is not a good fit, but Gloria, a friend from high school, indulged our passion and perhaps found an outlet for her own connection with words.

Gloria: Why did I join the group? Well, although I've been a somewhat avid reader of all types of literary genre, I found that reading can be quite isolating. When I lived in Connecticut near my friends and family, I thought it rather natural to discuss the latest Grisham novel with anyone who had read it or even to talk about what was written in the newspaper with my mom. Since I moved to Rhode Island by myself, I have come to realize that having no one to talk to about reading is like watching a television sitcom alone—it's not much fun laughing by yourself. So when Sandy kept talking about her "book thing with Becky," I invited myself to join, hoping once again to take part in that great human experience of sharing thoughts and ideas with others without the restrictions of rules and deadlines that can bog one down.

What have I gotten out of book group? Some really great apple pie! And I have received what I was looking for: wonderful new friends, enriching discussions of a variety of authors' works and styles, and a better understanding of the power of the written word. We all have been moved at some point either by a description, viewpoint, or something unstated by an author. I have learned that although the words can't move on the page, they will forever remain liquid in interpretation by those who read them.

Becky: Gloria joined us just as we were beginning Adrienne Rich's *What Is Found There: On Poetry and Politics*, a book that could make you cry for the skill of it. While this selection edged more toward literary criticism, we never lacked for images or incredibly crafted phrases to discuss. Perhaps more than with any other book, the conversations around this book happened on a grander scale, on a deeper level, with a broader sweep. The feeling that each word had been specially selected, never carelessly dropped on the page, stayed with us throughout this reading.

Sandy: With Rich's book, it was as if our wish to be moved by a book, to be able to quote it to our friends and go back to it year after year was granted. I knew instantly that this was a book that would be with me for a long time and help me sort out life in these complicated, media-drenched times. The reason? Part of it is her insight into the artistic community as it tries to survive on the fringe of modern society and part is Rich's achingly beautiful prose. To be in the hands of such a master was an unexpected and well-remembered joy.

Gloria: Rich's book is definitely my favorite so far.

Becky: Unfortunately, such favorable reviews were not in order for our next selection, *Dakota* by Kathleen Norris. This book has become our whipping post and a standard against which almost anything will excel. Many other reviewers wearing the mantle of respectability from famous journals and newspapers would disagree. However, we found it to be one of the most strident works we'd read, written by someone we felt did protest too much. This was definitely a discussion starter; our critique of Norris's work is the closest we've ever come to an outright flaying.

By July, we had recovered from the barrenness of *Dakota* and our group had added another member, Erika. As we took our books and iced tea to the beach and outdoor cafés, Sandy and I congratulated ourselves that the group had doubled in size in less than a year.

Erika: When Becky told me about the nonfiction book group she and Sandy had started, I was intrigued. Even as we spoke, I had twenty or so (and I only wish I were kidding) nonfiction books lying around my house waiting for me to pick them up and start reading. The problem was that although all of those books contained topics of interest to me, it was just too hard. It required too much discipline to put down that really great murder mystery or that fantastic science fiction book and pick up something that would actually require some thought and concentration.

Here was my opportunity. If I had a deadline, and if I had people with whom I could discuss these and other nonfiction works, then perhaps I could muster the motivation to crack those previously uncracked bindings.

It worked. I have found a way into the world of nonfiction. Good discussion and flying ideas lead me toward books that I would ordinarily never have stopped to peruse; and, yet once I begin to read, all kinds of worlds, thoughts, and personalities open up and I am, more often than not, delighted!

Becky: One of the books that delighted some, but not all of us, was *The White Album* by Joan Didion, which, like *Soul of a New Machine*, served a historical purpose, as a primer on the sixties since all of us are too young to have been a real part of the events of that time. We marveled over Didion's ability to select just the right details for her lists and her tendency as a Californian to be driven to distraction by the ebb and flow of water.

Next we methodically picked our way through Kansas and *PrairyErth* with William Least Heat-Moon. A few things set this book apart. The size, at 622 pages, was daunting and required us to think more than usual about where we should try to be in the book by our next meeting. The pace of this work was different too, more measured and even, like every Kansas county mile.

Presently, we're in the midst of *Surprised by Joy* by C. S. Lewis. Among us are a divinity school graduate with Unitarian leanings, a devout Catholic, a comfortably committed Congregationalist, and a former atheist making her way back into the spiritual fray. This mix should provide a rich and interesting context for discussions of this spiritual autobiography. Already we've wrangled with the definitions of joy—Lewis's and our own.

Sandy: One thing Lewis's book is teaching us is that four is not too few people to support wide-ranging views and lively discussions. Also, while our book group has some fairly specific aspects to it, like reading nonfiction, that other groups may not want to duplicate, there is a more basic concept that anyone can employ. When we did not find an established book group that would satisfy our interests and personal motivations, we simply started our own—something anyone can do.

Becky: As for me, did I find what I was searching for through this book group? You bet. I've surrounded myself with people who aren't put off by an animated, intense discussion about how a writer selects details. I am with individuals who know what it's like to read with pens in hand. I belong to a group whose members savor a well-proportioned trim size the way some people swill brandy in the light. I am among friends.

For the future, I'm confident that our group will thrive beyond its first anniversary, although the four of us now face the struggle of finding the point where our divergent schedules meet. The time spent together, when we can find it, is always rewarding. Everyone contributes equally. Each person brings a different perspective to the books while maintaining a common commitment to the group. As such, this book group is truly a chorus of voices, and the result is richer than the sum of the parts.

For this group's reading list, see page 267.

The Meta-Corporate Book Club

BRIAN W. VASZILY   ARLINGTON HEIGHTS, ILLINOIS

THE CORPORATE WORLD drones. Often causes groans. Inspires clones. Most enter the glass doors looking for bucks, at least bucks bigger than the small bucks to be scraped up repeating "Welcome to Home Depot, may I help you?" or "Let's have quiet now, class," or "I am Artiste! May I help you?" Many of the most who enter end up throwing all of their energy into the commerce winds, pushing day and even night to learn some new software, burn some old competitor, and earn some heavy raise.

But among the ranks of every corporation are the unincorporated. The resisters.

These people are not the same beings as the slackers or the sonofabitchin' anti-capitalist punk rebels that sometimes find temporary homes in air-conditioned cubicles. Indeed, the resisters are often among the most comfortably positioned in the company, precisely because of what they realize and what they do in response to the realization. They realize that their careers—the bottom lines, Gantt Charts, flights at 7:40 A.M., e-commerce, 401Ks, acquisitions, and PowerPoint presentations—are but one puff in a life full of profound gusts.

Such resisters are the stuff our Meta-Corporate Book Club is made of. We Meta members are not all female or all male, we do not all possess the same socio-politico-religiouso palettes, and we do not always fall in splendid submission at the altar of the same authors. We do, however, share three important things: we love to read, we work at the same behemoth company, and we know there is so much more to life than working at the behemoth company to make more and more and more. For instance, there is reading. Reading to understand the human condition, to reach beyond this condition, and—gasp!—to be entertained. And so our essential rule is to read and discuss books that are not tracts designed to Advance Your Career. No resume building, project managing, Internet developing, "working your way to the top" slop with us. We spend far too many business hours sludging our way through business goop as it is.

Instead, we read books that put us in landscapes far removed from cubicles, boardrooms, or the interiors of our Accords and Caravans. Salman Rushdie's *Midnight's Children*. Willa Cather's *Oh Pioneers!* Gloria Naylor's *Mama Day*.

We read books of the dispossessed and disenfranchised, who could have had it even worse and got a job in the mailroom. Russell Banks's *Rules of the Bone*. Nathaniel Hawthorne's *The Scarlet Letter*. Kate Chopin's *The Awakening*.

We read books whose subject, tsk tsk, one should never discuss in the workplace. Pablo Neruda's *100 Love Sonnets*. Julian Rios's *Loves That Bind*. And—big ooooh—*The Story of O* by Pauline Reage.

We read fantasy books. Not the sword-and-sorcery fantasy— although we did read and were uniformly captivated by Marion Zimmer Bradley's *The Mists of Avalon*—but moreover the fantasy of the little people standing up to and sometimes beating the big shots. Especially if the big shot resembles our boss's boss's boss or some prominent CEO. (I would say my boss, too, but I love my boss. He reads, and that may include this book.) Upton Sinclair's *The Jungle*. Leslie Marmon Silko's *Almanac of the Dead*. James Thurber's juvenile fiction masterpiece, *The Wonderful O* (a vastly different O than Reage's).

And we read books about those who have really done fantastic things with their lives, or recognized the fantastic in everyday life. *Let the Trumpet Sound: A Life of Martin Luther King, Jr.,* by Stephen Oates. Hayden Herrera's life of the famous Mexican painter, *Frida: A Biography of Frida Kahlo.* Eva Fogelman's *Conscience and Courage: Rescuers of Jews during the Holocaust.* Annie Dillard's *Pilgrim at Tinker Creek.* Thoreau's *Walden.* And we relate it to our lives, how maybe we could have been that brave, maybe we still can be, maybe our kids will be.

Because we are busy reading, or otherwise living our lives, we try not to spend our leisure time discussing the books. Instead, we offer our interpretations, views and reviews, and favorite moments, characters, and passages via company E-mail or outside our offices and over the cubicles. And, yes, even at the water cooler. When the conversation gets particularly good, we may even cut into our beloved lunch breaks. We have even been known—but not by those who would snitch—to carry on after working hours at a bar and grill down the street. All in all, though, we try to keep the book discussions in the workplace, to ensure a productive workday.

And now on to the how-to. Or, how to form a meta-corporate book club in your corporation.

The most important thing is to be yourself. That means you should continue eavesdropping on the conversations at the front desk, in the cafeteria, behind the closed doors of the executive conference suites, or anywhere the talk most likely has nothing to do with work. Based on what is being said, and how it is being said, you can get a pretty reliable fix on who is most likely to jump into the book club with you. If it is an endless loop of banter about the loopholes in the latest tax law, or a heated debate about the greatest spark plugs ever built, move right along. If, however, the talk swirls around everyone's first kiss, or how everybody got the scars on their flesh, or if there is a God then why do we have to shave our legs and faces, or why smoking is terrible— awful, yuck yuck, phooey—but three-fourths of everyone at the table sneaks one now and then, then maybe you've found some meta-corporate book club mates. Proceed casually.

Don't say, "Hi, I'm Sally from sales. You guys seem interesting, fun, and open-minded. Wanna share a book?"

You'll receive stares colder than the afternoon coffee in the break room.

Instead, politely interrupt by telling them you couldn't help but overhear their conversation, and then add something to it. Tell them how you got that scar in your armpit. Offer them a smoke, even if you don't have one. Over the course of this and perhaps subsequent conversations, you can assess who among them is a truly worthy meta member. When they seem comfortable with you, catch them alone and gently lure them into the club: "Hey baby, you seem so deep, wanna book with me?"

Or you could just invite your current friends at work into the club.

Of course, you can also attempt the conventional: advertise in the company newsletter or Intranet bulletin board. I don't recommend it, but you can attempt it. If you try to be low-key and simply state that "a company book club is forming," every Tom, Dick, and Mary in accounting will assume the intent is career-oriented. "This is, after all, the workplace for God's sake!" They'll have their *Valuation: Measuring and Managing the Value of Companies* in hand at the first meeting and just you try convincing them how Shakespeare's *Measure for Measure* is a more profound piece!

You can instead try to describe the true purpose of the book club:

"Our purpose is to read books with the intent of lifting our heads off the corporate grinder, to acknowledge that we're actually humans who simultaneously love and despise our families, who have pointless to profound sex, who lift our heads to the stars and wonder how far, when, who, and why? We don't, in short, read Tom Peters or anyone like him."

But don't count on publication. You'll likely be told by somebody, or somebody else who sounds just like that somebody, that corporate communications are for much more important things. Like the investment in some new technology that will fix all the problems caused by the old technology. Or the vice president of human resources' latest company bowling score. Drone drone drone.

Groan.

Don't be discouraged. For all the how-to advice, resisters most often tend to attract the other resisters just naturally, without much effort. Especially in enclosed spaces dominated by neutral hues and utterances. They're the ones taking the deep breaths of life and exhaling color. You are, of course, already a member of one club with them—the living. And if they like to read, perhaps they'll also become a member of your meta-corporate book club.

But even if you never find another living person among your corporation's dead, take final solace in this—you alone can be your meta-corporate book club. For there are thousands of truly worthwhile books out there for you to sneak under your desk or into the washroom stall. What's more, not one of them has "For Dummies" in the title.

PART IV

Follow the Leader (Though in a Book Group, She's Probably Following You)

Book group leaders come in all forms—paid, unpaid, elected, unofficially appointed—and, as evidenced in this section, group members and their leaders tend to be fiercely loyal to each other. One of the many benefits of a group with a leader is that it cuts the time spent on unrelated issues. A bigger benefit is that your book group leader just may have insight into the book that escaped you. If you're short on cash, but want a leader, check out your library or local bookstore. Library-sponsored groups (you'll find four in this section) are perhaps the most democratic book groups around—they're free of charge and open to everyone, even those who snooze through the discussion or don't read the book.

Saying Nay

Diane Leslie   📖   Los Angeles, California

RECENTLY, WHEN LEADING a newly formed book group, I encountered
a woman who I, in my kinder moments, can only refer to as a literary
naysayer. (Some facilitators believe there is one naysayer in every book
group, but I've never experienced such widespread virulence.) She
detested the book I'd chosen. "It's just a bunch of random incidents that
add up to one big zero," she hissed, emitting a mist of spit that settled
on the brownies and lemon bars that garnished the coffee table.
Unfortunately for me, her incontestable negativity induced a quasi-
accord among the other book group members.

As it happens, I've read *So Long, See You Tomorrow* by William
Maxwell about ten times. I find this novel so intricate and masterful
that every reading reveals even more profundity in its 135 pages. But
while I contemplated some snappy verbal abuse of the naysayer, I
recalled the very first contact—catastrophic contact—I'd ever had with
a book group.

A perfectly content, solitary reader, I had allowed myself to be
talked into attending my friend Ivy's group. She'd been raving for
months about the depth and breadth of the discussions and the prowess
of the leader. Giving in to her desire to "share," I prepared, as any
responsible book group participant should, by carefully reading that
month's selection, *Sophie's Choice* by William Styron. I'd already read

the novel in hardback with great admiration and found the second reading all the more enlightening.

The meeting took place at Ivy's synagogue. Refreshments were served in the lobby where I met the other book group members—all of them women—very nice, bright women I soon learned as we chatted about our jobs, hobbies, and families.

"We're not supposed to discuss *it* until the official discussion," Ivy explained the lack of mention of the novel. Finally, a man appeared on the balcony above us and signaled that it was time to join him. "That's our leader, Rabbi Taitz," Ivy said. "Isn't he amazingly good looking?"

We followed him into what appeared to be a schoolroom full of desks with attached seats that were meant for middle-sized children, not middle-aged adults. Rabbi Taitz could have moved his chair anywhere, but he chose to sit on the desk in front of us.

Before he could officially begin the discussion, one woman, then another and another, blurted out, "I loved it. I simply loved the book." "I cried for three days straight." "The suffering of that poor woman, making a choice like that." "But what a great writer because, look, there was still so much humor." "Laughing through tears." "And what insight into the human psyche." "And the difference between those who've survived and those who haven't."

The women couldn't contain themselves, they were so excited; they kept turning their heads and their bodies to see each other, spinning uncomfortably in their molded plastic chairs. When I glanced at the Rabbi, I couldn't help notice the look of disapproval that contorted his handsome face. His objection, as we soon learned, centered on the fact that he believed William Styron had no right to write about the Holocaust.

Now *I* couldn't restrain myself. "Why?" I asked.

"William Styron is not a Jew," the Rabbi said ruefully.

Since I am a writer who often writes about characters of religions, creeds, and a sex other than my own, I bristled.

The regular group members did more. They all talked at once. They yelled. "What difference does that make?" "He captured the feelings!" "He moved me!" "He understood!" "It's like saying a man can't write about a woman!" "Or a woman write about a man!"

"The Holocaust is different!" the Rabbi yelled back. "Only a Jew has the prerogative to write about it! No one else!"

It was lucky the refreshments had been left downstairs because, I felt certain, had they not, the book group members would have thrown chunks of brie and fistfuls of cracked-wheat crackers at Rabbi Taitz's perfect, though slim, target. As it was, the group's constituents extricated themselves from their diminutive desks and noisily slammed out of the room.

Now, many years later, sitting in a pretty living room with a teacup and saucer balanced on my knees, I didn't want to turn into a Rabbi Taitz. Nevertheless, I felt the necessity of defending this perfectly marvelous book. I'm a writer, after all, and I feel deeply saddened when readers don't notice or appreciate what some writers achieve with nothing more than words.

"Did you notice William Maxwell taking any risks in this book?" I asked in a nonjudgmental tone.

"What do you mean risks?" a voice asked skeptically.

"Well, I'd say that quoting the artist Giacometti about an abstract work of sculpture that seemingly has no connection to the characters in the novel is taking a risk akin to hang gliding in the Himalayas. Why would this ingenious novelist, an editor at *The New Yorker* for forty years, stop the flow of his plot to describe a work of art, ostensibly allowing a famous artist to usurp the narrative for a page and a half?"

A fruitful conversation ensued, and I hadn't resorted to Rabbi Taitz's method. I'd just posed one of the questions I'd been asking myself. Questioning as I read other writers has informed my own writing considerably. As a rule, members of book groups haven't taken literature courses, but given suitable questions they often respond with amazing insight. I've surely learned more from the book groups I lead than they have from me.

The naysayer, by the way, didn't betray her nature by telling me, as the other members did at the end of the discussion, that she now truly appreciated having read *So Long, See You Tomorrow*. She did me a great kindness however—she kept quiet.

A Community Place to Gather and Grow

CHRISTINE POSINGER AND
MARTHA SLOAN

DES PLAINES,
ILLINOIS

MY WONDERFUL EXPERIENCE running a book group in a public library of an upper-middle-class Chicago suburb led me to start a book group in 1996 when I took a new job in a very different library. The Des Plaines Public Library, located at the edge of Chicago, is in a more urban, more ethnically-mixed, and larger community than the library where I had worked previously.

But though I drive to a different place to work, I brought with me my same love of books and book groups, and my firm conviction that it is one of the missions of the public library to reach out to the community, share good books, introduce new authors and ideas, and provide a forum for discussion. Therefore, one of the first directions that I gave the Des Plaines Library Adult Services staff was to start a monthly book discussion. I felt certain that though this community was different from the suburb I had left, every community has a core of dedicated and interested readers. I gave Chris, the librarian responsible for the fiction collection, the task of starting the program. This experience is her story.

I have to admit that when Martha gave me the assignment of organizing a book discussion group for the library, I was apprehensive. But as I read an earlier edition of *The Book Group Book* and made plans, I became more enthusiastic. Over the past three years I have come to recognize that book groups are an integral part of the library's mission.

The six librarians in the adult services department decided to share the responsibility for the discussions. Each librarian selects a book to discuss and then leads that discussion. As in many book groups, the discussion leader is responsible for researching the author, reading reviews, and preparing questions for discussion. Because librarians have so many different duties, I felt that spreading out the responsibility for the discussions would prevent burnout and keep us all involved. We could support each other and give advice. My job was to coordinate the programs. We selected a fixed time and date to ensure continuity—the first Tuesday morning of the month—and we serve coffee and cookies.

In the spring of 1996, I placed flyers in the library lobby advertising this new venture. The first group met in April. Five people came and I led a lively discussion of Terry McMillan's *Waiting to Exhale*. I thought we were on the way to success. However, in May, my worst misgivings were fulfilled. Only one person came to the discussion of *The Plague* by Albert Camus, and that person had not even read the book.

But at least we learned a valuable lesson about the need to select the right book for our participants. This group was not ready for Camus. Though I held on to my hope that in the future they might be willing to stretch and try such an unfamiliar work, early in the book group's life I found it necessary to choose books with broad appeal. One of the next books we chose was Barbara Kingsolver's *The Bean Trees*.

From the start we made it a rule that books are chosen by the discussion leaders. I learned from the experiences of other librarians that if group members select the titles, they often suggest books they like, but ones that may not be very discussible. The leaders are then stuck trying to find something to say. Romances, mysteries, and other genre writing usually fall into this category.

When it's my turn to choose, I look for books that explore characters with different ethnic backgrounds. I like to use our discussions as an opportunity to expose us to ideas and lifestyles that are unlike our own. Another librarian makes her selections from the book group guides that have been produced by Vintage and other publishers. A third focuses on historical fiction like *Cold Mountain*. We all, however, experience an adrenaline rush when we hit a home run: Everyone loves the book and discussion is engaging and multifaceted.

An early challenge was attracting the larger community to the group. I realized that to attract more participants we would have to promote our program more heavily. The flyers were a start, but we needed something splashy. The library had recently purchased a color copier, and we used it to copy the covers of upcoming book discussion books. The titles for the next four months were arranged on a large poster that invited the general public to attend the discussions, and the poster was displayed prominently in the entry hallway. The library's public information officer also sent out press releases to the local newspapers advertising the monthly discussion. These efforts slowly led to a viable group of participants.

One of my jobs was to obtain the books for each month's discussion. I established a routine for purchasing a number of paperback copies of the books that could be supplemented with additional books sent through interlibrary loan. Therefore, the books we discuss are always more than six months old. After the discussion, I add the paperback copies to a new special collection that we call "Book Group." These multiple copies are available to other libraries for their book discussions. We are also pleased that some local, independent book groups have discovered our collection and will often choose to discuss books from it. In addition, we have sent copies to the local high school where they also have a discussion group.

As the numbers grew, the group began to take shape. A core group of twelve to fifteen women became regulars. The complexion of our group is largely senior women with a handful of stay-at-home moms. However, we have noticed that nonregulars are drawn by specific book titles. When we discussed Amy Tan's *The Joy Luck Club*, a Japanese man came for the discussion, and an Indian woman brought a fresh point of view to *The God of Small Things* by Arundhati Roy.

In the past year and a half, a stable number of eighteen to twenty-five people has attended each discussion. The members who have been together for three years now have bonded with each other and with the librarians. The increased number of participants, however, has created some challenges. When twenty-five people gather at a table, side conversations arise, and the discussion leader often has to be firm and reign in the talkers to keep the group focused on the book. The leader also walks a fine line between permitting participants to share personal experiences and strictly adhering to the book.

Recently, we have also been plagued by another problem that is common to many book group: participants aren't finishing the book. In the beginning, our members were very good about reading the entire book even if they found it hard going at first. They felt challenged by the books that were new to them, like *How the Garcia Girls Lost Their Accents* by Julia Alvarez. After those discussions, members would comment that, while they may not have chosen the book on their own, they were glad for the exposure. We librarians were encouraged to select a wide variety of different kinds of books that we felt could lead to a lively discussion.

However, as one or two newer members have not been finishing the book, others have begun to follow suit. Group members continue to be enthusiastic about the group, sign out each new book, and attend each meeting, but the discussion has suffered. Next month I plan to give the group a friendly but firm reminder that a discussion relies on the contributions of all its members and that no fruitful conversation can take place if people haven't read the book.

Book group Tuesday has become a welcome event in our library. The participants begin arriving around 9:30 A.M. for our 10:00 A.M. discussion. Their first stop is to sign out the book for the next month. They then spend some leisure time in the meeting room, drinking coffee and chatting with others. After the discussion they linger, and I have the satisfaction of seeing that they've enjoyed themselves and have been intellectually stimulated by the morning's discussion.

The group now has a life of its own, and I enjoy my part in it. Beyond keeping track of the program logistics, I make sure that the library continues to offer a lively and meaningful discussion each month on a book of singular interest. Book discussions are a wonderful way to build good will and enthusiasm for any library as well as to enrich the lives of its members. I am pleased that our book group has provided a place in our community where people who love reading and books may gather and grow.

For this group's reading list, see page 339.

Contemporary Books Discussion Group— Bettendorf Public Library

HEDY N. R. HUSTEDDE   📖   DAVENPORT, IOWA

IN MANY WAYS, a book discussion group sponsored by a library is the best of all worlds. It tends to carry on as long as a library staff member is assigned to be its liaison, despite fluctuations in membership. Publicity is no problem; a meeting place is no problem; special deals on the purchase of books can often be arranged; audiovisual equipment is available; and participants are likely to be diverse in viewpoint, age, and background, making for lively discussions.

The Bettendorf Public Library's Contemporary Books Discussion Group officially began in 1961. I didn't join until 1989, when I also joined the library staff as a part-time circulation clerk and felt the need to broaden my reading experiences. After a couple of years as a member, I was promoted to being the group's library liaison. I also began working on my master's degree in library science, which made for a fine mesh between my personal and professional life.

Currently, the group has thirty-one members, but that many have never shown up at any one meeting. Usually the number of participants hovers around twenty. Some of these people are what we call "found-ing" members, who have stuck with the group for more than thirty years. Members range in age from their twenties to their seventies and three-quarters of the group is female.

Participants come from all walks of life: journalist, minister, engi-neer, orthopedic surgeon, laboratory technician, parent, business teacher, English teacher, kindergarten teacher, special education teacher, sales-person, consultant, business executive, student. Naturally, many points of view are reflected in members' interpretations of what they read. This is a most valuable circumstance. When it was suggested that per-haps two groups should be formed from the one to prevent overcrowding the library's small conference room, the idea was soundly defeated—nobody wanted to miss out on what anybody else had to say.

As long as I've been in the group, we have met on the second Wednesday evening of the month, September through May. Discussions have been known to continue out in the parking lot or at a local restau-rant for those not satisfied at the conclusion.

Choosing books is a group effort. First, a volunteer committee of three to five members browses bookstores, reads reviews, asks friends and colleagues for recommendations, and devises a list of twenty titles that are available in paperback. The list is usually half fiction and half nonfiction, and despite the adjective "contemporary" in the group's name, it often includes classics like Mark Twain's *Roughing It* or Willa Cather's *My Antonia*. We also often include a play or a book of poetry, and we almost always read a prizewinner (Nobel, Pulitzer, National Book Award, or Booker).

After the list is compiled, the entire membership is then invited for a potluck meal at a member's home, where we read the annotated list of titles. At this time, members voice objections or make support-ing statements for particular books. We vote for nine books by a show of hands.

Formerly, one infamous item was always included on the potluck menu—Artillery Punch, a mixture of, among other things, claret, bour-bon, bitters, rum, and Rhine wine. I was given the recipe along with this admonition, "If you file it in the book group archives and don't serve it, I'm sure you're all better off." At recent potlucks, liquids of considerably less alcoholic nature have been the beverages of choice.

The potluck is usually well attended. While there, we get to know each other on a more personal basis, each member has a say in the choices for discussion for the next year, and we have yet another chance to talk about one of the loves of our lives—good reading.

Despite our attempts to be democratic, not everybody is always happy with the book choice. One person was disgruntled when we voted to read Rush Limbaugh's *The Way Things Ought to Be*. She came to the discussion, however, and got a rousing round of applause because it happened to be her seventy-fifth birthday. Her next statement, which we expected would acknowledge the applause, went something like this, "I have to say . . ." We nodded in encouragement, "that I am still ashamed that this group chose that book to read!" We were somewhat deflated but had to laugh in appreciation of her stubborn honesty.

Another member always reads the book aloud to her husband and said that there was a period in the seventies when the group was reading books that were so sexually graphic and so seemingly unnatural and immoral that her hair stood on end. Either the group's tastes have changed somewhat, writers aren't quite so graphic, or she's become immune, because, of late, her hair has always been in place.

I'm fond of remembering how some members initially didn't think Diane Ackerman's *A Natural History of the Senses* was so good, but after the discussion, some decided to purchase their copies. This same change of opinion has occurred with several titles and indicates the power of discussion.

At this time, books are paid for through the library's gift fund. Participants may purchase the books at a substantial discount or return them in as-good-as-mint condition to be sold in the library's semi-annual book sale or to other local book discussion groups, of which there are several. The theory behind this generosity is to emphasize our library's dedication to free services and participation in programs. No one will be turned away from our discussion group because of not being able to afford to buy the books. Funding a book discussion group also helps fulfill the library's function of promoting lifelong learning.

New members are welcome at any time. Some stay for just one discussion and some become regulars. Sometimes students show up to take notes or tape the discussion because they happen to be studying the book we've read. This happened with Deborah Tannen's *You Just Don't Understand*.

Whenever the local colleges and arts council bring a major writer to our area for a series of readings, lectures, and workshops, we always read something by that writer. This was the case with Kurt Vonnegut, E. L. Doctorow, Marge Piercy, and Bharati Mukherjee, among others. Knowing something of them and of their work ahead of time enhanced their visits for us.

Periodically, we've enjoyed having a local expert lead a discussion on a book of choice (as happened with *My Antonia*, *The Great Gatsby*, and *Balkan Ghosts*). They are usually teachers who gladly share their special knowledge. In watching them, we are also given hints on how better to lead discussions ourselves.

For the most part, the discussions are led by volunteers from within the group. I rarely lead a discussion. But I always help the prospective leaders find information about the author, book reviews, or other information from the resources in our library. I also encourage them to check out Ted Balcom's exceedingly useful *Book Discussions for Adults*.

Members also appreciate props of all sorts. We snacked on Indian cookies (*nankatai*) and sesame crunch during the discussion of Bharati Mukherjee's *The Middleman and Other Stories* and on Czech *kolaches* during *My Antonia*. We've used transparencies with overhead projectors, shown short videos (for Michael Carey's *Honest Effort*), listened to audiotaped segments of author interviews (for Jonathan Kozol's *Savage Inequalities*) and of programs conducted by authors (for Rush Limbaugh's *The Way Things Ought to Be*). One group leader treated the group to a simple and informative slide program on cell division as an introduction to Evelyn Keller's book about Barbara McClintock, *A Feeling for the Organism*. The person leading the discussion of Ralph Leighton's *Tuva or Bust!* brought a compact disc of incredible Tuvan throat singing and he also managed to collect a whole set of oddly shaped Tuvan postage stamps for us to examine. That bit of extra effort is truly effective.

I do all the bookwork and scheduling and lend support in a number of ways. I cannot imagine not being a member of a book discussion group. It has been advantageous to me professionally and personally. I've heard other members make similar comments. We learn so much about ourselves from each other and from this literature, which is enhanced by our comments. What's more, we laugh a lot.

In the beginning, I think we joined a discussion group because we cared about literature. We keep coming back because we care about each other. In the end, the literature becomes us and we become the literature. That's what makes it great.

For this group's reading list, see page 269.

Hard Work and Rich Rewards

CLARE PETERSON AND
MARIE DENCH

PHILADELPHIA,
PENNSYLVANIA

BOOK DISCUSSIONS BEGAN at Northeast Regional Library in 1966. At our library, the book discussions have both social and intellectual functions. The group members look forward to the time spent together, and the librarians who lead the discussions can interact with the group in a relaxed manner, in contrast to the hectic pace of reference transactions elsewhere in the library. The chance to share and enjoy ideas attracts the staff, even though the book discussions involve responsibilities above and beyond an already heavy workload.

How the Group Is Organized

The library is a logical setting for a book group. At Northeast Regional, librarians volunteer to plan and lead the discussions. There are two book discussion series—fall and spring. Planning for each begins roughly six months in advance to allow time for publicity, placement of book orders, and other organizational tasks. The librarians discuss themes and titles, brainstorm about problems, and plan approaches to the material.

Anyone interested in starting a group should think seriously about how formal the group's operations will be. Obviously, the less formality, the less work. In a library setting, which involves intricate scheduling of staff and facilities, as well as advance orders for materials, the book discussion process demands an orderly routine.

At Northeast, two librarians lead each discussion. Pairing people has many advantages. Two people working together share ideas, split up the workload of background research, and give each other moral support if a problem comes up during a discussion. If one leader becomes ill, or cannot work the discussion because of some other emergency, the other is able to keep the series on schedule. Barring the inclusion of a partner, anyone working alone needs to keep arrangements fairly simple and the group fairly small. Book discussions, for all the enjoyment and stimulation they provide, involve a lot of work.

Anyone wanting to establish his or her own group, outside the library, should ask friends, coworkers, and neighbors about their reading interests—this will give you a roster of eligible candidates from which to determine how much interest these people have in meeting to discuss what they read.

To find an established group to join, inquire at libraries, community centers, churches, or colleges that offer special workshops or noncredit courses.

Special Reading Interests

As it turns out, Northeast's book discussion patrons enjoy reading plays. Our members will try anything—not that they necessarily like it—but they are willing to win a few and lose a few. However, in a book discussion questionnaire distributed nearly three years ago, the respondents made a point of asking for more plays.

Book Discussion "Bests"

Our most successful choices come in a variety of categories for us.

Best gamble on an unconventional book: *Lammas Night* by Katherine Kurtz. This story of the efforts made by England's White Witches to use their occult powers to ward off the Luftwaffe and save their country had the potential to upset people, but the group members took the book on its own merits and enjoyed two thoughtful discussions of it.

Best book that almost didn't make the cut: *Windwalker* by Blaine Yorgason. The leadership of the committee at the time hated this book, but a determined committee member held on to it. Her perseverance paid off handsomely, with two groups of satisfied patrons unable to stop discussing this moving story.

Best discussion of a book that no one (even the leaders) really liked: *In Search of Melancholy Baby* by Vasily Aksyonov. For a series on immigration, this book gave a perspective on the experiences of a latter-twentieth-century Russian immigrant. We were lucky to have such a book (especially since many newly arrived Russians use our library), but the author's smug, know-it-all attitude put everyone's teeth on edge. Nevertheless, we had fun imagining how we would function as newcomers to a strange country.

Best comment ever made about the book discussion series: This would have to be the compliment paid by a gentleman who told the leaders of the discussion of *Elmer Gantry* that he had attended another library's discussions but was switching to Northeast Regional's because we were "more intellectually challenging."

Support Materials

Where appropriate, the book discussion leaders use other media to enhance the discussions. For instance, when we read *To Kill a Mockingbird*, we used scenes from the film (shown on video) to illustrate certain points. When appropriate, one discussion leader displays paper dolls that show what the characters in the book would have worn. Books related to the discussion theme are always on display for further reading.

Other specific instances where we've used support materials include:

1. A clothesline art exhibit of van Gogh and his contemporaries helped illustrate *Lust for Life*.

2. A full-length video showing of *The Great Impostor* complemented a similar book *Catch Me if You Can*.

3. Needleworked scarlet *A*s were given to those who attended discussions of *The Scarlet Letter* so that they could better understand the experience of wearing a badge of shame.

4. Selections from P. D. Q. Bach's *Oedipus Tex* gave the *Oedipus Rex* groups the real lowdown (literally) on Sophocles.

Tales of Woe

It hasn't been all smooth sailing. Several problems have plagued Northeast's series from time to time.

Low attendance has been one problem. We have adjusted both our scheduling and choice of material to attract a slightly younger group. With all due respect to the wonderful older readers who have supported the book discussions for nearly thirty years, we must acknowledge the need for new blood, particularly since we face the loss of our older patrons through illness, relocation to nursing homes, and, ultimately, death. If we can lure a few fresh kids in their forties and fifties into our group, we can anticipate more years of meaningful discussions.

Pushy members can be a problem. Most of the attendees are assertive enough to regain the floor from those who don't wish to yield it. Also, the leaders have developed a knack for seizing on comments made by the disruptive persons and using these remarks to segue back into the group discussion.

Those who haven't read the book are sometimes a problem. In most cases, those who are unprepared have enough sense not to draw attention to themselves. Frequently, these "auditors" simply want to sample the discussion to see if they want to participate more fully in the future. However, one woman who attended the discussion of Andrew Morton's *Diana: Her True Story* had not read the book, but came to the discussion for the sole purpose of proclaiming her vehement hatred for Prince Charles. One of the leaders later dubbed this woman the Energizer Bunny, in honor of her persistence.

Then there are bodily functions. An evening discussion of *Mourning Becomes Electra* came complete with its own inebriated Irishman—an O'Neill soulmate, perhaps. Two women slept through an afternoon discussion of *Fried Green Tomatoes at the Whistle Stop Café*, one of them snoring like a locomotive. And then there is a regular attendee who arrives promptly, greets everyone pleasantly, settles down, and, at regular intervals, emits thunderous belches. At the end of the discussion, he says a cordial goodnight. He rarely comments on the books, unless the belches mean something that the rest of the group cannot comprehend. However, this man did speak very eloquently during a session on Edith Wharton's *The Custom of the Country* and belched only once. Forget Wharton's Legion of Honor and Pulitzer Prize—this is the tribute that really counts!

Organizational details gone awry can also muddle things up. Books sometimes go out of print, publicity flyers occasionally come back with major errors, and procedural questions can filter up or down from the library system's chain of command. These problems occur spontaneously and we deal with them on an ad hoc basis.

Nuts and Bolts

As mentioned above, the volunteer librarians select a theme and flesh it out with appropriate books, which we both borrow from the library system and purchase in bulk in paperback. For this reason, we only use titles that are in print and in paperback. We schedule the use of two meeting rooms for the discussions, which occur at three-week intervals. The discussion dates cannot conflict with civic or religious holidays, library closings, or the vacation plans of the leaders.

Discussions last about ninety minutes, and begin with some background on the author's life and a few critical reviews of the book. The evening groups have a time constraint. They start at 7:30 P.M. but must end in enough time for the librarians and patrons to leave safely at the building's 9:00 P.M. closing time.

The discussion patrons sign in upon arrival and obtain the books for the next discussion. The setup resembles a relay race, with patrons checking in the books they have finished for that particular discussion, and checking out what they will need for the next discussion, three weeks away. The normal library borrowing period is three weeks; if the discussion patrons had to read their books in less time, they would complain bitterly. The afternoon patrons get a break in that they may remain behind after the discussion ends. The staff members must leave to go to desk duty in their departments, but the patrons often remain behind, sometimes for as long as an hour to share their thoughts about some of the more stimulating books.

Fulfilling a Personal Need, Too

No one has yet come forward with a story of how the discussions have saved them during a personal crisis, but we know that several of the regulars have lost spouses or others close to them, have retired, or have made other fundamental changes in their lives. We feel confident in saying that the discussions help these people keep active, maintain contact with other people with similar interests and tastes, and give them something to anticipate.

Frick and Frack at the Library

LAURA LUTERI AND
JUDY BENNETT

MOUNT PROSPECT,
ILLINOIS

WHY IS IT that high comedy is usually delivered in pairs? Abbott and Costello, Laurel and Hardy, Edgar Bergen and Charlie McCarthy . . . Laura and Judy at the library?

For the past ten years, we have been bringing our brand of comedy to our Friends Evening Book Discussion Group on the third Wednesday of every month. Our regulars come each month for entertainment as much as to talk about the book, I think. We aren't sure what we're doing right, but we're having a lot of fun doing it. And, to my way of thinking, that's what makes it all worthwhile.

In the beginning, the library hosted an afternoon book discussion, but it was losing momentum. Judy was president of the library board and I was the neophyte trustee. The library staff morale was low and the Friends Group was suffering from terminal burnout after two unsuccessful referenda campaigns. It had become necessary to reduce library hours and jettison programs and services. When people requested a book discussion group that would meet in the evening, there was just no way the library was going to be able to fund it.

As I remember, it all started, as so many of the things I get myself into do, with the statement, "You know what would be neat . . . ?" The next thing I knew, Judy and I had been volunteered to lead the book discussion sponsored by the Friends of the Library.

We meet in the library's conference room. Our books are borrowed through an interlibrary loan program from neighboring libraries and are checked out for one month. The discussion is advertised through the Friends' newsletters, as well as through the library's publicity.

We have a core group of about a dozen who come regularly, and new Friends are always welcome. Sometimes we have people who come just to see what we're about and other times new people come to discuss a specific book. We've had as few as four and as many as twenty attend. Because it is a quasi-library program, we are always open to the general public and we always try to make newcomers feel welcome. I usually start by making the introductions while Judy and the rest make side bets that I won't be able to remember everyone's name.

When Judy and I started the group it was the blind leading the partially sighted. I had gone to the afternoon discussion group just a couple of times. I don't think Judy had ever been in a book group. Our first choice was Robert Fulghum's *All I Really Need to Know I Learned in Kindergarten*. This book was a terrific icebreaker because we went around the circle and encouraged participants to talk about how each of Fulghum's little pieces reflected their own lives.

Our second book was Tom Wolfe's *Bonfire of the Vanities*. This was the first of our "Frick and Frack" routines. I liked the book and Judy hated it. Judy and I share a sort of dynamic tension. When all else fails and the discussion lags a little, we square off. The group quickly takes up on one side or the other and the discussion takes on a life of its own. The fun part is that we're never sure who is going to side with Judy and who is going to side with me. Although there's a lot of good-natured teasing back and forth, we're all very careful to listen to each other's point of view and not to hurt feelings. We laugh a lot together.

Some of our best discussions have been on books one of us loved and the other hated. But we both agree on our outstanding successes

(*Cold Sassy Tree* by Olive Ann Burns is now assigned reading for anyone who becomes a regular) and our total failures (*Thomas Jefferson* by Fawn Brody is our group's benchmark for our worst choice). Judy and I work with our library's readers' advisors and put together a list of books we think the group would like to read and we also ask for suggestions from the group. We pirate information from anyone who will share it with us. We are very fortunate that Dee, one of our most loyal members, has a daughter who works in a bookstore in Seattle. She keeps coming up with great books for us to add to the list. It took Dee almost two years (Judy and I vetoed it originally) to convince us to read *The Bone People* by Keri Hulme, but it turned out to be a terrific discussion.

We read both fiction and nonfiction, but the group seems to enjoy fiction more. We try to set up the schedule about six months ahead so the library staff can line up the copies we need. Judy and I usually alternate months for choosing, which makes for better variety. If the selection is a success, I picked it. If the discussion is a dud, old-what's-her-face picked that one. Funny how it works out that way.

Our discussions are usually rather free-form. I come with a list of discussion questions, but on good nights I might not even look at the paper. Originally we were supposed to alternate months, but our schedules soon broke the order. Most months we touch base the afternoon before and ask, "Is it your turn or mine?"

Quite often if the story is one which most of the members have enjoyed and it has cinematic quality, we'll spend a few minutes casting the movie. We did this with *Bonfire of the Vanities*, and it was amazing. Not one of us thought of Tom Hanks as the lead. When a book we talked about is made into a film, we take a road trip to see it and discuss the film over dessert afterwards. Our verdict on *Jurassic Park—read the book*. Except for *The Name of the Rose* we usually agree that the books are better.

The average discussion runs an hour to an hour and a half. We then open up the floor to book reports. Each member is asked to tell us about what other books she has been reading since we last met. Some months this discussion of other reading matter is just as interesting as the book we came to discuss. We have discovered we have varied tastes, but we encourage each other to try new genres and authors. After Dee told us about the book, we all read *Bimbos of the Death Sun* by Sharyn McCrumb. I think someday we're going to have to discuss it just so we can see the public reaction when the book is advertised on the library's marquee at the intersection of two major highways.

I realized a while ago that we've all become close friends. When one of our regulars had the lead in a community dinner theater production that kept her from coming to the discussion, we surprised her by turning up as a group in the audience. We discuss our December selection over a potluck at Judy's house. When some scheduling conflicts and an illness in my family made me miss a couple of months in a row leaving Judy to fend for herself (with books I had picked), I realized how much I missed my friends.

This group may have started out as a Friends project, but it has become a project among friends.

For this group's reading list, see page 309.

Brown-Bagging and Mind Stretching

RUTH H. KUEHLER   📖   SAN ANTONIO, TEXAS

OUR BOOK DISCUSSION group started in 1979 under the direction of
Dr. Coleen Grissom, who at the time was a professor of English and
dean of students at Trinity University in San Antonio, Texas. It was her
idea to structure the group as a noncredit, continuing education project for social and intellectual needs. Since then, Dr. Grissom, still an
English professor, became president for student affairs and continues
teaching one advanced English course each semester. She says she
won't give up our reading group, if for no other reason than we keep
her from being afraid of old age (many of us are senior citizens). She
was born in 1934 and I'm afraid if she ever retires the group will never
be the same.

We meet on Mondays from noon to two. There are six Mondays
in each session and we have three or four sessions a year, depending
on Dr. Grissom's schedule.

Twelve to fifteen participants showed up for the first class in 1979,
and we sat around a large conference table in the Gold Room of the
Chapman Center to share books and coffee. Now we have grown to
approximately one hundred members, and we meet in a large room
and sit at round tables in groups of six or eight.

Three original members still come to meetings, others have died and some have moved away, but the ranks keep filling up with women in their forties and fifties. And some of us oldies are still hanging on. One of our members, who has attended for years, was the first woman pathologist in the United States and another the youngest woman to have ever graduated from Vassar. Almost all of the women are college graduates, many from Trinity University.

Our attendance is high all the time, and this is strictly due to Dr. Grissom. She is an accomplished leader and keeps everything moving at a fast pace, calling on one after another as we raise our hands. She's a great show woman, putting on a performance of the highest quality. Everyone leaves class still energized and continuing the discussion nonstop with each other.

Dr. Grissom begins meetings by give interesting tidbits of information. Then she tells us something about the author of the day, always having done her homework thoroughly. Next, she may say something such as "I would like you to talk about the style of the author and whether it enhances the novel and if so, how? I know from experience most of you will decide to talk about what you want to talk about, but I'll do my best to keep you in line."

Then, as a show of hands quickly comes up, she calls on individuals, repeats their comments, and writes snatches of what they say on the blackboard.

She gave us the study sheet that runs at the end of this essay, and though she doesn't follow it during the discussion, it's very helpful for home reading.

Ours is a brown-bag meeting, since we meet during lunchtime. The University furnishes drinks. Dr. Grissom grabs a bite before she comes; she tells us that she stands in front of her microwave shouting at the potato in it to hurry up. The two hours fly. All of the women in the class are interesting—I haven't heard a dull one yet.

Dr. Grissom and the university take care of receptions for visiting writers and we all get invited to these and sometimes even to a master class. Over the years I've met many authors at these events, including Margaret Atwood, Joyce Carol Oates, John Updike, Jane Smiley, Toni Morrison, May Sarton, Susan Sontag, and John Irving.

Dr. Grissom chooses the books for our group and she tries to intro-duce us to new authors, as well as the classics. Sometimes she has a theme for a session, but often her selections are based on which books of value are available in paperback and can be readily obtained. She's also open to suggestions from members, but doesn't adhere to our choices too much.

Over and over I hear members say, "I didn't think the book this week was very interesting when I was reading it at home, but after hearing the discussion, I thought it was the most fascinating book I had read in years," or, "When Dr. Grissom had the discussion moving, I was sure I had read the wrong book. The one we were talking about was really great—once I learned how deep it really was."

What a mind stretcher this book group has been for me. I have met numerous interesting women and through them have enriched my life in other fields. Some have become very dear friends through the years.

Questions to Help Analyze Literary Style
Illustrate your point by direct reference to the text.

1. Is there anything strikingly different about the author's style?

2. Does she or he often use figures of speech?

3. Is there much wit and/or humor? Pathos?

4. Is there anything unusual about her or his methods of description?

5. Is there much dialogue? Is it natural? What is its purpose?

6. Do you feel the author is a close observer of life? Is she or he sensitive to life?

7. Does she or he ever moralize or seem didactic?

8. Is she or he particularly interested in moral problems? Social problems?

9. Does she or he succeed in evoking an emotional response on the part of the reader?

10. What are the themes? Are they universal or shallow ones?

11. Is the title related to the theme? Is it appropriate? Effective?

12. Is the setting essential to the story, i.e., are the particular times and places especially important?

13. Is an unusual amount of space devoted to establishing the setting? If so, what seems to be the reason?

14. Are the descriptions important either in establishing mood or atmosphere?

15. Is nature used to increase the effect of a scene?

16. Are there many changes of scene? Why or why not?

17. What is the basic conflict of the plot?

18. How is the exposition handled?

19. How is suspense created and maintained?

20. Is each chapter a unit? How does it begin? End? What keeps it going?

21. Is the hand of the author apparent in the plot or is what happens the natural outgrowth of the circumstances, the characters, and their interactions?

22. Can the character development of the protagonist be readily traced? How and why did she or he change?

23. What use is made of minor characters?

24. Could any characters have been omitted? If so, why has the author included them?

25. What are the author's methods of character portrayal?

26. Who are the "essentially evil" characters? Do they have any redeeming qualities?

27. Who are the "essentially good" characters? Do they have any detracting qualities?

28. Do the characters seem more important than the action? Is what they are more important than what they do?

29. Is there foreshadowing? Is it signposted by the author?

30. What is the method of narration? (Chronological, flashback, diary, letters, parallel events)

31. Are there episodes, incidents, or chapters that might have been omitted as far as the plot is concerned? If so, why did the author include them?

32. What makes the first scene a fitting beginning? Or isn't it?

33. What makes the last scene a fitting (or unfitting) ending?

34. Is the basic conflict of the plot completely and logically resolved?

35. What do you learn or assume to be the author's sense of morals or moral values?

36. Is there close integration of plot, character, setting, and theme?

37. What have you learned that will help you to live more finely (to paraphrase Arnold Bennett)?

A Conversation Among Friends

JANET TRIPP   MINNEAPOLIS, MINNESOTA

BOOKS HAVE MORE to say to me since I joined my book group. Previously, the conversations I held with my books were a quiet dialogue. There were just two voices, mine and the book's. It was nothing like the communion that goes on now—full of exclamations, impassioned pleas, confession and campaigning, enlightenment, and exchange.

Our many voices open a dialogue between book, author, and reader that takes reading beyond a private intellectual endeavor. It places us all in a relationship, interconnected in a reading community. In the companionship of the group, my appreciation of the text is amplified and my relationship with the book transformed.

My book group is full of friends now, people who nineteen years ago were strangers in a continuing education for women class at the University of Minnesota. The class was offered to women interested in an education but not in working on a degree. Our focus was women's autobiography and our teacher was English professor Toni McNaron. At our last class meeting we read portions of our own autobiographies and came to a decision: This was too good to end.

Through our reading, we have become good friends. Nineteen years and 228 books after our original class we continue to read, discuss, and share our own writing each month. We do this self-consciously. Our lives as women are formed by our culture and by the books we read. After twenty and forty and eighty years of shaping by male eyes, we are searching for a different pattern. In our reading we seek a balance to the outside world where men's words dominate the printed page and men's voices dominate the conversation. To this end, we read only books by women and every six months we choose, at our leader's insistence, at least one poet, one writer from an earlier generation, and one author of color. Each member nominates one book and a vote is taken on which six books we'll read.

Book group keeps me abreast of the times. It leads me to books I'd never choose by myself. On one hand is the book and the author. On the other is me with my own history and expectations. In the middle is the book group—the balancing fulcrum. It is the ground on which my interpretation of the book is balanced with that of the others. I come away from group with an altered perception of the book—altered and enlarged as I see it through twelve sets of eyes and not my own alone.

Opening a new book is like the excitement of a flirtation. Something new, unknown, and appealing yet unconsummated, promising endless pleasures. There is exhilaration in the feel of the book—its smooth surface, the small audible moment as the cover is opened and the pages first turned. The title sets up a question in my mind. It invites me in. On the jacket, admirers promote its virtues. I am hooked. Not yet in love, but attracted and willing to enter. Sometimes the promise is fulfilled.

Sometimes I am disappointed. There are books I haven't liked. But I'm never sorry for the investment of time. Each book has offered something. I've dealt with issues that did not concern me until I've found they mattered. I've read books about women who seemed like foreign creatures from another planet and ended up calling them friends. I've read books on subjects too painful for me to have chosen them and, consequently, have been moved to see things in a new light.

I open book group selections with a small reverence. It is a member's choice, meaningful to that woman and therefore deserving my attention, although it may not appeal to me and although it may be full of disappointment, frustration, and displeasure. I read it all. Then I go to group waiting to see what it is I missed, what it is the others saw, and where inside was the pleasure—the word or phrase so carefully placed it brings a shiver to my spine or a tear rolling down my cheek. It is a revelation to go to book group, a whole new conversation, different from the one I myself had with this book.

Sometimes these conversations have moved me into the larger world. They have prompted letters to the editor, donations to worthy causes, and on one memorable occasion even led me to a daughter.

Over the years we have read many books, such as Tsitsi Dangarembga's *Nervous Conditions*, Toni Morrison's *Beloved*, and Mariama Ba's *So Long a Letter*, in which the position of black women made me cringe for my privilege. It was at this juncture that I was offered the opportunity to help. The insight from these books and the empty room vacated by my college-bound son primed me to say yes when our pastor asked if we would consider taking in a young Ethiopian woman. She was stranded in this country with no support except an uncle who viewed her as a possession to be locked in for the summer and controlled in every aspect of her life. She lives with us now— proof that in a very real sense my book club has expanded my world and my family.

Some group conversations are memorable events in themselves: volatile and mind shattering. I remember the argument over *The Bone People* and the distaste of members whose personal experiences with alcoholism and child abuse pinpointed its romanticization in the novel. It led Toni to review the book critically for a local feminist journal and it prompted Libby to write a letter to the editors rebutting Toni's critical reading. I remember the discussion after reading the Norwegian *Kristin Lavransdatter* when Toni, who is from Alabama, said it helped her understand Minnesota, where the culture is so intertwined with its Scandinavian heritage.

Many of us remember one dramatic response to Margaret Drabble's *The Waterfall*. Janet was so disgusted with the alienated, neurotic, passive characters and their despairing, dreary, listless lives that at her turn in the circle, she tore what she felt was the one worthwhile page from the book and deposited the remainder into the fire that was roaring in the hostess's fireplace. There was shocked silence: We're not the kind of women to go in for book burnings. She had made her point.

Though we have strong feelings, we are a civilized group. We have a few rules. We don't wear white gloves, flowered hats, and nylon stockings with seams snaking up the backs of our calves, but we are a polite group, well mannered and orderly. We are careful to show respect for the ideas in the book and for one another. There is no one correct interpretation of the book. We disagree often, but agree that these disagreements add zest to the discussion. We enter with an equality—one member with another. In the world outside our conversation, we are vastly different in age and station in life, in experience of inclusion or exclusion in mainstream culture. In group, we are equal. Though some of us live in exclusive neighborhoods in homes full of fine art and some of us cannot afford to replace a broken furnace, each opinion carries equal weight and is treated with respect. Books such as *Bastard Out of Carolina* deal with class issues and touch sensitive nerves. At this meeting women spoke with deep feeling and many with pain.

Two elements are key to our longevity. One is our leader, Toni McNaron, who keeps us on track. This is a paid position and she diligently monitors the time, moving us along and seeing to it that there is time at the end to read our own work. She contributes information about the author and literature of the period.

The other element is our structure of going around the circle, which gives each woman uninterrupted time to speak. We explain our responses to the book and list our problems, disappointments, connections, and pleasures we found within the pages. We read favorite passages aloud. Each woman has her time. She is forced to speak up, but the clock is ticking and no one is allowed to dominate. The time is shared.

Reading favorite passages aloud adds to our appreciation of the book. When we are in general agreement and everyone loves the book, reading aloud enlivens a discussion, which could otherwise be brief and without revelation. Hearing these passages, chunks of the novel are fixed in the reader's voice in my memory. Passages are framed like a jewel in its setting. I remember Ruth reading from *The Dollmaker* of the "icy-hearted refrigerator." I remember the image it created for us of the cold-hearted industrial world. Ruth has now moved to New York to care for her grandson, walk the streets like Grace Paley, and write and conduct walking tours of the neighborhoods. Still, when I describe the book to people, it is Ruth's voice I hear in my head reading lines to our circle of women.

My group puts me in a new relationship with the book. It extends the dialogue that is begun by the writer, continued in the text, heard by myself in the reading, responded to in the group discussion, and answered as we read our own work. We put ourselves in the position of writer.

The readings we share at the end of our group mark us as different from most book groups. These written responses increase the experience of dialogue we feel as we move back and forth between the book and our group. The conversation deepens. Toni believes it is in this reading that the most empowering experiences occur. She says, "Every woman has a story. Our task is simply to create forums in which more and more women can get out more and more parts of their stories."

The first time we read together was the last day of our continuing education class for women. Instead of discussing a text, we went around the circle and each woman read in turn from her own story.

Helmi, in her eighties at the time, read about her romance with her husband of many years. Helmi was a Finn from the Minnesota Iron Range and Isadore, her husband, was a Russian Jewish furrier who had come to New York to escape the Russian army. Helmi was headstrong and independent, and free with her money. Isadore was a practical, business-minded young man who was aghast to learn that Helmi had not one penny saved despite her jobs in the St. Paul and Minneapolis libraries and at a private social agency for "wayward girls."

Money wasn't the only problem between the young married couple. She wanted a dozen children; he didn't care if they ever had any. He was troubled that Helmi was a gentile and that his beloved mother would not be able to accept her. He decided to take a long trip to Cuba to think things out. Helmi went home to visit her family.

She read to us, "So he went and I went. My parents were calm, unruffled Finns who took things as they were without any hoopla and

I had a lovely visit. When I returned to Minneapolis, my brother-in-law and I met the thinker at the train, came home, and had a gala lunch opening gifts brought by the traveler. As soon as my brother-in-law left, I was thrown on the bed with great joy and no protection and no discussion of should we or should we not have a family. Nine months later there was Libby—a gift of love, and later two more gifts of Sara and Arnold."

This cycle of communication—author-book-reader-group-writer—is completed when we trade seats with the author, write, and then read our own work to the group. We hear letters to children and friends, letters to the editor, essays, short stories in progress, poems and memoir, personal reflections, and, occasionally, a published piece. From this new perspective, as writer, we enter our reading on another level. We hear with a finely turned ear.

There are many large problems in this world and not many large pleasures. My book group, however, is one such pleasure. The books that we read link us one to another, a small experience of the joyful dialogue that is life.

For this group's reading list, see page 378.

Confessions of a Book Sniffer

NATALIE KEMMITT   📖   LAFAYETTE, INDIANA

I SPEND MORE time deciding which books to take on vacation than I do planning my holiday wardrobe, and I'm currently searching for a woodworking class that will allow me to skip the chopping board phase and go straight to building large and sturdy bookshelves. Books are taking over my house and my life. I wouldn't have it any other way.

I am a book sniffer. I have to admit it. And a stroker, too. I can't pick up a new book without indulging in a little literary foreplay. I find the solidity of a book comforting in my hand as I imagine what lies within and then there's the frisson of excitement as I crack back the covers and reveal the title page.

I come by it naturally. I was three years old when my mother plunked me defiantly on the counter at the local library and declared that she didn't care what the rules said: Maybe I wasn't five years old, but I could read and therefore I should have a library ticket. Apparently (I have no recollection of this), by way of demonstration I read *Noggin the Nog* and *The Whale* (a children's favorite in England thirty years ago) in a loud and piping voice from my perch until the librarians surrendered.

Years later, as a high school English teacher in Britain, I was paid to read lots of books and to pass on the torch of my enthusiasm to youngsters so that they would leave school inspired about great writing and with a lifelong reading habit. Sounds good? It was. Nobody

165

could have asked for a better way to spend their working life and nobody missed that life more than I did when it abruptly ended.

Ambitious teacher in Britain one day; unemployed newlywed in Indiana the next. Very Kafkaesque. It seems when I chose my husband, I also elected to leave my career, my family, and my friends several time zones behind me and to become a stranger in a strange land. It wasn't an easy transition to make. My husband was now embarking on an exciting new career with good prospects whilst I had no job. (Nor was I allowed to have a job until my humiliating "trailing spouse" status was upgraded.) When it looked like I might actually start climbing the walls, it was clearly time for action.

I came up with "The Plan." I got myself a library card, located the nearest bookstore, and slowly and surely began to work my way along the fiction shelves, absorbing everything that I hadn't had a chance to read during my frenetic teaching days. Whilst I had a good working knowledge of eminent Victorians, Shakespeare, various modern poets, and books written for under-fifteens, I hadn't much of a clue about the literary outpourings this side of the Atlantic. So beginning with A, I binged on Margaret Atwood. Then I swooped on Maya Angelou and Dorothy Allison and headed to Olive Ann Burns and T. Coraghessan Boyle, operating somewhat like a literate vacuum cleaner sucking up stories.

Soon I found it impossible to be so systematic, especially since some uncooperative writers wrote new books. Should I go back and read Atwood's latest or catch it on my second pass through the alphabet? And since I was now in B, why not reread all the Brontë novels? And though The Plan was really about American and Canadian writers, if I were to allow the Brontës, why not A. S. Byatt, whose works had been far too demanding to read between lesson planning in my former life? And why not writers from any country? Why not throw the gates open to all comers? To Vikram Seth and Jung Chang, for instance, whose books *A Suitable Boy* and *Wild Swans* had been sitting reproachfully on my shelf for longer than I cared to admit. And so it went until I was forced to take hold of myself. That day, The Plan was formally abandoned, and though I still read and read as if my life depended on it, I now flitted about like a fly at a buffet. I read Wallace Stegner before I sought out Toni Morrison. I discovered Tim O'Brien after I sampled Anne Tyler.

As I read, I heard the voices of North America. The heart of the land opened up to me like a magician's box. I heard the voices of pioneers. I heard Jewish voices, African American voices, and songs from the reservations. I heard the voices of immigrants, farmers, loggers, and slaves. My reading ranged from bayous to sierras, from great cities to small towns, and somewhere along the way, I became excited about my new home. The more I read and the more I entered into American life through books, the more settled I became.

But when I closed a book, the silence was palpable. I wasn't so much lonely—a life of reading never really allows loneliness—but I felt as if I had been struck mute somewhere along the way. I missed interacting with others about books—I remembered all too vividly how stimulating it was to ask a class questions and then listen as ideas flowed. I missed seeing the expression on faces as things clicked. I needed to be with booky people: I needed to connect.

At around this time I joined a wonderful group of international women and plucked up courage to attend their book discussion. I wasn't at all sure what to expect—you have to appreciate that the group thing is not typically done in England. That day is still vivid in my mind: I didn't know a soul and I'm not good at small talk, but I did know how to engage in an interesting literary discussion and I did know what I thought about Marguerite Duras's *The Lover*.

That first book discussion saved me. Even in those pre-Oprah days, the whole book discussion phenomenon I saw blossoming across the country gripped me. I tried groups here and there and made lots of new friends and was exposed to marvelous writers, but still I wanted more. Sometimes the discussion was disappointing. I was frustrated when ideas were left hanging in midair and when certain members dominated while quieter members didn't stand a chance. It annoyed me when members turned up with only half the book read and flimsy excuses for the other half. I began to wonder if our reasons for being in a book group were too different. I was there to feel intellectually alive. But instead I found myself practically acting out the second half of *The English Patient*, waiting for people who hadn't got around to reading it, much less thinking about it. I finally realized that the only way to be a member of the kind of group I searched for was to start one myself.

My local library was surprisingly accommodating when I marched in armed with book lists and references and told them that if they provided a room and publicity, I would lead a book discussion group for them. I look back with fondness at those early days when a small band of enthusiasts gathered nervously around a large library table and talked about books, venturing a remark here and a shy opinion there. At first, everyone looked to me for answers. What could I tell them about a writer, the period, the genre? What does the third line on page eight mean? I asked probing questions, and half the time, I ended up answering them myself, but little by little people began to pipe up and offer ideas, until, finally, we were having a lively group discussion.

Forging links between members in a brand new group is a slow and delicate process, but with tolerance, time, patience, and respect, strangers become friends. We don't worry about silences any more; I don't rush to fill them up. Members need thinking time, and as the group's ability to look deeper into texts becomes more sharply honed, I am aware that I need to devise better and better questions to shape our discussions. Sometimes we still take time to make sure that we've all got the story straight, but we're far less likely to dedicate time to a novel's plot than we are to looking at the writer's purpose and evaluating his or her techniques.

Now that the first group I started is well established, it is a far easier task to choose the books that will get discussion going. Our methods are perhaps not as democratic as they could be, but the system works and it makes my life easier by allowing me to keep some hold on the reins and to schedule the same book for several of the different groups I currently am involved with.

For a book to make my selection list, it needs to be available in paperback and it needs to satisfy certain literary criteria. Simply put, it has to have some kind of magic. Maybe the writer's language is amazing or maybe the writer's take on the world is so original that it deserves to be talked about. We choose books with interesting plots, unusual structure, strong characterization and settings, and ideas worth discussing. For the first meeting of the year (when we discuss a very short book), I prepare a selection sheet of twenty or so titles with blurbs and we talk them through one by one. I have a checklist in mind as I put this sheet together to ensure that it reflects a balance of male and female authors and protagonists and as wide a representation of cultures and time periods as possible. I usually have at least one prize winner and a couple of books that nobody has ever heard of (with fingers crossed that Oprah won't blow the surprise in the meantime).

In the last two years, we've done something a little different with our choices. I wanted to take things a step further and actively encourage comparisons between the texts we were reading. To this end, I've proposed books loosely connected by themes: Weird and Wonderful, Magical and Marvelous, The Human Face of War, and Fascinating Families, and we select three or four books to discuss under each heading. For each theme I distributed a list of open ended questions to encourage thinking about more than one title at once. Now even when comparisons are not so deliberately engineered, they are still forthcoming. I often begin discussions by asking whether the book we are discussing reminds anyone of anything else they've read and I almost always hear something I haven't bargained for. This is what I relish most—where I get my buzz—this energetic exchange of booky ideas and swapping of booky enthusiasms. This year we've focused our choices on books about interesting people in interesting places and we are considering how writers evoke settings in novels and the effect landscapes and places have on characters.

A while ago I looked around my home study at the heaps of notes, ideas, and clippings about books and book groups, and I decided to take the connection one step further and publish a newsletter, *Fiction & Friends*, for readers and book group members. I think of *Fiction & Friends* as a book group on paper. Whenever I think that I've heard of every good book and that there's nothing new under the sun, a reader's letter will arrive from Tennessee or California raving about a writer we simply cannot live without. And the booky buzz is back.

A teaching friend from England telephoned me recently because she thought I was probably bored and lonely, stuck at home, and missing teaching. What a bizarre idea. I've never been busier, and I've got friends all over America.

For this reading list, see page 291.

PART V

See, It's Really More than Just a Book Group

You don't have to dig too deep to uncover all the things besides thoughtful discussion that book groups offer their members. Book groups can be personal and political. For instance, in this section you'll find a piece about why Eastern Europeans don't join book groups, one that illuminates how American teen moms can benefit when they do, and one that shows how an ex-wife and a then-current girlfriend forged a twenty-five-year friendship over books.

Literature for All of Us

KAREN THOMSON   📖   EVANSTON, ILLINOIS

LITERATURE FOR ALL of Us began as a pilot program in October 1996 when I met a group of teen mothers enrolled in a G.E.D. program run by Malcolm X College at what is now called the Teen Parent Services Department of the Illinois Department of Human Services. About fifteen young women sat in a circle with me that first day and agreed to try a new idea. I noticed that the group warmed up as they read poems by Maya Angelou. The young women started making eye contact and they sat up straighter. They were engaged and interested. By the second week, they buried their heads in *The House on Mango Street* by Sandra Cisneros, and were doing the business of book groups. I was hooked and so were they.

Within a year, Literature for All of Us was created as a nonprofit organization with a mission to bring the rewards of reading and writing to low-income teen mothers and younger girls through weekly book groups that combine literature discussions with poetry-writing exercises. The organization currently serves four groups and is expanding to serve more. It also offers training to representatives of other organizations who want to replicate this book group model.

As founder of Literature for All of Us and a long-time book group leader, I offer this series of vignettes that tell some of the stories of the young women who are the heart and soul of the program.

In the Beginning

It's a Friday morning and I arrive at the welfare department on the near south side of Chicago for the teen-mother book group. It's week four of the eight I agreed to do as a pilot project funded by my long-established adult women's book group. Angel arrives without her book. She has a black eye. She says her brother beat her up last night and then tore up her book. I give her another copy of *Their Eyes Were Watching God* by Zora Neale Hurston. I am sure the funders would approve.

A Beautiful Book

We have run out of initial seed money for books and journals, so I bring copies of a chapter from *How the Garcia Girls Lost Their Accents* by Julia Alvarez. It's about a young girl who writes an essay for a school speech that is inspired by Walt Whitman's poem "Song of Myself." To further illuminate the story, I read several long stanzas of Whitman's poem aloud.

Afterward there is silence. I wonder if I've bored them. Finally, someone says quietly, "Could we read more of that kind of stuff?" Someone else chimes in, "Yeah, I like this. Could we read Shakespeare, too?" Someone else asks me where I got that beautiful book. I restrain myself from giving it away on the spot. It's a good book group day.

Book Group All Day Long

I notice today that when we read aloud in a circle, everyone counts the length of the segments so that no one gets a bigger share of reading time. They like the sound of their voices, even if they stumble over some of the words. The eagerness to read aloud, discuss, write poems, and read to the group, is palpable. When asked what they would change about the book group program, the chief complaint is that it is too short. Many wonder why it can't last all day.

The Program Grows

Tuesday afternoon and it's time for book group at a social service agency in West Humboldt Park. This neighborhood reports the highest incidence of murder in Chicago, or so I've heard. Today's book group comprises young women who have come to this agency from various referrals. Many are former foster children or girls who have been on the street and homeless before finding their way to a shelter. All have at least one child and are under twenty-one. One has three children and is pregnant again. I am here to provide one of the agency program offerings, a book group. This particular day might be a difficult one.

I come in and distribute books around the table. I've brought copies of *Shabanu* by Suzanne Staples, a book about a Muslim girl in western Pakistan who is forced into an arranged marriage. I've been trying to get these teen mothers to engage with this book for a few weeks, with little success. They complain that it's hard to understand. They are stopped by the strange words in Pakistani interspersed in the text, even though the author had provided translations. This book is highly recommended for junior-high readers, but for these young women, it doesn't help them connect to themselves . . . yet. I'll probably have to scrap this book as a selection, but for today I'll finish by reading aloud the last few chapters and getting a discussion going.

I start the group with an introduction around the circle. We give our names and our mother's and grandmother's names as an attempt to realize a sense of self through our matrilineal lines. It warms up everyone. Next we go to the book. The young women groan, but I persevere and take them to the last chapters. We read most of it aloud.

It's depressing. The main character has been captured by her father and beaten for running away from the arranged marriage that will be her fate. She had wanted to be free. We discuss it. We need to do something to cheer us up.

"Isn't it wonderful how free we are as women in this country?" I ask. Then the reality of their lives stops me. Are they free? Saddled with babies, with G.E.D. certificates at best, with troubled families, with poverty, what am I asking them? But I'm in too deep to stop now. "Here's some paper. I want you to write 'I Am a Free Woman' at the top of the page and write a poem below about how you're free. When you're done, if you want, write another poem about the cages you're in, or the cages you've left." Before too long, everyone is engaged. Everyone has written a poem. One by one, they read their poems aloud.

When we've finished, the mood has changed. We're all smiling. Hope abounds.

Finding Balance

The teen mother group begins to study Maya Angelou. We've just read about her grandmother in *I Know Why the Caged Bird Sings*. We discuss grandmothers, Angelou's two strong ones and our own. We talk about smells in our grandmother's houses. We write poems about our grandmothers. One girl freezes up. She finally writes that her grandmother is a witch. She fills the page with these letters. She won't say more. Another sweet-faced sixteen-year-old writes about her grandmother and cries. She was raised for her first six years by this grandmother in Honduras, then sent to be with her parents in the States, and still feels the loss. The discussion moves to mothers, good and bad, and everyone is in tears. On the way out of the group, one young woman stops me and says she will not come back if we are sad again. I remind her that last week we wrote poems about being free women and laughed. I remind her that life is both, that we hope for a good balance. She comes back.

A Reluctant Circle

I am at a south-side Chicago welfare department office where teen mothers go for a G.E.D. program as a requirement for receiving financial assistance for themselves and their children. We're discussing *L'il Mama's Rules* by Shaneska Jackson. Twelve young mothers gather around a conference table and our book group begins.

Today I get to observe because I have found two young women who are unbelievably good at this book group business, especially with teen mothers. Tricia Hersey and Amanda Lichtenstein come prepared for the discussion. They begin by making everyone get up from the table, form a circle behind their chairs, and hold hands. Each is then instructed to state something she is grateful for that day.

It's a reluctant circle, but it gets going after Amanda starts by being grateful that she had clean underwear to put on that morning. They all laugh and get into the spirit of the thing. After the circle, we pass a squeeze from hand to hand. Everyone sits down energized and we open our books.

They start with chapter one, reading aloud. The book is about a young woman named Madison who had broken one of her many dating rules designed to protect herself from emotional involvement and the trouble of relationships. Madison is a teacher and she's been in love with a young doctor. The young women who are reading in turns around the circle stop often and laugh and exclaim about the book's humor and Madison's strong spirit.

I marvel to myself how wonderful this moment is. Young women, some of who have never finished a book before, are sitting around a table reading and sharing laughter and opinions about a young woman whose problems are ones they can relate to, although they themselves are preparing for a G.E.D. test and few will go on to college. Reading about Madison, relating to her as a character they can talk about as if she were real, is a step toward imagining themselves in college, or dating doctors, making choices and rules for themselves that will help them stay out of trouble. The miracle of connection made possible through reading is happening. They write lists of their own rules for dating and share them with each other. They are very clear in their desire for decent partners. Perhaps they'll remember their rules even better for having written them and spoken them to each other.

A Tri-Lingual Group

It is February and it is cold, but these brave souls come to the overheated, ugly building for classes. Today is the start of the book group for the year. I have brought a book of short stories by J. California Cooper, *Homemade Love*. The girls are pleased when they find out they get to keep these books. They put bookplates in them, our dancing, reach-for-the-stars-girl logo. But the real fun starts when they begin to read.

Devon starts and stops abruptly at the first sentence. She laughs. "What is she saying? Why does she write like that? This is how we talk. How can she write like that? Is she allowed?" I explain that this writer prefers to write in southern vernacular, which fits the characters in her stories. They laugh and laugh and are eager to get back to the text and try out the words in this book. It is another language, but one which is familiar. This freedom is a revelation.

I learn that these young women consider themselves to speak three languages: rough, ghetto talk; regular, soft, homey girl talk; and standard English. I listened to Chantella perform all three in sequence. They love these stories, all ones of triumph over odds by not losing faith and belief in one's values, even while people around you betray you. We are united over this book from the first day.

How Book Group Changes Lives

After book group today, Agripina asks for a ride to her daycare center. I say yes. It's not that far and it gives me a chance to talk to her one-on-one. She tells me that she had always loved reading, but one of her many foster mothers had thrown out all her books as punishment since she knew that Agripina loved to read. She said she hadn't wanted to join my book group at first because she distrusted the idea of books being given to her, as it could cause pain again. But she was glad she chose to do this. The book group had changed her life. Did I know that she had started to read to her two-and-a-half-year-old boy because of me?

"What do you mean?" I said

"Well, I used to think that if I kept the baby clean, dry, and fed that was enough. Then in book group, you gave us books for our kids. I took them, but I wouldn't read them to him."

"Why not?" I asked.

"Because it was too painful. But finally one day I took that one you gave me, and I did what you said to do in book group. I put him on my lap and put my arms around him and I read to him. And guess what? Before, I have to admit that I didn't really like him—he would run around and make messes and want things. But when I read to him and discovered that he would sit with me, I calmed down inside and then I liked him better. Now when he sees me getting into a bad mood, he goes and gets a book off the shelf and says, 'Read, Mommy.'"

I stopped the car, tears in my eyes. I told her that's how I made it through raising three little boys, that the same thing happened to me when I could get them to sit with me and listen to a story. Doing so helped me relax and feel the love I had for them. She had discovered this fact at age seventeen! I learned something that day.

Something Really Special

My calling as a book group leader has always been a joy. But this new opportunity to do book group circles for teen mothers and to watch them begin to relate to books as important to their lives, often for the first time, is something really special. It's a fulfillment of E. M. Forster's dictum in *Howards End*: "Only connect." When one of these strong, young women, herself a testimony to hope and determination, tells me that this is the first time she has ever liked reading (a common occurrence), I realize that this is a gift of love all around. I go to books for solace and adventure, for escape and enlightenment. To open this world of literature to others is to watch lights of connection appear.

There is no failure possible in these book group circles. The girls help each other with difficult words and are quick to support each other in reading their poems. We practice listening and relating to the best in each other. Connections are made across race, class, and age. One participant told me once that the young women often get into fights in other settings, but that in book group they find what they have in common. Another young mother said that before on the bus the girls talked about hair and nails, but now they talked about books.

Now, they see themselves as vital and valid people, not only as teen mothers on public assistance. The subjects of the groups are sharing, love, and connection to imagery, ideas, and character growth in good books. It is literature for all of us, including young women who have little access to many of the resources available to most book group members. It is book group work that creates lifelong inner connections, like any other true artistic activity. And the exhilaration of a really good book group can't be topped. Book groups are for all of us; it's got to be right.

For this leader's reading list, see page 371.

Meeting Bill

KATHERYN KROTZER
LABORDE

RIVER RIDGE,
LOUISIANA

THIS STORY STARTS with three single, bored, twentysomethings looking for intellectual stimulation and a reason to gather on a regular basis.

I doubt we would have met Bill any other way.

One muggy September night, Doug called out of the blue, saying he wanted to form a book discussion group. At about the same time Gina, claiming her brain was turning to mush, came upon the same idea. The three of us got together, added some others, and our group was born.

Altogether there were about ten of us all with liberal arts educations we failed to use in occupations that bored us. We decided to meet every other Tuesday and drew up a preliminary book list. We agreed to read Kate Chopin's *The Awakening*—something short to get us started—for our first official meeting, set two weeks from that night.

The big night came. Five people showed up.

"We need some outsiders, some new blood," Gina said, and we agreed. I designed eye-catching flyers that we placed in a few coffeehouses around New Orleans. They didn't go unnoticed: I received one death threat (complete with heavy breathing) and one query from a guy named Bill, whom I told to read Anne Rice's *Interview with the Vampire* for Tuesday.

I told the three who showed up that night of our solitary response. We ordered coffee and scones and agreed that should this Bill turn out to be weird—remember that death threat?—we'd change our meeting spot and conveniently forget to inform him.

We looked around anxiously. Doug eyed his watch and announced the newcomer was already fifteen minutes late and would perhaps never show. Then, as if on cue, the door edged open and a chubby man carrying a worn paperback looked around anxiously.

I called out to him and motioned to an empty chair. He sat, blinking several times as we introduced ourselves.

None of us were prepared for Bill, to be quite honest. For one thing, he was older by a good fifteen years and sported more than a few gray hairs. He was pudgy and soft and had an intense squint. As the night wore on, he rubbed his palms along his thighs frequently and constantly pushed up his glasses. When he got nervous, he stuttered. Softly.

But he knew books—the great and the insignificant, the classic and the just published. And while his ways bordered on timidity, his comments were insightful. "If you d-don't mind," he said after the third meeting, "we need to revise this b-book list. W-w-why should I read something suggested by someone who's not even here?" He was right, of course, since the group had already lost more than half of its original, enthusiastic core.

I opened my book and recorded the new list on the back cover. Some suggestions stayed the same: Deanne still wanted to read *Cold Sassy Tree*; Gina suggested *The World According to Garp*; Doug insisted we would love *Murder in the Smithsonian*; and I maintained that a discussion of *Edie*, accompanied by a viewing of the cult film *Ciao! Manhattan*, would give greater insight to a decade that most of us had seen through Mr. Rogers's eyes.

Bill looked to the ceiling before speaking. "W-well, those are OK, but there are a few books I know of that I think you'd like." *The Unbearable Lightness of Being. Justine. The Last Temptation of Christ.* ("The movie's coming out soon," Doug said. "Oh, but there's no way the movie could be as beautiful as the book," Bill countered, and, of course, he was right.)

Deanne left the group before we could get to her book, so we never read it. Nothing against Olive Ann Burns, but we found ourselves adding to and deleting from the official list so often that I never bothered to retype it. All Gina had to say was, "García Márquez's new book is in paperback," and we found ourselves adding *Love in the Time of Cholera* to the list. I can still remember the heated discussion over the success of that book's ending, with the men defending its romantic beauty, and Gina and I denouncing it as sentimental.

On more than one occasion, I noticed people staring as we debated a particular point. *In Cold Blood* led to a discussion of capital punishment. We couldn't pick a mutual favorite from the *Best American Short Stories* anthology. Bill was the only one to enjoy *Forrest Gump* (but now that it's made it to the big screen, I'm tempted to read it again). I recall being the lone defender of *A Cannibal in Manhattan*. And on one night, we were ten minutes into a discussion before realizing Bill had read Steinbeck's *Cannery Row* rather than *Tortilla Flats*, the book *he* had suggested.

As weeks passed, we got to know Bill better than we originally would have thought possible. He told us stories about a younger, thinner Bill who wore his hair long and hitchhiked across the country. Occasionally he would talk about how he had waited out the Vietnam War in Canada, or how his trench coat and bike were, at one time, his only possessions. He mentioned that while his estranged wife was living in Alabama, he still worked for his father-in-law as a roofer. Though we all hated our jobs, we felt the worst for Bill since his job was obviously tearing him apart. We saw him as a teacher. A wonderful teacher.

And a frustrated writer. I still can remember him telling us about living in a boarding house that was occupied, for the most part, by old people. It wasn't until one of the tenants—an old, lame man whom he used to visit—died that Bill discovered the man was the estranged husband of the woman who ran the house. "I've always wanted to write about that, but I've never known how," he said.

Actually, we all wanted to write, so in addition to our bimonthly book meetings, we added a few writing sessions. On these nights, each handed his or her notebook to another who would write an opening sentence. We would take these sentences and build upon them for an hour, then spend the next hour reading our work aloud over second cups of coffee.

Once, I handed my notebook to Bill, who wrote: *When I was a kid, I remember riding down the highways out west and seeing little white crosses on the side of the road where there had been an accident.*

It occurred to me that Bill, in many ways, was still that little boy traveling the highways of this country, not really settled or satisfied. Fiction must have offered an escape to him from a life I could barely imagine. I knew he wasn't what you would call a happy person, but I also knew that our group offered some sort of salvation to him. He looked forward to our meetings and was often not only the first to arrive, but the last to rise from his chair when we were through.

One night, Bill announced that the roofing company had gone bankrupt and that he was out of a job and broke. His wife was willing to take him back, he said, and he would be leaving at the end of the week. He was telling us good-bye.

Though it didn't have to be, that was the last meeting for all of us. Doug was considering a move to Miami, and Gina, a career change. I had been accepted to graduate school, which I knew would take me away from the group in time.

It was time to move on.

A good five years has passed since the group disbanded. My MFA diploma hangs neatly on the wall. I'm married now and a mommy to boot. I've lost touch with Doug, but Gina and I still get together to discuss books or life in general. We're ready to form another group—a new group. Sure, we have names of people we'd like to ask to join, but we're working on flyers to stick in our favorite bookstores.

We're hoping to find Bill.

I still half-expect to find him sitting on the coffeehouse porch, book open. Sometimes I think I see him in a crowd—quickly, peripherally—the way one sees someone who has passed away. I remember asking a limousine driver if his name was Bill, which he denied. Being drunk on champagne and the excitement of my wedding day, I decided that my eyes were playing tricks on me.

If I ever do see him again, I'll tell him that I've made the jump: I'm a writer now. That I'm still working on that story about the little white crosses on the side of the road. And that I'd like to write that other story for him, the one about the boarding house. It's a hard story to write, but I know one day I'll find the words.

And I'll name the main character Bill.

Dangerous Book Groups

SUSAN P. WILLENS   📖   WASHINGTON, D.C.

DURING THE YEAR I just spent as a Fulbright professor of literature in a small city in eastern Slovakia, I became close friends with several women who had lived there all their lives. Now in their early forties, these educated, English-speaking women are established in their professions and their family lives and ready to branch out beyond the doctor's practice, the interpreter's travels, the mother's schedule. "Bored, that's what I am," said Dagmar. "How much gossip can I endure? How many conversations with my sister-in-law?" Zuzana concurred. As much as they love their families and work, an intellectual void, which their sporadic English lessons did not quite fill, was yawning before them.

"Why not start a book group?" I asked and described how my long-running groups in Washington, D.C., had provided just the stimulation that they were looking for: to talk about books with interesting men and women. Blank faces. "No," they finally chorused, "no one would come."

In the conversation that followed, I discovered one more of the many differences between Slovak culture and American culture that grows from the long authoritarian domination of the East. No one would come to a book group meeting because for years, meetings were places where people observed each other's ideological development. Right thinking meant promotion, summer holidays, opportunities for one's children. Wrong thinking—even apathy—meant delayed privileges, thwarted plans, or quiet exile. Now, after the Velvet Revolution, the memory lingers, and people shun meetings.

Zuzana and Dagmar are both readers of fiction in several languages and loved discussing with me any of the writers whose works we'd all read, especially Steinbeck and Hemingway. But those discussions were with me—a safe outsider. Even if they could build on these conversations and persuade their friends that the thought police have relaxed, that book groups could be exploratory, open to conversations and tentative ideas, with no one reporting on anyone else, there was still a corollary holdover from the bad old days. They claimed that their friends had lost the habit—maybe had never had it—of expressing personal opinions in public. "Even the women I meet all the time at my children's school stop talking when I bring up anything beyond the teachers or the lunches," Dagmar complained.

In the United States, book groups meet in a particular psychological area, halfway between the private zone of household and family and the public zone where strangers conduct the affairs of the world, stores, offices, and civic services of all kinds. In between we have another region, where we meet acquaintances to discuss our children's play groups, the work of our church or synagogue, the safety of our neighborhoods, or the protest before the city council. This is where we attend to the work of the bar association, the alumni association, Alcoholics Anonymous, or the board of a charity; it is the home of the PTA and the political club, the tennis association, the AIDS awareness group, the ecology newsletter—and the book club.

The authoritarian system in Slovakia, and, I assume, most of Eastern Europe, spoiled this psychological area. Because a centralized planning structure was responsible for all the questions that citizens in a democracy manage in this middle region, people have neither the interest nor the skills to solve problems with others who are not family or friends on one hand or strangers on the other. Furthermore, the past makes them reluctant to confide in a mere acquaintance, for fear that, as in the old days, that acquaintance might report the confidence. Although the old system has died, its ghost haunts those who endured it for so long.

Book groups as we know them depend on the members' capacity to trust each other and to permit half-formed, unorthodox, revolutionary, and even wrong ideas to be stated, considered, debated, used, or discarded. Book groups depend on our comfort with acquaintances with whom we share not our whole lives, but just this interest of reading and discussing books.

Now, if anyone can shake loose from old habits, my Slovak friends can do it. As we talked about the possibility of their forming a small book group—maybe among those few who can read and discuss in English or maybe among those who want to read Slovak or other literature together, maybe with other women or other professionals—they seemed more hopeful that such an experiment was at least worth a try. I expect to hear from them in the fall that a few friends have gathered for the adventure of discussing their reading.

I am not suggesting a covert way for eastern Europeans to imitate us in the United States. They have many strengths in their culture and we have many weaknesses in ours. Not all the good is on the side of the West. At the same time, I learned—as I did all the time I was there—how precious are our patterns of democratic debate, informal assembly, and continuous learning, as evidenced by the thousands of book groups across the United States.

If my friends could overcome the hurdles on their way to a book group, they could gain access to ideas for debate and exploration now that their formal schooling is over. They might find a place to practice the skills of free assembly and open discussion that they have lost. And I find myself hoping that conversation about books can bring energy, excitement, and collegiality to areas of the world that have been deprived of them for so many years.

As a result of my being in Eastern Europe for a year, my book group in Washington, D.C., wants to read books that will teach us more about that part of the world. A partial list of our readings on this topic includes *Mendelssohn Is on the Roof*, Jiri Weil (Czech novel); *The Castle*, Franz Kafka (Czech novel); *The Captive Mind*, Czeslaw Milosz (Polish essays); *One Day in the Life of Ivan Denisovich*, Alexander Solzhenitsyn (Russian novella); *The Encyclopedia of the Dead*, Danilo Kis (Serbian stories).

My List, My Books

DAVE NARTER   CHICAGO, ILLINOIS

RECENTLY, OVER COFFEE, I told an artist friend about an experience I'd had putting together a book list for the Advanced Placement Language and Composition class I teach and she gushed about how lucky I must be to be able to share something so personal with so many eager minds and how she envied the experience. How wonderful to give such a gift and in turn be rewarded with my students' responses after they've explored the terrain I'd set out for them. I nodded my head politely and wondered if cappuccino tasted any differently on Planet Ridiculous.

I hated to be reminded that so much English instruction was perceived to be this affected sharing of one's own passions with a . . . disinterested audience. What an absurdly romantic notion to think that students would be any more interested in the books I like than in my father's home movies. I'm a teacher, not a giver of gifts. If there is a word for such a person besides Santa, I don't know it—and believe me, the days I distribute required reading are nothing like Christmas.

But it would be dishonest to pretend that there wasn't something personal about the list. All the titles are in my bookcases at home and I have to admit that I like most of them. However, my intention was never to share my treasures, only to prevent cheating. If I've read them, I can't be fooled by the Blockbuster version.

But I did sell this as a sort of gift. After the national AP test, a grueling, four-hour exam administered in May, I would let each of my students choose one book from the list and spend the remaining four weeks of the year leisurely reading it and researching criticism. The final class, a two-hour session, would be held outside where we would discuss our choices. Our own book group, I said. They said little. Merry Christmas.

So while the rest of the school was sweating out final exams, my ponderous book group slid out of exit four and onto the grass in front of Twenty-fifth Street. The sun beat down on us, the grass tickled our legs, and all around were the chaotic sounds of transit. Airplanes taking off from the nearby airport, semis off Twenty-fifth street making their morning deliveries, salesman hustling their two-door offices past our circle. And we sat, as solitary and determinedly stationary as words on a page. And then my students shared their thoughts on some American literature.

Michael, a quiet artist, brilliant and perceptive, so handsome and kind that girls were sure he was gay, went first. He had already been reading Arthur Golden's *Memoirs of a Geisha* (not on the list) when I gave the assignment and asked if he could just finish that. Here was a kid who the first week of the year, when we were studying Woolf's "Death of the Moth," remarked that Sylvia Plath seemed to be suffering the same sort of self-imposed alienation in *The Bell Jar*. That sewed up Michael's "A" for the rest of the year. It also sent me running to the library to read a copy of *The Bell Jar*.

Michael didn't like *Geisha*; he found the inconsistent tense distracting and Golden's penchant for figurative language juvenile. He shrugged his shoulders a lot while describing the book as if he'd just tried goat cheese or caviar for the first time and thought, "Eh. It could be better."

Good for me! Me too! I had given up on the book myself and felt vindicated that someone else, someone brilliant, hadn't liked it much either. I too hated the Tontoesque use of similes in *Geisha* . . . as the sun hates the black of night. I praised Michael for having stood up to popular criticism and developing his own opinion.

I later found that this concept of empowerment through contrary opinion, while part of the academic game, can be a dangerous one to publicize. As cool as academic rebellion sounds coming from a teacher, tell students to disrespect authority enough, they eventually will.

Vonnegut turned out to be the first problem. Maybe I pushed it too hard when I went through the list, but if there is a political cause I'd endorse in my classroom, the return of Kurt Vonnegut, Jr., would be it. Skylar, the coolest kid in the class, able to travel fluidly between all cliques (witness the contrasting pierced eyebrow and cheerleading outfit), kept her copy of *Slaughterhouse Five* tightly rolled in her grip. Skylar. She would set the opinion of Vonnegut for probably half the lemmings in the class with what she'd say next. She curled her lip, and expelled as if letting out a long drag off a Camel.

"It was confusing. I couldn't follow it."

Confusing? Confusing! It's not confusing; it's stylish. It's modernism. It's economical. Confusing? Surely Skylar would find the grace to express how she had mistaken the source of the confusion. It is not Vonnegut who is confused, but rather Kilgore . . . and Skylar. Tell them Skylar! Tell them!

Skylar sat looking . . . confused. Suddenly, I felt I didn't know her anymore. This cool kid with whom I thought I had struck a bond over the year, was rebelling against the very rebellion I'd allowed her. Her "confusion" became a very personal gesture of contempt and I stared at her a long time, trying to figure out her motives, her plan. She feigned ignorance. We left Vonnegut. I was sure everyone who read Tom Robbins would love him. Maybe not the book, maybe not his characters, but the writer himself. After so much that is alienating about English, over twelve years, students need to read an author who seems to really enjoy the process of putting words on paper and who wants you to enjoy reading them. A student once asked me if all great literature is depressing. I told him it isn't, but that his mother probably won't let him read the fun stuff. In fact, if students want to read Tom Robbins, they have to bring in a note from their parents.

Carmy, craving fun literature like a kindergartner craves paste, brought his permission slip scribbled on a paper plate. Carmy sat isolated from the rest of us by a firewall he'd created ripping grass out of the ground. In most classes, Carmy might be called the class clown, but to me Carmy was simply one of the funniest people I'd ever met. He spoke with a slight lisp and was far too thin, traits I'm convinced are possessed by all good comedians. Carmy signed his papers, "Huggy Bear" and among his essay titles were, "Chilly Willy Would Agree" and "Gatsby: A Gay Fantasia." His version of *Still Life with Woodpecker*, however, was flat and uninspired. He certainly read the book, but only politely gave in to its humor. He found parts of it too absurd, bordering on uncomfortable, he said. Growing agitated, I looked around for a contrasting opinion to put up against Carmy's. Kim had read Robbins's *Jitterbug Perfume* and I knew she liked it. She told me.

Kim was a shaky, angry girl (as Carmy would say, "full of angst"). Her slow burn had erupted recently when the left-brained debaters firmly contended that when Emily Dickinson writes about a snake, she is only referring to . . . a snake. The debaters used every trick in their arsenal, deducing and inducing, even resorting to obvious fallacious reasoning; but they were finally beaten by Kim's fierce, personal attacks and that she was right. I needed that kind of fighter on my side now; but as I looked around, I noticed for the first time that she was not present. Knowing that she needed as much grade help as she could get, I was surprised at her absence on this last class day. Honestly though, I was more concerned at losing my grasp on the intellectual rudder of the class. We drifted into the waters of nonfiction, but they proved no less perilous.

Leah read *There Are No Children Here*. She didn't like it. Leah is delightfully friendly, but shy. She'd often withhold her valid and accurate observations in class for fear that there might be a more correct insight out there. For once she was the only one who'd read the text in question and she baffled me.

"It's really sad. I was hoping they were going to get out. But everything that happens to them is worse than the last. Then it just ends."

"But it's nonfiction," I exclaimed. "That's how it happened. Would you rather he had made up a happy ending?"

She found this attack on her artistic sensibilities as uncomfortable as the book itself. So I backed off and changed course. I asked her if there was value in such a book, if chronicling the tragedies in our midst is a worthy endeavor.

"Of course it is," she said. "But . . . "

But it ain't a joy to read. Or is it? Is the quality of the book getting confused with the quality of the characters' lives? One would never say *A Midsummer Night's Dream* is better than *Hamlet* simply because one is happy and the other sad, but so many of the kids were ready to dismiss work based on these grounds. *Slaughterhouse Five*, *Nat Turner*, and *Deliverance* all had the stamp of disapproval for similar reasons.

I've been trying to figure out where this strange school of criticism comes from. Maybe it's Disney. Its template plot of birth, tragedy, and victory is fed to students from birth like colostrum. Perhaps such focus on the inevitability of external victory removes the appreciation for subtle character shifts or implied victories or the subtle beauty of defeat. Or maybe they just are losing the ability to see the intrinsic yet implicit beauty in the tragic or the ugly.

Or maybe I'm taking this all too seriously. Maybe nothing's really changing. There has always been a large audience for the simple and mundane. "Father Knows Best" is considered classic television, after all. But to put it in that context, I am talking to a group of kids who have been taught to appreciate the phony cheerfulness of Barney's perpetually sunny classroom instead of the gritty, chaotic urban landscape of Sesame Street. And Kotlowitz is no Grover, much less Baby Bop.

A couple of students shifted their legs looking for bugs in the grass. Things were not going well and we all knew it. Then Matt, three-sport athlete and Adam Sandler devotee, raised his hand high. His foot tapped and his face grew red as it became apparent that he intended not only to share his book, *Savage Inequalities*, but that he had to share it now. I knew he'd enjoyed the book, as Matt enjoys just about everything, but until he began, I'd no idea how carefully and passionately he'd considered Kozol's argument. Like a coach at halftime, Matt commanded our attention with his towering presence, neck bulging, hands shaping, as he described the pathetic condition of life in an East St. Louis school and then, with a shift of his shoulders, compared this to student life at wealthy New Trier High School. Matt had done further research to see if anything had changed and was disappointed to report that not much had. Any cynicism any of us had about literature, race, or politics evaporated as we realized this assignment, this book, had become something personal for Matt.

So it was for Jenny, a quiet, almost invisible blonde whom we called Whitey. When she shared *The Beauty Myth*, it was as if she had found poison in a well and had gathered us all around to share the brutal truth. I am a teacher of writing and literature, not social studies. Though I am politically minded, I am careful not to intentionally influence students due to my position of authority. But I could barely contain my pride for Jenny, Naomi Wolf, and public education when Jenny laid her book down before her like the final piece of evidence and said, "I think every woman ought to read this book."

So the tide turned and it never reversed. Title after title was enthusiastically presented to what became an excited and spirited class. Excited about literature. Jack on *A Farewell to Arms*: "So much better than *The Old Man and the Sea*. Why do they make us read that?" Maribel on *The Sound and the Fury*: "It sounds weird, but this book made me hate time." Sanji on *The Adventures of Huckleberry Finn*: "Did you ever notice how just about every movie is like this book?" Katie on *One Flew over the Cuckoo's Nest*: "I was thinking how much this school is like a mental hospital." Brian on *The Crossing*: "There are images in this book I don't think I'll ever forget."

Eventually the momentum died and with twenty minutes left, an uncomfortable silence took over again. Suddenly Matt jumped to his feet and ran toward the dirt and grass of the baseball fields yelling for the rest of us to follow. Perhaps since I hadn't yet filled in the final grade sheets, the students looked eagerly my way for some indication of permission. I closed my grade book and declared, "This class is over."

Pages, words scattered and fluttered in the wind as my students headed away from me and toward Matt. For the first time that day, I followed.

When I returned to my classroom later, balancing attendance sheets and books, I saw atop my desk the copy of *Jitterbug Perfume* I'd lent Kim. Sticking out from beneath the cover was a greeting card, an apple drawn on a blue background. Inside she'd written, "I'm sorry I've been falling behind in this class. I really love it. But things in my house have been very hard lately. My father's been sick and it's hard on all of us. But I wanted you to know *Jitterbug Perfume* is the best book I ever read. Thanks for suggesting it. Kim."

It made me feel like I'd given her a sort of gift. Something of myself that I thought she could use. Now how often does anyone get to do that?

For this reading list, see page 337.

Gentle Reader

NOËLLE SICKELS   LOS ANGELES, CALIFORNIA

I DO NOT belong to a book group. I was once a member of a short-lived, four-woman group in Philadelphia; we read three books before unraveling, not from lack of enthusiasm for our enterprise, but because we failed to see in time that our group needed conscious protection from the pull of the other strands in our lives.

In spite of the undeniable fact that I love to read and talk about books and although during a recent visit to Manhattan I sat in on a long-running group and found it welcoming, stimulating, and very enjoyable, I do not plan to start a book group, either, at least not in the foreseeable future. The New York group was discussing *Middlemarch* (before the television series), which coincidentally, I had just read a year earlier. Hence, I was able to insert my two cents worth about the irritability quotient of the pious Dorothea.

So what am I doing worming my way into a collection of essays on book groups? I am here to try to explain why it means so much to me to know that such groups are flourishing across the nation, creating their own nonelectronic Internet, complete with the hum of ideas and feelings aroused by the thoughtful and intricate perusal of books.

I am a writer. I have tackled every form of writing except the limerick, but my mainstay is fiction, both long and short. Writing is, paradoxically, both an extremely solitary occupation and an activity that presupposes the existence of an other—the unknown reader. As a writer, I do not write to seduce or even, necessarily, to please this reader; nevertheless, by the very nature of writing, I am constantly addressing her, inviting her to walk with me a while, to trust me enough to follow my map even if the ground is familiar, to see what I notice and listen to what I hear, to open her heart to invented pains and joys as fully as she does to those in real life, sometimes, perhaps, even more fully.

The kind of readers who choose to join book groups are a writer's dream come true, the perfect hiking companions through the writer's claimed landscape. Metaphorically speaking, they know enough of botany and geology to appreciate the curve of the hills, the shadowy undergrowth of the fens, and the sweep of the beaches. They see the forest and the trees. They have, too, a firm purchase on human nature, both their own and various fictional representations of it, so they are able to judge a story's people (and a person's story) with acumen and sympathy.

But above all else, they care. They take the time and the energy needed for caring and give it to a book as they would to a friend. They invest their reading and their discussions of what they have read with true passion. They are willing to spend their emotions and their intellect with openhanded generosity. A casual observer of one lively book group meeting remarked with amazement on the involvement of the members with the book at hand, the fervor of their opinions, as if, he said, the characters under discussion "were real people they knew." Though it was not meant as a compliment, I think that group can take it as such, for it is testimony to their success as readers.

It seems to me that the members of book groups think like writers. They are acute observers. To each book, they bring what they already know of both books and life, and, as importantly, they bring an openness to learning something new—not learning in a dull, moralistic sense, but learning as discovery. They are willing to let what is unformed within them well up and take shape in answer to words on a page. Indeed, they invite this to happen. For the writer, these things occur as the words come out; for the reader, they occur as the words go in. The book group member then takes an extra step, entering with a kind of joyous bravery the fray of explaining her reactions, harnessing yet more words—her own and those of her fellow members—to expand and extend the reading experience, and, in an intangible but substantial way, the book itself.

I have modest aspirations. I do not covet a place on the best seller list or the movie of the week. What I want for my poems and short stories and novels and essays is an engaged audience. (Not, perhaps, such a modest aspiration, after all.) Engaging them is part of my job, of course, but it is a great boost to my spirits to know that readers exist who fervently seek engagement—readers who will bring to my work as deep an attention as I spent in producing it.

I struggle to find the right words, the most effective sequence of events, the most appropriate form, and the essential truth of my characters because I must do so to satisfy myself. But close to that, so close as to be simultaneous, I do it to communicate my vision, to share my versions of storytelling and living and language.

I do not know who will pick up the anthology that contains my story, when someone will read my poem in a literary journal, or where someone will curl up with my novel. I cannot know, either, what secrets, bitter and sweet, those readers carry in their backpacks as they trudge through my contrived territory, nor how they will spread their own meanings on my tale—whether they will choose to lay their bedrolls on granite or moss. What I do know is that if this reader—this intimate stranger—is in a book group, half the battle is won, for my writing will have its day in court before a jury that weighs justice with both head and heart. Critical but patient ears and eyes will be turned my way. Private lives will be suspended for a brief span to make room for the lives I have devised. I couldn't ask for more. I don't.

So, to all book group members everywhere, leaning across crumb-strewn tables toward one another or circled in a living room with books open on your laps and arguments or laughter in the air, I say, keep up the good work. For it is work, and it is good, what you are doing. Even if the authors you discuss never know a single word of what you have said, even, in fact, if the authors are dead, you are contributing to their vitality and to the longevity and reality of their creations. You are patrons of the arts, spending the invaluable coin of your minds and your sentiments. Actions may speak louder than words, but words matter. They matter very much. You, gentle reader, stand witness to that.

A World Open to Chance

JOHN MCFARLAND   📖   SEATTLE, WASHINGTON

"YOU WALK DOWN the street. You see somebody that looks interesting. You strike up a conversation. You check it out," one of us said. The other three nodded in agreement. We'd all been there. "You clear a place for chance to operate with your men and you see where it takes you. Why would you want it to be any different with your book group?"

Who of us could argue with that? Thus it was that the four of us, all gay men, chose serendipity and experimentation as the guiding principles in forming our book group. We were convinced that being open to chance influences would protect us from what we saw as the forces that would doom such a venture. Just as they should be avoided in budding romances, the stodgy, the routine, and the pretentious were to be guarded against at all costs in book group. We trusted that diversity of membership, with the promise of new blood constantly recharging the mix, would be our insurance.

Our group had sixteen members at first: men and women, gay and straight, all voracious readers with eclectic tastes. Once that group assembled, of course, we established ground rules in the great tradition of participatory democracy. We would meet on the last Wednesday of the month. The meeting would start at 7:30 P.M. sharp and would include discussion of that month's book with time set aside for the selection of the next month's book. The meeting would rotate through our various residences and the only thing served would be brewed decaf coffee. We kept it simple.

Then, with the simple ground rules in place, the eternal dance of small group dynamics took over. It became clear very quickly that we had a strong and sizable literary contingent among us. These people knew their books, were up on the latest trends, and were passionate in their advocacy of certain books.

In a group that went whichever way the wind blew, this contingent took over from the get-go. But none of us argued with the fact that these people contributed an untold knowledge of books. They raised the level of books we read and held the discussions to a high standard. They also did everybody's homework since they had enough book suggestions to last us into the next century.

But on the whole, we all had to admit that the discussions of these high-caliber books weren't exactly hot stuff no matter how much we liked the books themselves. Louise Erdrich's *Love Medicine* was a prime example. Here was a rich and satisfying collection of short stories about Native Americans on and off a reservation in the desolate landscape of North Dakota—the electric private reading experience that we all pray for. But it left us with little to say to each other besides "beautifully written" and "profoundly affecting."

Love Medicine was not alone in our experience. Over and over again, we found that a praiseworthy novel or story collection did not stimulate substantive discussion. We were there to share our reading experiences not husband them like priceless jewels. We wanted debates and dynamics and explorations, not just consecration of high art that didn't need our added blessing. The trick was how to get to that sharing.

To solve our problem, we resorted to experiments. During one summer when everybody in the group was planning a trip, we decided to take a three-month hiatus from meeting to read a classic, the longer the better, to fill the months we were apart. We chose Leo Tolstoy's *Anna Karenina*.

When we reunited in the fall, the group did have a lively discussion, but not in the way any of us could have predicted. Though we didn't depart radically from the "liked it/didn't like it" trap that we fell into when it came to modern American fiction, people's passionate involvement with Tolstoy's masterpiece made them reveal aspects of their tastes that were news to the rest of us. "Next to this novel, every-thing else looks bland," was one comment. Another person enjoyed the portrait of Russian life but declared, to gasps of astonishment, "Anna is a shallow character." Yet another said, "I liked this, but I have no interest in reading another word he wrote."

Although people did reveal themselves in relation to *Anna Karenina*, we couldn't deny that novels were not the best basis for dis-cussion. Yet all of us were fanatic novel readers and wanted to include them among our selections.

It was time for another experiment. This time it was an attempt to mix in more nonfiction with our fiction choices. We selected Richard Rodriguez's *Hunger of Memory*, a book that addressed the issue of bilingual programs in U.S. education. As we assembled, people mum-bled that they hated this book. We felt that Rodriguez had been set up as a Hispanic spokesperson fronting for conservatives who wanted bilingual education programs to die. We wanted to put our fists through the wall at what a dishonest piece of work this was. Then the formal discussion began.

Much to our surprise, we found that the points Rodriguez made provided an excellent framework for thought-provoking policy debate whether we agreed with his point of view or not. The book inflamed readers in our group like no other one we had read so far, yet it was the basis for the single most exciting discussion in the first two years of our group.

Despite all the benefits the group reaped from the literary contin-gent, there was a very real downside to their dominance. We lost some of our members who didn't like the serious direction in which things were drifting. After the defections, there were new and healthy grum-blings that "certain people's" tastes were shutting out other valid alter-natives. Once again, it was time for an experiment.

To force people to voice their choice, we declared that those who had chosen a book recently should sit back while others proposed a book. Although this approach was unusually regimented for us, it did break up the sense of literary uniformity that was settling over the group.

Things went along fine with this method for a while. Until we chose Don DeLillo's *The Names*, that is. What appeared to many of us as the simple story of a vacation on an unnamed mysterious Greek island awash with spy like activities incensed others. The anti-forces declared that they found the novel not to be of interest—empty, silly, and macho posturing. That assault drove the pro-forces to defend their position. As the debate got ugly, opinions grew more polarized. And there we were, facing the reality that although our group itself was diverse, our choices of what to read were shutting down diversity in choice and response.

We kicked this problem around for a while. It seemed that people wanted guarantees. They wanted to know ahead of time that investing time in reading a book and coming to the two-hour meeting would be interesting. But as we all knew, gay men and lesbians especially, there are no guarantees.

After much wrangling, we settled on a device long used by *The New York Review of Books*: pairing books according to some common criterion and thus creating a de facto forum. This choice provided many options for our diverse membership: we could read one book and not the other; we could read some of one, hate it and close it, and then move on to read all of the other; or, we could read them both, be insatiable and studly, and compare and contrast them or generally lord it over our less energetic colleagues. By this time we were so used to experiments, what did we have to lose with another one? We went for it.

Since it was late September when we had this discussion and our next meeting would be just before Halloween, we put a seasonal spin on our experiment. We selected Anne Rice's *Interview with the Vampire*, the first installment of her vampire chronicles that nobody had read but many had heard was solid storytelling, and Stephen King's *Salem's Lot*, a tale of horror set in autumnal New England and a bone thrown to those members with less exalted tastes.

As it turned out, each novel was excellent on its own terms and full of surprises in the bargain. Anne Rice's was funkier than its literary reputation suggested, and Stephen King's was a lot more literary and well written than its trashy reputation implied. The discussion of how these two writers got their effects turned into one of our best about novels. It gave us hope that we wouldn't have to give up fiction as a group.

This successful combination, which happened by chance, seemed to make people less hesitant about suggesting titles. The burden of selecting a book to impose on everybody was lifted. Now you had only fifty percent responsibility and, as we would find out, often a less-than-sterling book set off its partner to great advantage. The key was selecting matches that would lead to creating a dynamic discussion. Now every time was an experiment. And since the selection process became interesting in its own right, people seemed more willing to come to meetings even when they had no interest whatsoever in the books being discussed. They came because the future always held promise and possibility.

It was a new variation of the reason why we all go out and why we give strangers the benefit of the doubt. It was as if each of us believed in the depth of our throbbing hearts that right around the corner there would be that one glorious book to change our lives.

The list section of this book highlights some of the books we paired together in experiments that paid off in ways that we all want our romances to pay off.

For this group's reading list, see page 326.

Transported

E. Shan Correa   📖   Honolulu, Hawaii

Once, when I wrote a science fiction story called "The End of the Road," I carried it along to my book group. That group was, I'm certain, the best book group in existence. We all loved reading and loved each other, so how could it have been otherwise? We had long since accepted that the first half hour of our discussions needed to be non-structured, a euphemism for "we'll never get down to business right away anyway, so why try?" This half hour was when we shared news, triumphs, rejections (Angie and I were both writers who shared most of those), support, and kindness. Sometimes Angie and I tried out new poetry or short prose during our nonstructured time. That morning I read "The End of the Road."

Now when I wrote that story, I hated it. Not the story. I'm still fond of the short-short about an elderly, childless couple who found a baby, took it home, then faced some very strange circumstances when the infant spoke to them. What I hated was myself for writing in a genre I found unfamiliar and, I'll admit, slightly inferior to the more "literary" fiction I fancied I wrote. I blamed my new computer for enticing me into foreign territory and myself for relishing the way my characters reacted to the extraordinary events in their tired, ordinary lives.

Our unofficial group leader loved my little fantasy. Helen, a bulky woman with straight hair and a plain face adorned only by constellations of freckles, was our most perceptive reader. Her ordinary appearance masked an extraordinary mind and her insights into our readings sometimes left us shaking our heads. Helen's tastes in literature were eclectic, encompassing ancient tomes and, it turned out, future worlds. I especially admired her quirky sense of humor, so I preened mightily when she laughed at what she termed the "whimsy" in my story.

Helen immediately suggested that we read the science fiction anthology she'd just finished, *Writers of the Future, Volume V*. As she dug about in her capacious rattan beach bag for the book, the other five of us exchanged weak smiles. We didn't read science fiction and fantasy. "I vaguely remember liking some Ray Bradbury and Isaac Asimov a hundred years ago in junior high," Angie admitted, "but I think I grew out of it."

"Speculative fiction can be a real kick," Helen countered. She produced a thick, slick, black-and-silver paperback with a white butterfly-like creature on the front. At closer glance, the creature centered between gossamer wings and beneath three antennae was a comely, nude woman. A moon of some sort floated on the black behind her, and a space traveler gazed up at her from his newly-downed craft. Definitely alien stuff.

Angie squinted at the cover's large white letters: "L. Ron Hubbard presents the best new SF of the year . . ."

"Forget it," we said. The name on the cover held no pleasant associations for us. "No way, Helen," we said. "You can give sci-fi a fancy name, but it's still juvenile and stupid."

We took a vote.

And in spite of our protests, we agreed to read the anthology of "speculative fiction."

Why? Maybe because we realized that our criticism was shallow. Or because our group was, at last, ready to give more than lip service to the premise that no literary genre was inferior in and of itself, that the author's creativity and skill mattered, not the subject matter.

More likely, the reason for Helen's prevailing was Helen herself, who smiled and nodded, her gray-blue eyes sparkling as she waited for each of us to have our say. She had never steered us wrong, not even when she decided we should read a western and Walter Van Tilburg

Clark's *The Oxbow Incident* blew away our preconceptions about bloody, mindless cowboy sagas.

I voted yes for reading sci-fi. But I also bought a floral-quilted book cover for paperbacks when it appeared auspiciously at a craft fair—I bought it to cover *Writers of the Future*. On the bus, I kept the book closed when a friend sat down close enough to peek at the pages. And I felt something akin to guilt when, late at night, I read one of the book's stories and let myself be transported by a magical healer into the Realm of Mistrel.

"She died just before dawn," the tale began. "I closed the book I had been reading—*Estavio's Moral Tales*—and placed it atop the pile of volumes that leaned perilously against my chair." Damiano, the old queen's attendant in Mark Matz's fantasy "Despite and Still," drew the drapes. "We had wanted to see the sunrise, but now I had no affection for that sight." He smoothed the queen's hair with her favorite carved rosewood hairbrush, pulled the satin quilt to her quiet breast, and left the room. In the antechamber were lords, ladies, and Prince Giovan, the firstborn and heir: "The boy's face was frozen in a perfect mourning mask, but how his eyes were rich with exaltation!"

Damiano was bereft but not witless. He knew that he, "the queen's whore," was in danger. He left immediately for remote Salentina and chimerical adventures as the thrall of a marauding sea king. I followed him, transfixed by his escapades and his healing magic, delighted by the author's lyrical style and skill.

While reading other selections in the book, I was transformed into a bag lady named Maude who found a magical wallet; a courageous Jewish woman named Rachel in an artificial world; and a fledgling attorney encountering gothic adventures on the Iowa farm of the grotesque Nomaler family. Reading earlier and later volumes in the series transported me into the body and soul of a vampire (what a lonely soul that was!). I survived in a world of ice and devastation. I shuddered when a red-eyed thing howled in the night for me.

Although each story in the series was not as captivating as "Despite and Still," the overall quality was excellent, especially considering that the authors were not professionals. (For instance, author Marc Matz "supervises the financial management of his family's cosmetics company.") The works were selected each year from the winners of an open contest. I knew better than to submit "The End of the Road." Helen's encouragement to the contrary, I was quite humbled.

When our group met again, I found I was not alone in my enthusiasm for our latest reading. The discussion that day was one of the richest ever. Helen never gloated over our conversion; instead she suggested an Ursula LeGuin novel for a later time and a romance novel that had captured her fancy.

Reading, we're told, is broadening. Yet on my own I had always selected books that roamed within the borders of the prose and poetry land where I felt comfortable. True, I had come to enjoy the best in music and art from all eras and all genres, but I was snobbish when it came to certain literary types. It took a beloved book group—and a Helen—to stretch me out of my complacency, to beam me up, to transport me to new and exotic realms.

Tonight Is Book Club

LEE STRICKLAND   📖   CHICAGO, ILLINOIS

SPRING 1976. MY boyfriend, Paul, was golfing, and I had done some shopping in preparation for a peaceful Saturday afternoon sprucing up his house. He'd lived in it with his wife before she left him, and, in my opinion, the place desperately needed an overhaul. Officially, I had my own apartment, a tiny studio affordable to a former English major surviving on temp jobs. But, for three months, I'd been hanging out unofficially at Paul's. With a bountiful potted fern under each arm, I sidled from the garage, where I had parked my car, through the back door. From the kitchen, I heard noises, loud and unrestrained, like a raccoon ransacking the garbage. Metal things clanged and lightweight plastic things bounced and fell to the floor. Warily, I tiptoed in and saw a woman sitting cross-legged on the floor beside piles of kitchenware, her head and hands deep inside the cabinet under the range. This had to be the ex-wife, or, more precisely, the soon-to-be ex-wife. I'd never met her, but I'd heard plenty. Paul, poor thing, had been suffering through the unpleasant finalities of a divorce that she had initiated but wasn't making easy. Now, here she was in the kitchen I'd been treating as my own, demonstrating all her characteristic unreasonableness and greed.

I lowered the ferns to the floor, inching them with my foot toward a discreetly dark place under the kitchen table.

She looked up and introduced herself cheerfully. "You must be Lee," she said. So she'd heard about me, too. Her gaze zoomed in on the fern forest bulging near my feet. She was prettier than I had expected, and her smile, despite the way Paul had described her, did not seem the least bit phony. "I just stopped by to pick up a few of my things."

"Go right ahead," I said, my face stretching into a wide, saccharine grin of hospitality. I realized too late that she didn't need, nor was she waiting for, my permission. I was at a disadvantage, caught red-handed in the act of redecorating her house. On the other hand, what was she doing stealing my pots and pans?

"Cup of tea?" I asked. At exactly the same moment, both of us reached to open the cabinet where the cups were kept. This made us laugh. After I'd known her for a while, she told me I'd seemed calm and gracious that day; not one bit—how had she put it?—intense or neurotic. Even my decorating instincts were ones she shared. She liked the idea of brightening the place up with the sort of greenery then fashionable in singles bars. By moving out, she'd been fleeing an environment that had become to her dull and uninspiring, a kind of prison.

I put the tea kettle on and she located the tea bags. As she emptied cabinets, we chatted, skirting the subject of him, and exchanging information about jobs and interests. Paul hadn't told me she'd spent a few years teaching high school English. And she hadn't heard I'd been an English major. "I can't believe it," we squealed, excited and girlish, though we were in our late twenties. We pretended to suspect some strategy in Paul's withholding these facts, but we both knew it was more serious than that. He was missing some fundamental something in his understanding of the world. He didn't realize how important it was to be an English major, to love books enough to want to teach English. He didn't see how these choices defined us. Over our second cup of tea, I confided a secret, one Paul did not know: I wrote poems, scribbled in my journal. Delighted, she reciprocated. She, too, wrote daily in a journal, and he had never seen it.

"Bet those would be interesting to exchange," we joked. But it occurred to me that there were precious few entries in mine about Paul. He hadn't touched my soul, and, strangely, it was in talking to Karin that I realized it fully.

A few weeks later, I saw Karin again. The divorce was nearly final, and the house was to be sold. By some elaborate, lawyer-facilitated agreement, she was to paint the guestroom in preparation for putting the house on the market. She came by on a Sunday. Paul, who had recently been promoted to vice president of a large ad agency and was irritatingly preoccupied with his clients, stayed in the living room, hunkered over his papers. I snuck off to the guestroom where Karin was painting. From my perch on the bottom rung of her ladder, I kept two Dixie cups constantly brimming with pink zinfandel. We got right to the subject of books. She liked Thomas Hardy and the Brontës. I liked the Romantic poets. Aviation had figured largely in both our literary developments: Erica Jong's *Fear of Flying* and Anne Morrow Lindbergh's diaries.

"This sure is fun," she said, as if it had been a long time since she'd had fun in that house.

"Beats talking about advertising," I said. "Or golf."

Karin and I were talking from the heart, enjoying a meeting of our deep, spirited, authentic selves, parts of each of us that, sadly, neither boyfriend nor husband had yet figured out how to tap.

"Did you ever think of starting a book club?"

Twenty-three years later, I can't remember which of us actually said that.

We each invited four or five female friends. By then, months had passed and I had gone on to another boyfriend; Karin was divorced and dating. Our first official meeting took place at my studio apartment in Chicago. I served soup made from a dry mix, cheap jug wine, and Oreos. The women were excited to meet each other, eager to be pioneering members of a book group. In the mid-seventies, the idea was still unique. We tried to be serious and purposeful, vowing that night to read only books written by women. (That vow, along with the simple menu, never took. This year alone, we've read John Irving, Stephen Millhauser, Caleb Carr, James McManus, and Bernhard Schlink.)

We thought then that it mattered what we read. We thought procedure mattered: someone should lead discussions; there should be a system for choosing books; and, if someone dropped out, we should have a method in place for evaluating new prospects. We'd been in sororities, on committees and boards. We'd had jobs in hierarchical organizations, been martinet camp counselors. Women's groups—and other groups—were held together by deadlines, tradition, by-laws, autocracy, organization charts. Wouldn't we need these to hold our book club together?

Now it is 1999. We've been meeting every month for twenty-three years. Just short of a quarter century. For the five of us founding members, this is nearly half our lives. We are and have always been called simply "Book Club." As in, "Sorry, I can't go. Tonight is Book Club." As in, "Start the invitation list with Book Club." We have shared weddings, births, adoptions, nanny problems, graduations, cancer, business starts, career changes, delinquent teens, divorces, parents' illnesses and deaths, and, most recently, menopause. And, of course, several hundred books.

We meet once a month, rotating houses. We send invitations and insist on an RSVP. We arrive with small hostess gifts—a bottle of wine, flowers, an hors d'oeuvre, a dessert. The hostess serves dinner-sitdown, not buffet. One or two people will usually clear dinner plates in preparation for dessert, but rarely do we offer to stay after and help with the dishes. Book Club tends to feel more like a casually elegant dinner party than a women's meeting.

About once a year, usually at the holidays, we evaluate what we've read and how we're doing. Someone will complain about the food preparation or how hosting Book Club is time-consuming and expensive, to which someone else will say, "Don't sweat the food. Just order a pizza." All around the table, heads will nod in sensible agreement, women pretending that the food doesn't matter and offering up creative, convenient solutions.

"Just get Chinese."

"Throw some lettuce and tomatoes in a bowl. Don't fuss."

"Deli sandwiches from the Jewel."

But, as the years go on, no one ever orders pizza or Chinese; no one brings sandwiches from the grocery store. A curried couscous dish prepared by Whole Foods, maybe. A large entrée salad, but garnished with roasted red peppers, hearts of palm, dried Michigan cherries, smoked salmon. You don't have to cook, but you must show respect for food and for the venerable traditions of Book Club. And, since membership stays around twelve women, hosting responsibilities only fall on each of us once a year. Better to switch dates with somebody during a pressured month than to risk providing a disappointing culinary experience.

Our format is the same each month. We arrive between 7:00 and 7:30 P.M. to sip wine and enjoy a variety of hors d'oeuvres for at least an hour. During this period, we exchange updates; shriek like school girls over someone's new hair color or a hilarious report of a blind date; hug and wag our heads over a parent's illness, a job loss, a kid's disciplinary problem. Children and husbands are rarely in evidence. From time to time, a pre-teenager may take coats, then discreetly disappear. A husband, returned too early from his evening exile, may poke his head in during coffee, say hi, and go up to bed. And, in the old days, a nursing baby would occasionally sleep silently in a new mother's arms. Book Club is a women's night, the high-brow equivalent of girl's night out, a special time to commune and have fun without children, without men.

Some time after eight, we sit down to dinner. At this point, we make efforts to focus, moving the dynamics in a direction that will allow for discussion of the book. But we don't rush into the book. There is still much to catch up on. Some piece of news delivered to one or two during the cocktail hour will have to be repeated so all can absorb and comment upon it. Questions must be asked, stories fleshed out and shared with everyone. Then and only then will we discuss the book. Typically, most-but not all-members have read it. Not reading the book is never a reason to stay home.

This is the first year we have decided on all the books ahead of time and assigned a discussion leader for each selection. We like this new procedure. It gives us more time to read the books, and makes for a more lively, focused discussion. The discussion leader comes prepared with book reviews culled from the Internet, and adds to—but does not dominate—the discussion. The most serious portion of book discussion occurs over decaf and dessert, usually platters of cookies or pastry or fruit, which can be passed around without distraction. We don't get up from the table and move somewhere after dinner. No brandy or cigars. The evening ends directly from the dinner table, at about 10:30. We all say goodbye and depart at the same time.

Book Club get-togethers are predictably smooth and without conflict. We are happy to see each other. For the most part, this harmony, our traditions, have simply evolved. But, there was a time, a decade or so back, when some people felt the evenings were too chatty, too little related to discussion of the books. Our dinners were buffet in those days, promoting noisily diffused conversation. There was a feeling that some people dominated, while others were seldom able to make themselves and their thoughts heard. One member routinely played the devil's advocate, to the irritation of some others.

This was in 1989. The group had been together for over a decade, and we were restless and cranky, wondering: "Are we doing this right? Can this group last forever?" So, in the spirit of the times, and as an adjunct to our first and only retreat, we spent a weekend in Wisconsin and one of the members suggested bringing along a therapist. (This member's own therapist just happened to be an expert in "group dynamics," and would agree, for a reasonable fee, to share the weekend with us.) A majority of us were interested and set off to Lake Geneva for a weekend of scrutiny and facilitated communication.

Observing our interactions up close, the expert concluded that we weren't very good listeners. We all talked at once. She recommended that we work on having one conversation at a time. We nodded our heads solemnly, like children admonished to be quiet, and, having paid for this feedback, we felt obliged to try out some changes. Henceforth, there would be no more buffet suppers, trays balanced on knees, conversations splintered as we grouped ourselves willy-nilly in threes and fours. No longer would the noise level be deafening, the children upstairs kept awake. We would sit at a table. The serving of the main course would signal that it was time to begin discussing the book. We would speak one at a time. We would remember our original purpose: to focus on literature.

The changes over the past decade have been helpful, but I don't know that Book Club would have fallen apart without them. We have been a remarkably stable group. Over the twenty-three years, only a couple people have dropped out, and a few others have moved from Chicago. Karin remarried and moved to Savannah. Kathy married and moved to France. Jane's family was transferred to St. Louis. Laura and her husband sold their home and took off for an extended cruise on their sailboat. Evadene now lives in Kansas City but flies in four or five times a year for meetings. They all keep in touch. We have found that the best way to add new members is what we call "self-selection." Anyone can bring a guest. And, if we're down a member or two, they are welcome to join if they enjoy us. We have found that the ones who like us end up making good, longstanding, contributing members.

Why, when so many groups begin, flicker, and die, has Book Club lasted? I asked the group this question, and we discussed it.

"We're so diverse."

"We're all alike."

"We keep growing and changing."

"We've kept to the same traditions."

Our longevity is a mystery, even to us. Socio-economically, we aren't very diverse. But we are diverse in terms of lifestyles, interests, and jobs. Among us are the owner of a travel company, a nurse, a corporate sales consultant for Marshall Field's, a mortgage broker, a market researcher, an organizational development consultant, a painter, a flight attendant, a homemaker. We are, at present, about half married and half single, more city than suburban.

I believe we are particularly strong women who take our lives seriously, changing when we need to change. Several of us went back to graduate school later in life. Others have changed careers and partners. At the same time, we are all solid and Midwestern, and perhaps that accounts for our duration. Two or three core members have put in consistent energy and participation over the years, a factor that cannot be overlooked.

Though we wouldn't be together without books, Book Club is, I believe, more about "club" than "book."

"Book Club isn't really about books anymore," Susan said. "It's just a group of women who truly care about each other."

That's the theory I subscribe to. During these twenty-some years, Book Club members have experienced and shared all kinds of pedestrian travails: heartache, weight gains and losses, depressions, and job, marital, and parenting frustrations. Some have had more serious crosses to bear. Mary developed cancer and had a successful liver transplant. Karen went through a painful divorce after the birth of her third child. Janet lost her mother and her French boyfriend in a three-month period. Karin's husband died suddenly. For me, since 1976, I have been married and divorced; started and grown a business; obtained a graduate degree; been reunited with a son I'd given up for adoption; become a grandmother; lost a parent; had my heart broken; bought and sold several homes; and "become" a writer, publishing short stories in literary journals. Karin has had a son; lost a husband; established and dismantled a life in the South; obtained a degree in design; started and sold a successful business; and, most recently, begun writing a memoir. When her husband died, who was on the next plane to Savannah to help her but three members of Book Club.

When I moved earlier this year, who was there to unpack boxes, to organize my new kitchen? When I got married, graduated, mourned at my father's funeral, who was there? And who, like a circle of eager children, begs me to read my stories out loud?

After a quarter century, I can say with confidence that this is a commitment for life.

For this group's reading list, see page 365.

PART VI

What to Read: Book Groups Share Their Reading Lists

rom *Augustine's Confessions* to *The Liars' Club*. From Susan Faludi
to Robert Bork. From Louisa May Alcott to Sigmund Freud. From
Oprah's book group choices to anything but. What do book groups
read? To find thirty-five answers, take a look at the thirty-five lists (in
alphabetical order by contributor) that follow.

Vicar's Landing Book Club Reading List

JEAN ARMSTRONG   📖   PONTE VEDRA BEACH, FLORIDA

I BECAME CHAIR of the book club here at Vicar's Landing, a continuing care retirement community, quite unexpectedly when our original
leader left for the summer. I suggested to the other members that we
continue to meet in a casual way, and we did. Our group consists of
women aged seventy-five and older. Our normal attendance is sixteen,
but we have had as many as twenty-four and as few as six. We meet
once a month and we discuss books being currently reviewed as well
as those that we've recently read. This casual approach has been well
received and I was recently asked to continue as leader. We don't expect
everyone to read the same book. We don't use the Internet. The Oprah
book club is quite new to most of us, but we find more and more that
her selections are well worth reading. In the summer our attendance
drops off, as members are away. Currently we are talking about *The
Reader* and *East of the Mountain*, the latter not too well appreciated by
our group, it being a far cry from *Snow Falling on Cedars*. We have discussed many fine books that are well worth reading, as you'll see in the
selected list below.

Under the Tuscan Sun, Frances Mayes
A Live Coal in the Sea, Madeleine L'Engle
Love in the Time of Cholera, Gabriel García Márquez
The Cunning Man, Robertson Davies
Alias Grace, Margaret Atwood
Body and Soul, Frank Conroy
Charming Billy, Alice McDermott
The House of Mirth, Edith Wharton
The Children, David Halberstam
Beach Music, Pat Conroy
Cold Mountain, Charles Frazier
Evening Class and *Tara Road*, Maeve Binchy
Patchwork Planet, Anne Tyler
You Belong to Me, Mary Higgins Clark
Brunswick Gardens, Anne Perry
Divine Secrets of the Ya-Ya Sisterhood, Rebecca Wells
Madame Curie: A Biography, Eva Curie
Memoirs of a Geisha, Arthur Golden
The Greatest Generation, Tom Brokaw
The Reader, Bernhard Schlink
The Pilot's Wife, Susan Shreve
Jewel, Bret Lott
Midwives, Chris Bohjalian
Voyage of Discovery, Stephen Ambrose
Ulysses and *Portrait of the Artist As a Young Man*, James Joyce
The Simple Truth, David Baldacci

Shirley's Book Club

JEANNE BAY AND SHIRLEY R. JOHNSON   OBERLIN, OHIO

THIRTY-SIX YEARS and 412 books ago, Shirley's book club started. (It was so named by the Oberlin Cooperative Bookstore because Shirley did all the arranging with them for selecting and ordering books.) Of our current nine members, two original members remain (death and moving away happen), five have been members for ten to twenty-five years, and two joined in the past one to two years. Enough continuity exists for us to agree on certain observations.

We have always been eclectic; we try to maintain a balance between fiction and nonfiction, classics and current authors, and authors from or writing about other countries and cultures. In recent years our best discussions included the Muslim world and women of *Nine Parts of Desire* by Geraldine B. Brooks and the history and tragedy of gypsy life in *Bury Me Standing* by Isabel Fonseca. We learned a lot from these books. *Hole in the Sky* by William Kittredge and *All the Pretty Horses* by Cormac McCarthy, in our own geographic area but of a different culture, were also of great interest.

There's almost no way to tell in advance whether a book will lend itself to a good discussion. *Ladder of Years* by Anne Tyler, a fairly innocuous choice, *Dakota* by Kathleen Norris, and *The Riders* by Tim Winton brought out real differences of opinion about the themes and messages of each book. Widely read books like *Possession* by A. S.

Byatt, *A Civil Action* by Jonathan Harr, and *Shipping News* by E. Annie Proulx stimulated good discussion. Doris Kearns Goodwin's *Wait Till Next Year* appealed to even those who were leery of "baseball stuff." Other books, perhaps less widely read, that had quieter but considerable discussion were *Ancestral Truths* by Sara Maitland, *Wild Swans* by Jung Chang, *Obasan* by Joy Kogawa, and *Alva Myrdal, A Daughter's Memoir* by Sissela Bok.

Certain authors interested us so much that we read more than three of their works: Camus (5), Cather (6), Conrad (5), Faulkner (6), Forster (4), Hardy (4), James (9), García Márquez (4), Smiley (4), Stegner (4), A. Tyler (4), Wharton (4), and Woolf (4).

We echo the view of book clubs all over the country and quote Shirley again: "Book groups transform the solitude of the reading experience in much the same way as reading itself broadens the individual mind. In sharing our reading we reveal something about ourselves and broaden our palates intellectually and culturally."

Woman in the Dunes, Kobo Abe

A Natural History of the Senses, Diane Ackerman

Second Chances, Alice Adams

Twenty Years at Hull House, Jane Addams

A Death in the Family, James Agee

Who's Afraid of Virginia Woolf?, Edward Albee

Of Love and Shadows, Isabel Allende

I Never Sang for My Father, Robert Anderson

Winesburg, Ohio, Sherwood Anderson

I Know Why the Caged Bird Sings, Maya Angelou

The Lark, Jean Anouilh

Surfacing, Margaret Atwood

Powers of Attorney, Louis Auchincloss

Dog Beneath the Skin, W. H. Auden and Christopher Isherwood

Emma, *Northanger Abbey*, and *Pride and Prejudice*, Jane Austen

Good Times and *Growing Up*, Russell Baker

Père Goriot, Honoré de Balzac

Kepler: A Novel, John Banville

Nightwood, Djuna Barnes

End of the Road and *Steptime*, John Barth

Love Always, Ann Beattie

Virginia Woolf: A Biography, Quentin Bell

The Victim, Saul Bellow

Love Is Not Enough, Bruno Bettelheim

Alva Myrdal: A Daughter's Memoir and *Lying*, Sissela Bok

Lost Honor of Katharina Blum, Heinrich Böll

A Man for all Seasons, Robert Bolt

Ficciones, Jorge Luis Borges

Miracle at Philadelphia and *Yankee from Olympus*, Catherine Bowen

The Death of the Heart, *Friends and Relations*, and *The Little Girls*,
   Elizabeth Bowen

The Desegregated Heart, Sarah P. Boyle

Three Short Novels, Kay Boyle

Joan of the Stockyards and *Mother Courage*, Bertolt Brecht

Tenant of Wildfell Hall, Anne Brontë

Jane Eyre and *Shirley*, Charlotte Brontë

Wuthering Heights, Emily Brontë

A Closed Eye, Anita Brookner

Nine Parts of Desire, Geraldine Brooks

Leaving Home, Art Buchwald

Possession and *Still Life*, A. S. Byatt

Women in Fiction, Susan Cahill, ed.

Caligula, *The Just Assassins*, *Exiles*, *The Plague*, and *The Stranger*,
   Albert Camus

The Homemaker, Dorothy Canfield

The Education of Little Tree, Forrest Carter

House of Children, Joyce Cary

Death Comes to the Archbishop, *Lucy Gayheart*, *My Antonia*,
Oh Pioneers!, *The Professor's House*, and *Sapphira*, Willa Cather

Wild Swans, Jung Chang

Three Sisters and *Uncle Vanya*, Anton Chekhov

The Awakening, Kate Chopin

Taipan, James Clavell

The Life and Times of Michael K., J. M. Coetzee

Cheri, Colette

Family Happiness, Laurie Colwin

Mrs. Bridge, Evan S. Connell

Lord Jim, *The Secret Agent*, and *Three Short Novels: Heart of Darkness, Youth, Typhoon*, Joseph Conrad

Stop Time, Frank Conroy

The Road from Coorain, Jill Ker Conway

Great Short Works, Stephen Crane

A Woman's Place, Anne Crompton

A Reporter's Life, Walter Cronkite

Madame Curie, Eve Curie

Memoirs of a Dutiful Daughter, Simone de Beauvoir

Year of the Zinc Penny, Rick Demarinis

Moll Flanders, Daniel Defoe

White Noise, Don DeLillo

Having Our Say: The Delany Sisters' First 100 Years, Sarah and A. Elizabeth Delany with Amy Hill Hearth

American Notes for General Circulation and *Bleak House*, Charles Dickens

White Album, Joan Didion

An American Childhood and *Pilgrim at Tinker Creek,* Annie Dillard

Out of Africa and *Seven Gothic Tales*, Isak Dinesen

The Tiger in the Grass, Harriet Doerr

Lincoln Reconsidered, David H. Donald

Crime and Punishment and *The Idiot*, Fyodor Dostoyevsky

Sister Carrie, Theodore Dreiser

World Without End, Francine du Plessix Gray

The Physicists and *The Visit; Traps; The Pledge*, Friedrich Durrenmatt

A Matter of Principle, Donald Dworkin

Disturbing the Universe, Freeman Dyson

The Solace of Open Spaces, Greta Ehrlich

Middlemarch and *The Mill on the Floss*, George Eliot

The Invisible Man, Ralph Ellison

Silence, Shusaku Endo

The Trojan Women, Euripides

Five Smooth Stones, Ann Fairbairn

Absalom Absalom!, Go Down Moses, Light in August, Sartoris, The Sound and the Fury, and *The Unvanquished*, William Faulkner

Memoirs of My Ghost Brother, Heinz Insu Fenkl

Joseph Andrews, Henry Fielding

The Great Gatsby, F. Scott Fitzgerald

Madame Bovary, Gustave Flaubert

Mary Wollstonecraft, Eleanor Flexner

Conscience and Courage, Eva Fogelman

Bury Me Standing, Isabel Fonseca

The Good Soldier, Ford Madox Ford

Howards End, The Longest Journey, Passage to India, and *A Room with a View*, E. M. Forster

Love in Full Bloom, Fowler and McCutcheon, eds.

The French Lieutenant's Woman, John Fowles

Thais, Anatole France

Man's Search for Meaning, Victor Frankel

My Mother, Myself, Nancy Friday

The Feminine Mystique, Betty Friedan

The Art of Loving, Erich Fromm

Overhead in a Balloon, Mavis Gallant

Dreaming in Cuba, Cristina Garcia

The Queen of the Tambourine, Jane Gardam

Nickel Mountain, John Gardner

North and South, Elizabeth Gaskell

The Balcony, Jean Genet

Lafcadio's Adventures, Andre Gide

The Trouble in One House, Brendan Gill

The Odd Women, George Gissing

Electra, Jean Giraudoux

Schools Without Failure, William Glasser

The Inheritors, *Lord of the Flies*, and *The Spire*, William Golding

The Vicar of Wakefield, Oliver Goldsmith

No Ordinary Time and *Wait Till Next Year*, Doris Kearns Goodwin

A Sport of Nature and *World of Strangers*, Nadine Gordimer

Final Payments, *Men and Angels*, and *On the Other Side*, Mary Gordon

Personal History, Katharine Graham

The Keepers of the House, Shirley Grau

In This Sign, Joanne Greenberg

I Never Promised You a Rose Garden, Hannah Greene

Praying for Sheetrock, Melissa Greene

Reef, Romesh Gunesekera

Snow Falling on Cedars, David Guterson

The Best and the Brightest, David Halberstam

Snow in August, Pete Hamill

In Search of Salinger, Ian Hamilton

The Growth of the Soil, Knut Hamsun

The Mayor of Casterbridge, *Jude the Obscure*, *Tess of the D'Urbervilles*, and *Under the Greenwood Tree*, Thomas Hardy

Seduction and Betrayal, Elizabeth Hardwick

The Other America, Michael Harrington

Decision, Richard Harris

The Go Between, L. P. Hartley

A Civil Action, Jonathan Harr

The Marble Faun and *The House of Seven Gables*, Nathaniel
  Hawthorne

The Transit of Venus, Shirley Hazzard

Stones from the River, Ursula Hegi

Writing a Woman's Life, Carolyn Heilbrun

Catch-22, Joseph Heller

Pentimento, Lillian Hellman

No Man's Land: The Last of White Africa, John H. Heminway

Siddhartha and *Steppenwolf*, Herman Hesse

The Deputy, Ralph Hochhuth

Private Memoirs: Confessions of a Justified Sinner, James Hogg

Hazards of New Fortune and *The Rise of Silas Lapham*, William
  Dean Howells

A Doll's House, Hedda Gabler, and *Rosmersholm*, Henrik Ibsen

The Remains of the Day, Kazuo Ishiguro

Soledad Brother, George Jackson

*The Ambassadors, The American, The Aspern Papers, The Golden
  Bowl, Portrait of a Lady, Spoils of Poynton, Turn of the Screw,
  Washington Square*, and *Wings of the Dove*, Henry James

Pictures from an Institution, Randall Jarrell

Country of the Pointed Firs, Sarah Orne Jewett

Heat and Dust and *Out of India*, Ruth Prawer Jhabvala

Foxy Baby, Elizabeth Jolley

Fear of Flying, Erica Jong

Riding the White Horse Home, Teresa Jordan

Dubliners and *Portrait of the Artist as a Young Man*, James Joyce

The Trial, Franz Kafka

Sound of the Mountain, Yasumari Kawabata

Girl, Interrupted, Susanna Kaysen

Freedom or Death, Mikos Kazantzikes

Annie John and *Lucy*, Jamaica Kincaid

The Bean Trees and *Pigs in Heaven*, Barbara Kingsolver

China Men and *The Woman Warrior*, Maxine Hong Kingston

Hole in the Sky, William Kittredge

A Not Entirely Benign Procedure, Perri Klass

National Advisory Commission Report on Civil Disorders,
  Koerner Report

Age of Longing and *Darkness at Noon*, Arthur Koestler

Obasan, Joy Kogawa

On Death and Dying, Elizabeth Kübler-Ross

Laughing Boy, Christopher LaFarge

The Leopard, Giuseppi de Lampedusa

The Quest, Elizabeth Langgasser

The Plumed Serpent, *Sons and Lovers*, and *Women in Love*,
  D. H. Lawrence

The Golden Notebook and *Martha Quest*, Doris Lessing

Balm in Gilead, Sara L. Lightfoot

Moon Tiger, Penelope Lively

Only Children, Alison Lurie

Miramar, Naguib Mahfouz

Ancestral Truths, Sara Maitland

The Natural, Bernard Malamud

The Autobiography of Malcolm X, Malcolm X with Alex Haley

Man's Fate, André Malraux

The Watch That Ends the Night, Hugh MacLennon

Death in Venice, Thomas Mann

Nectar in a Sieve, Kamala Markandaya

The Autumn of the Patriarch, *Love in the Time of Cholera*, *No One
  Writes to the Colonel and Other Stories*, and *One Hundred Years
  of Solitude*, Gabriel García Márquez

Bird of Life, Bird of Death, Jonathan Maslow

The Folded Leaf and *They Came Like Swallows*, William Maxwell

The Color of Water, James McBride

All the Pretty Horses, Cormac McCarthy

Memories of a Catholic Girlhood, Mary McCarthy

Angela's Ashes, Frank McCourt

School for the Blind, Dennis McFarland

Principles of American Nuclear Chemistry, Thomas McMahon

Testing the Current, William McPherson

Blackberry Winter, Margaret Mead

The Confidence Man, Herman Melville

Growing up Female in America, Eve Merriam, ed.

Death of a Salesman, Arthur Miller

Spring Snow, Yukio Mishima

Dangerous Dossiers, Herbert Mitgang

Love Among the Cannibals, Morris Wright

The Bluest Eye and *Song of Solomon*, Toni Morrison

I've Been Meaning to Tell You, Alice Munro

The Flight from the Enchanter and *The Severed Head*, Iris Murdoch

Speak, Memory, Vladimir Nabokov

A Bend in the River and *India: A Wounded Civilization*, V. S. Naipaul

The Vendor of Sweets, R. K. Narayan

Portrait of a Marriage, Nigel Nicholson

McTeague and *The Octopus*, Frank Norris

Dakota, Kathleen Norris

Expensive People, Joyce Carol Oates

Three Plays, Sean O'Casey

White Lantern, J. Leonard O'Connell

A Good Man Is Hard To Find, Flannery O'Connor

Tell Me a Riddle, Tillie Olsen

The English Patient, Michael Ondaatje

Mourning Becomes Electra, Eugene O'Neill

Keep the Aspidistra Flying, George Orwell

My Michael, Amos Oz

Close Company: Stories of Mothers and Daughters, Christine Park
   and Caroline Heaten, eds.

I Remember, Boris Pasternak

A Short History of a Small Planet, T. R. Pearson

Manchester Fourteen Miles, Margaret Penn

Naked Masks, Luigi Pirandello

The Bell Jar, Sylvia Plath

Presidential Elections, Nelson W. Polsky and Aaron Wildavasky

The Old Order, Katherine Ann Porter

My Name Is Asher Lev, Chaim Potok

The Shipping News, E. Annie Proulx

Swann's Way, Marcel Proust

Excellent Women and *Quartet in Autumn*, Barbara Pym

The Negro in the Making of America, Benjamin Quarles

Beyond Vietnam, Edwin Reischauer

Smile Please, Jean Rhys

Rabble in Arms, Kenneth Roberts

Survive the Savage Sea, Dougal Robertson

Housekeeping, Marilynne Robinson

Jean Christophe, Romain Rolland

Parallel Lives, Phyllis Rose

The God of Small Things, Arundhati Roy

Boss, Mike Royko

Autobiography (Volume 1) , Bertrand Russell

Home, Witold Rybczynski

An Anthropologist on Mars, *A Leg to Stand On*, and *The Man Who
   Mistook His Wife for a Hat*, Oliver Sacks

History of a Man and *Mrs. Stevens Hears the Mermaid Singing*,
   May Sarton

Memoirs of a Fox-Hunting Man, Sigfried Sassoon

An Explanation for Chaos, Julie Schumacher

A Fine Romance, C. P. Seton

Heartbreak House, Major Barbara, and *St. Joan*, George
  Bernard Shaw

And Quiet Flows the Don, Mikhail Sholokhov

Ceremony, Leslie Marmon Silko

Orphans: Real and Imaginary, Eileen Simpson

Spinosa of Market Street, Isaac Bashevis Singer

Walden Two, B. F. Skinner

Duplicate Keys, Moo, Ordinary Love and Good Will, and
  A Thousand Acres, Jane Smiley

Power Game and *The Russians*, Hedrick Smith

The Expedition of Humphry Clinker, Tobias Smollett

Cancer Ward and *The First Circle*, Alexander Solzhenitsyn

Electra, Sophocles

Curriculum Vitae, A Far Cry from Kensington, and *Memento Mori*,
  Muriel Sparks

Salt Line, Elizabeth Spencer

The Education of a WASP, Lois M. Stalvey

Angle of Repose, Crossing to Safety, The Spectator Bird, and *Where
  the Bluebird Sings*, Wallace Stegner

Three Lives, Gertrude Stein

Miracle Under the Oaks, William Stevens

Rosencrantz and Gildenstern Are Dead, Tom Stoppard

Never Done, Susan Strasser

Pioneer Women, J. S. Stratton

Alice James, Jean Strouse

Lie Down in Darkness, William Styron

The Kingdom and the Power, Gay Talese

The Joy Luck Club and *The Kitchen God's Wife*, Amy Tan

Angel, Elizabeth Taylor

Old Forest and Other Stories and *A Summons to Memphis*,
  Peter Taylor

The White Hotel, D. H. Thomas

Lark Rise to Candleford, Flora Thompson

The Eco-Spasm Report, Alvin Toffler

Anna Karenina, *The Kreutzer Sonata*, and *War and Peace*,
  Leo Tolstoy

Middle of the Journey, Lionel Trilling

Barchester Towers, Anthony Trollope

A Connecticut Yankee in King Arthur's Court, Mark Twain

The Accidental Tourist, *Breathing Lessons*, *Dinner at the Homesick
  Restaurant*, and *Ladder of Years*, Anne Tyler

Kristin Lavransdatter, Sigrid Undset

Morality Play, Barry Unsworth

On the Farm, John Updike

A Far-Off Place, Laurens Van der Post

Galapagos and *Slaughterhouse Five*, Kurt Vonnegut

The Color Purple and *The Third Life of Grange Copeland*,
  Alice Walker

American Originals, Geoffrey C. Ward

All the King's Men, Robert Penn Warren

Decline and Fall and *A Handful of Dust*, Evelyn Waugh

Marat/Sade, Peter Weiss

The Hearts and Lives of Men, Fay Weldon

Golden Apples, *The Optimist's Daughter*, and *Thirteen Stories*,
  Eudora Welty

The Devil's Advocate, Morris West

The New Meaning of Treason and *The Real Night*, Rebecca West

The Age of Innocence, *The House of Mirth*, *Old New York*, and
  Roman Fever, Edith Wharton

Points of My Compass, E. B. White

Solid Mandela, Patrick White

One Generation After, Elie Wiesel

Incline Our Hearts, A. N. Wilson

The Riders, Tim Winton

The Quest for Christa T. , Christa Wolf

Look Homeward Angel, Thomas Wolf

Mrs. Dalloway, *Three Guineas*, *To the Lighthouse*, and *The Waves*,
    Virginia Woolf

Biography, Volumes II and III, Leonard Woolf

A Coin in Nine Hands, Marguerite Yourcenar

The Masterpiece, Émile Zola

Book List

ELLIE BECKER   SANTA FE, NEW MEXICO

1988

The Unbearable Lightness of Being, Milan Kundera. Men, women, love, freedom, necessity, political repression, moral truth. Elicited either strong like or dislike.

Beloved, Toni Morrison. Haunting. Deep discussion of humanity, mother, dignity, truth, the black woman's experience. Profound.

In a Different Voice, Carol Gilligan. Questions about dividing up and determining moral choices on the basis of gender.

Love in the Time of Cholera, Gabriel García Márquez. Lost in the magic of García Márquez, surreal. Where will Fermina and Florentino end up? Or will they end?

1989

The Drama of the Gifted Child, Alice Miller. Implications for our own children, for all children. How do we raise whole human beings?

The Woman That Never Evolved, Sarah Blaffer Hrdy. Why are female reproductive organs hidden? Does the female primate choose the father of her offspring? Which tends more toward monogamy, male or female? Who's in charge here, anyway?

A Room of One's Own, Virginia Woolf. Difficult, but worth it.

Jacob's Room, Virginia Woolf. Almost incomprehensible.

Breathing Lessons, Anne Tyler. Disappointing. Superficial. As one member noted, doesn't say much for the Pulitzer.

1990

Ceremony, Leslie Marmon Silko. Extraordinary. Moving. Violent.

Caring: A Feminine Approach to Ethics and Moral Education, Nel Noddings. Better scholarship than Gilligan. Cogent. Moral choices. Are imperatives ethical?

The Road from Coorain, Jill Ker Conway. A pleasing biography. The effects of constraint, bias, education, and harsh landscape on a woman of courage.

The Bone People, Keri Hulme. Strange, almost eerie. Unusual style—the literal part is difficult, but a deeper level is experienced.

Woman at Otowi Crossing, Frank Waters. Uninspired by the writing; intrigued by the time, place, history, and woman. Desire to read other versions by other authors.

Sons and Lovers, D. H. Lawrence. Vintage Lawrence: mother, woman, love, violence. Is anyone likeable in this book?

The Mill on the Floss, George Eliot. Dissatisfying. Inferior to *Middlemarch*. Cop-out ending.

1991

Crossing to Safety, Wallace Stegner. Sensitive and perceptive writer. We know the people Stegner wants us to know.

Ake: The Years of Childhood, Wole Soyinka. Lukewarm. Somewhat engaging story of a childhood, a confusing place.

Composing a Life, Mary Catherine Bateson. Rather self-righteous, self-justifying. Only relatively affluent women portrayed.

Madame Bovary, Gustave Flaubert. Another woman with circum-scribed choices, who has to die for being distinct, for doing what men do.

Anna Karenina, Leo Tolstoy. See *Madame Bovary*.

Their Eyes Were Watching God, Zora Neale Hurston. Dialect, gut-level speech and action. Deceptively simple. Had to read more Hurston.

A Midwife's Tale: The Life of Martha Ballard, Based on Her Diary 1785–1812, Laurel Thatcher Ulrich. The forming of America, with families as production units. Primarily work, more work, and death. Realization: at this same time, Mozart was composing in Vienna.

1992

Mrs. Caliban, Rachel Ingalls. A little book, a deep discussion. Is Larry real? Does it matter? Mysterious, frightening, unforgettable. Had to read more Ingalls.

Stones for Ibarra, Harriet Doerr. Intelligent and perceptive. A little too sparse to be entirely satisfying, but that's probably the point.

Mama Day, Gloria Naylor. Unusual. Told from varying points of view and it works. Magic and love. Had to read more Naylor.

The House of Mirth, Edith Wharton. Wonderful portrayal of New York turn-of-the-century society and constraints on women. See *Madame Bovary* and *Anna Karenina*.

The Charterhouse of Parma, Stendhal. Love and politics. No one was much impressed.

Mrs. Dalloway, Virginia Woolf. One of Woolf's more accessible works. Discussion about Clarissa's happiness, sincerity, marriage.

As I Lay Dying, William Faulkner. Grim. Rough. Hopeless. Clearly a master.

Eichmann in Jerusalem, Hannah Arendt. Profound questions. Ultimately, who is morally accountable?

Iron John, Robert Bly. Terrible scholarship. Sloppy writing. Almost humorous. The same old story—men, take charge, be "real" men, don't take any crap from women.

Women Respond to the Men's Movement, Kay Leigh Hagan, ed. Anthology of responses from varied and articulate women. Diverse points of view. Lively discussion.

1993

A Thousand Acres, Jane Smiley. A brilliant undertaking. This one *deserved* the Pulitzer. We can never know the why of meanness, of blind ego; we can only witness the devastation it sows.

King Lear, Shakespeare. Read in conjunction with *A Thousand Acres*. Those who have taught Lear for years began to look at him and his daughters in a different light.

Angle of Repose, Wallace Stegner. The title reflects a metaphor that wraps itself around intricately interwoven past and present stories. Rest and repose are not easily found. An engaging read, a sweeping story.

The Mismeasure of Woman, Carol Tavris. Feminist critique of the consequences for women when man is the measure of all things. A pretty thorough examination of the beauty myth, the medical/psychological professions, and women's sexuality. In the end, we wished for more clarity about where Tavris lands on the gender sameness/difference question.

The Messiah of Stockholm, Cynthia Ozick. It is post-Holocaust Europe. A Jewish man may or may not have reinvented his past. Engendered a difficult and ultimately illuminating discussion.

Villette, Charlotte Brontë. A dark book with an unusual point of view and an oddly modern aspect. As one reader put it, "Who is this woman and why would anyone love her?"

The Spoils of Poynton, Henry James. It's about furniture and love, but also about the corruption of money, the power of art, and the poisonous influences of the two on the principal characters. A stroke of other-than-human justice ends this tale.

The Abyss, Marguerite Yourcenar. A philosophical novel that describes, in often-beautiful prose, the life of a medieval physician/scholar/alchemist who is not limited by the thinking of the church or that of the era he moved within.

The Book Group Book, Ellen Slezak, ed. Yes, we really read this as a group. It changed the way we thought about ourselves as a group, broadened our perspective, and gave us new direction.

1994

The Things They Carried, Tim O'Brien. There you are, wherever O'Brien wants you to be: immersed in a heavily mined jungle quagmire; crossing a Canadian river; watching your nine-year-old best friend die. Yet all the stories are the same story—trying to remember the same truth. In this book, the coward is the one who goes to war.

Ordinary Love and Good Will, Jane Smiley. An aching restlessness pervades these tales of two very different families, forever changed by single jarring incidents. Illusion clashes with the realities of intention, commitment, and love. What can we give our children? What do they inherit?

The Lost Honor of Katharina Blum, Heinrich Böll. An attractive housemaid falls in love with a wanted criminal she's just met—and things are definitely not as simple as they seem.

Girl, Interrupted, Susanna Kaysen. Personal narrative account of an eighteen-year-old woman's sojourn in a psychiatric hospital in the late sixties. Riveting descriptions illustrate the thin line between sanity and madness. Beautiful prose. The book asks difficult questions.

Paris Trout, Peter Dexter. Despite its genteel complexion, the small town of Cotton Point, Georgia, contains an undercurrent of violence and greed. A senseless crime launches the story of a paranoid psychotic—otherwise known as one of Cotton Point's best—and the shattering of a town that will never be the same.

Listening to Prozac, Peter D. Kramer. Thinly disguised paean to Prozac, ostensibly exploring the concepts of self, mood, and personality. Lots of dense text regarding research and biochemical processes. Importance and discussion value lays in the implications of Kramer's perspective for the malleability of the human personality.

Woman in the Dunes, Kobo Abe. A man hunting beetles is held captive in a town of sand. Sensual and existential.

1995

A Lost Lady, Willa Cather. Before we could figure out why she was lost, we tried to figure out what it was that caused every male in her sphere to be so taken with Mrs. Forrester. She was strong and full of life, yes, but she was also reckless, full of artifice, and linked romantically with a scoundrel. Her fall paralleled the end of the era of western expansion.

The English Patient, Michael Ondaatje. A multitextured novel with stunningly beautiful prose. This is a rich work of art: compassionate portraits of damaged people, poetry, romance, mystery, and philosophy.

The Histories, Herodotus

Kim, Rudyard Kipling

The Handmaid's Tale, Margaret Atwood

Peripheral Visions, Mary Catherine Bateson

Refuge, Terry Tempest Williams

1996

Saint Joan, George Bernard Shaw

The Idiot, Fyodor Dostoyevsky

Justine and Balthazar, Lawrence Durrell

The Mayor of Casterbridge, Thomas Hardy

Medea, Euripides

Tender Is the Night, F. Scott Fitzgerald

Cousin Bette, Honoré de Balzac

1997

Tristes Tropiques, Claude Levi-Strauss

The Dispossessed, Ursula K. LeGuin

The Princess of Cleves, Madame de Lafayette. A familiar theme: the (lack of) options open to women. The layers of deception: was Madame being needlessly chaste or did she know a good thing to avoid when she saw one?

Between the Acts, Virginia Woolf. As in Mrs. Dalloway, the action takes place on a single summer's day. The characters carry on a silent dialogue (not just thoughts) throughout. What stands out is Woolf's haunting lyricism, so expressive of loneliness, sorrow, and pain; her vulnerability is on the pages.

The Cloister Walk, Kathleen Norris. Permanence; commitment; belief; the Rule; and knowing where you will die, as the monks do.

An American Childhood, Annie Dillard. An extraordinary person. An extraordinary family, whose privilege and protection allowed her the luxury of being able to be left on her own to follow her pursuits.

Othello, William Shakespeare

Three Lives, Gertrude Stein. Two German servants, one happy and one not, and an almost-tragic black woman: their lives in America.

The Shelter of Each Other: Rebuilding our Families, Mary Pipher

"Good Country People" and "Everything That Rises Must Converge," Flannery O'Connor

Angela's Ashes, Frank McCourt. Imagine carefully transporting a single egg for your family's treasured meal. Imagine watching your siblings die from the effects of poverty you live every day. Cold, hunger, grinding despair, and yet in reading this story, at times you laugh so hard the tears run down your cheeks. McCourt's triumph is in surviving his childhood with wit and grace.

1998

Hedda Gabler, Henrik Ibsen

The Songlines, Bruce Chatwin

Things Fall Apart, Chinua Achebe

Out of Silence, Russell Martin

Divine Secrets of the Ya-Ya Sisterhood, Rebecca Wells

Of Woman Born, Adrienne Rich

1999

The Stone Diaries, Carol Shields

Three Books from the Bible: *Judith, Ruth, Esther*

Stones from the River, Ursula Hegi

The History of Sexuality, Volume 1: An Introduction, Michel Foucault. Paragraphs two pages long, sentences half a page long. Circular arguments. No answers. And yet the point seems to be that we are asking the wrong questions. Why do we endlessly dissect sex? Is sexuality real?

Selected Book List— Takoma Park and Bowie, Maryland, Book Clubs

BARBARA BERNSTEIN   BOWIE, MARYLAND

Fiction

Map of the World, Jane Hamilton. Two women trade babysitting, and tragedy sets in motion a chain of events with profound effects on everyone.

Other Women's Children, Perri Klass. The events in a pediatrician's life as they interweave with and affect her work at the hospital.

Of Such Small Differences, Joanne Greenberg. Profoundly moving novel about a community of people who are both deaf and blind.

Before and After, Rosellen Brown. When a teenage boy is suspected of murder, his mother wishes to hide nothing and his father tries to protect him. Members discussed how they would react to this situation.

When Nietzsche Wept, Irvin Yalom. Description of a therapeutic relationship between Nietzsche and Joseph Breuer, a doctor in the late nineteenth century. Describes how psychotherapy feels and might have been invented.

Family Pictures, Sue Miller. The impact of an autistic child on the rest of the family, set in an era when mothers were largely blamed for a child's autism.

The Thanatos Syndrome, Walker Percy. Story about a criminal plot involving psychoactive drugs—led to a fascinating discussion about the use of drugs in modern life.

Waiting to Exhale, Terry McMillan. Female bonding runs deep in this story about four professional black women and their lives, loves, and searches for men.

The Joy Luck Club, Amy Tan. A look at the relationships between several Chinese mothers and their daughters in a culture of close-knit family bonds.

Animal Dreams, Barbara Kingsolver. A beautiful story with a Native American theme about maturing and finding happiness in one's own backyard.

The Beans of Egypt, Maine, Carolyn Chute. Offbeat story about lives of poverty and squalor in America.

The Accidental Tourist and *Dinner at the Homesick Restaurant*, Anne Tyler. A travel writer who hates to travel and a restaurant for people who'd rather not eat out. Tyler's twists and eventful plots make both these novels fascinating reading.

Cold Sassy Tree, Olive Ann Burns. An excellent coming-of-age story about a teenage boy in a small town and his relationship with his grandfather.

A Thousand Acres, Jane Smiley. A slice of life on a midwestern farm. Beautifully written, but depressing.

Nonfiction

City of Joy, Dominique LaPierre. In Calcutta, India, the human spirit surmounts incredible physical hardships and dire poverty. Squalid, depressing, and uplifting at the same time.

Life and Death in Shanghai, Nien Cheng. The hardships of a well-educated Chinese woman jailed for more than six years in solitary confinement during the Cultural Revolution.

From Beirut to Jerusalem, Thomas Friedman. The history of the Arab-Israeli conflict and the efforts to resolve it.

Home Fires, Donald Katz. A troubled family with children growing up during the sixties.

Common Ground: A Turbulent Decade in the Lives of Three American Families, J. Anthony Lucas. By following several Boston families through many generations, Lucas sets the stage for the conflict surrounding integration of public schools.

You Just Don't Understand: Women and Men in Conversation, Deborah Tannen, Ph.D. Men use language to establish independence and status while women use language to establish intimacy and connection. With this premise the author explains some classic gender conflicts such as why men don't want to ask for directions and women do.

Living in the Labyrinth, Diana Friel McGowin. A woman recounts early descent into Alzheimer's.

Lost in Translation: A Life in a New Language, Eva Hoffman. A psychologically rich autobiographical account of a youngster who moves from Poland to Canada (and ultimately to the United States). The language and culture were so different that the author couldn't find English words for her "Polish feelings."

More recent reads include . . .
Cry of the Kalahari, Mark and Delia Owens
The Liars' Club, Mary Karr
The Alienist, Caleb Carr
Independence Day, Richard Ford
Zenzele: Letter for My Daughter, J. Nozipa Maraire
A Civil Action, Jonathan Harr
The Sparrow, Mary Doria Russell
Into Thin Air, Jon Krakauer
An Italian Education, Tim Parks
A Lost World, Wendell Berry
The Perfect Storm, Sebastian Junger
Memoirs of a Geisha, Arthur Golden

God Is a Verb, David Cooper

The Weight of Water, Anita Shreve

Stones from the River, Ursula Hegi

The Way of the World: From the Dawn of Civilization to the Eve of the Twenty-First Century, David Fromkin

A Yellow Raft on Blue Water, Michael Dorris

Father Melancholy's Daughter and *A Mother and Two Daughters*, Gail Godwin

Hot Flashes, Barbara Raskin

A Prayer for Owen Meany, John Irving

Fortunate Lives, Robb Forman Dew

Growing Up, Russell Baker

Emotional Intelligence, Daniel Goleman

One True Thing, Anna Quindlen

Gift of Hands: The Ben Carson Story, Ben Carson with Cecil Murphy

The Prince, Niccolò Machiavelli

Divine Secrets of the Ya-Ya Sisterhood, Rebecca Wells

Long Way to Go, Jonathan Coleman

Tuesdays with Morrie, Mitch Albom

Room Temperature, Nicholson Baker

This Boy's Life, Tobias Wolff

Refuge, Terry Williams

Charming Billy, Alice McDermott

Breath, Eyes, Memory, Edwidge Danticat

Hystories: Hysterical Epidemics and Modern Media, Elaine Showalter

Leaving Home: A Memoir, Art Buchwald

A World Lit Only by Fire, William Manchester

Damage, Josephine Hart

She's Come Undone, Wally Lamb

The Bonfire of the Vanities, Tom Wolfe

Presumed Innocent, Scott Turow

Bemidji Book Club
Reading List

ALICE V. COLLINS　　　　　BEMIDJI, MINNESOTA

NEW BOOK CLUBS are springing up all over the country, helped along by the efforts of Oprah Winfrey. However, there have been several clubs in Bemidji for a number of years, and ours has a relatively long history.

The Bemidji Book Group has roots leading back to the sixties when it was an offshoot of the Bemidji State University Faculty Wives Club. When the faculty became a much more equal mixture of genders, and many wives joined the workforce, clubs for faculty wives died out.

The book group faded from the scene for a few years and many of the members joined with another fledgling club that went through a number of metamorphoses and now is a mixture of women from a variety of backgrounds. Several women come from careers in education and a number of us are retired.

A major project each year is selecting a list of books for the next season. Many in the group are avid readers and come to the April meeting ready to lobby for a list of their favorite recent reading experiences. We record the suggestions and a short synopsis of each so that one of the members with computer skills can print the information for the group to pore over during the next month. We used to try to come to some kind of consensus at the May meeting, but there are way too many strong opinions in our bunch to make that work. Now we actually take a ballot vote and choose the eight or nine books that get the most votes.

No one is ever too disappointed if a favorite loses out because there is always some member of the group who decides to read a suggested book that doesn't make the list and share reactions with those who had plugged for it to be included. It is not unusual for there to a big difference in those reactions. We all love books but not necessarily the same ones!

Books are a special love of our lives and two years ago we made a major project of raising funds to send to East Grand Forks, Minnesota, following a tragic flood that wiped out the entire resources—books, records, and computers—of both the school and public libraries.

We enjoy the summer months here in our northwoods area that is a vacation destination for many people from cities farther south. But we also look forward to the coming of fall and the first gathering of our book group cronies to talk about all the exciting new reading experiences we've had along the lakeshore during the summer.

1985
Wuthering Heights, Emily Brontë
Growing Up, Russell Baker
Lutefisk Ghetto, Art Lee
Love and War, John Jakes

1986
Hunt for Red October, Tom Clancy
Iacocca, Lee Iacocca
A Distant Mirror, Barbara Tuchman
Ironweed, William Kennedy
Walking Drum, Louis L'Amour
The Agony and the Ecstasy, Irving Stone
On Wings of Eagles, Ken Follett
The Diary of a Provincial Lady, E. M. Dellifield
The Adventures of Huckleberry Finn, Mark Twain

1987

Strange Encounters, Mike Wallace

The Haj, Leon Uris

Nutcracker, Shana Alexander

Common Ground, J. Anthony Lucas

The Beans of Egypt, Maine, Carolyn Chute

1988

Pride and Prejudice, Jane Austen

The Red and the Black, Stendhal

Grand Opening, Jon Hassler

Silent Partner, Judith Greber

1989

Taming of the Shrew, William Shakespeare

Hatchet, Gary Paulsen

Walden, Henry David Thoreau

Vanity Fair, William Thackeray

Accidental Tourist, Anne Tyler

Les Misérables, Victor Hugo

Cold Sassy Tree, Olive Ann Burns

Lonesome Dove, Larry McMurtry

84, Charing Cross Road, Helene Hanff

1990

Killing Time in St. Cloud, Judith Guest

Spring Moon, Bette Bao Lord

Crossing to Safety, Wallace Stegner

Love Medicine, Louise Erdrich

Love in the Time of Cholera, Gabriel García Márquez

Indian Givers, Jack Weatherford

The Sun Also Rises, Ernest Hemingway

Type Talk, Otto Kroeger

1991

Jubilee, Margaret Walker

Billy Bathgate, E. L. Doctorow

Big Rock Candy Mountain, Wallace Stegner

Once upon a Time on the Banks, Cathie Pelletier

Pilgrim at Tinker Creek, Annie Dillard

A River Runs Through It, Norman Maclean

When Rabbit Howls, Trudy Chase

The Power and the Glory, Graham Greene

A Cup of Christmas Tea, Tom Hegg

1992

Necessity of Empty Spaces, Paul Gruchow

Death in Venice, Thomas Mann

Rabbit Run, John Updike

Ashana, E. P. Roesch

A Is for Alibi, Sue Grafton

The Oldest Living Confederate Widow Tells All, Allan Gurganus

Walking Across Egypt, Clyde Edgerton

Mark of the Maker, Tom Hegg

Secret Garden, Frances Hodgson Burnett

1993

Callander Square, Anne Perry

Bridges of Madison County, Robert James Waller

The Firm, John Grisham

Follow the River, James Thom

H Is for Homicide, Sue Grafton

A Thousand Acres, Jane Smiley

My Antonia, Willa Cather

Rising Sun, Michael Crichton

1994

Gulliver's Travels, Jonathan Swift

Trinity, Leon Uris
Twelfth Night, William Shakespeare
Honor Among Thieves, Jeffrey Archer
The Odyssey, Homer
The Age of Innocence, Edith Wharton
Mousetrap, Agatha Christie
I Know Why the Caged Bird Sings, Maya Angelou

1996
As We Are Now, May Sarton
Henderson the Rain King, Saul Bellow
Night Sins, Tami Hoag
Call No Man Father, William Kienzle
Plain Speaking, Merle Miller
Coming Home, Rosamunde Pilcher
Snow Falling on Cedars, David Guterson

1997
Song of Solomon, Toni Morrison
Burr, Gore Vidal
Cruel and Unusual, Patricia Cornwell
The Book of Ruth, Jane Hamilton
Mamma Makes Up Her Mind and Other Dangers of Southern Living, Bailey White
The Rosewood Casket, Sharyn McCrumb
Stones from the River, Ursula Hegi
Remains of the Day, Kazuo Ishiguro

1998
Mary Todd Lincoln, Jean Baker
The Horse Whisperer, Nicholas Evans
A Long Fatal Love Chase, Louisa May Alcott
Mother Voices: Essays, Traci Dyer, ed. (includes an essay by club member Alice Vance Collins)

Cold Mountain, Charles Frazier
Midnight in the Garden of Good and Evil, John Berendt
Angela's Ashes, Frank McCourt
Undaunted Courage, Stephen Ambrose
Snow in August, Pete Hamill

1999
Animal Dreams, Barbara Kingsolver
A Tree Grows in Brooklyn, Betty Smith
Memoirs of a Geisha, Arthur Golden
The Life of Andrew Jackson, Robert V. Remini
Colony, Anne Rivers Siddons
An American Requiem: God, My Father, and the War That Came Between Us, James Carroll

Between the Covers Book Club List

NANCY J. COURT   GRAND RAPIDS, MICHIGAN

BETWEEN THE COVERS began in 1980. Our thirteen female members have read more than 160 books. Although we focus on recent fiction, our yearly book choices have also included nonfiction, classics, humor, and autobiographies. The following list includes those books that provided stimulating discussions and hours of joyful reading.

Classics

East of Eden, John Steinbeck. Monumental novel of good and evil and the passionate lives of two turbulent American families. One of Steinbeck's best. A favorite.

Rebecca, Daphne du Maurier. Successful novel of romance and mystery. The author is a virtuoso at conjuring up suspense, tragedy, and romance.

Maurice, E. M. Forster. A must-read classic in our homophobic age. Written around 1913, this novel of a young homosexual in the elegant world of Cambridge University was not published until 1971. Very moving.

My Antonia, Willa Cather. Story of a pioneer woman and life as an early settler. Author's anger at loss of earlier values sets the tone.

Lady Chatterley's Lover, D. H. Lawrence. World-famous love story is a masterpiece. Want to read more Lawrence.

Pulitzers

A Thousand Acres, Jane Smiley. Shakespeare fans will love the *King Lear* parallels in this twentieth-century version of tragic family passions. Exposure to large-scale midwestern farm life.

The Color Purple, Alice Walker. Issues of racism, child abuse, and universal truths about intimate relationships in another time and culture. Memorable.

A Confederacy of Dunces, John Kennedy Toole. Unforgettable slob, extraordinary Ignatius Reilly, has been told by his mother that it is time to get a job. Comic and tragic. Toole committed suicide in 1969 at age thirty-two. His mother had his novel published in 1980.

Lonesome Dove, Larry McMurtry. Epic masterpiece of the American West. Wonderful characters and story. Read this book.

About Women

The Road from Coorain, Jill Ker Conway. Thoughtful autobiography of the first woman president of Smith College. Set in the harsh Australian landscape and a male-dominated society. This author's reflections are highly recommended.

Written by Herself, edited by Jill Ker Conway. Collection of autobiographies of American women. Why weren't these women mentioned in our American history classes? Inspiring.

West with the Night, Beryl Markham. Autobiography of a female pilot in Africa in the early thirties. Beauty, humor, and wisdom pervade this lovely book.

Libby, Betty John. This extraordinary book is presented by Libby Beaman's granddaughter. Through Libby's diaries and letters (1879–80), we travel with the first nonnative woman to explore the Alaskan Pribilof Islands, just outside the Arctic Circle.

Life and Death in Shanghai, Nien Cheng. Who needs fiction? Nien Cheng's autobiography of imprisonment during the Chinese Cultural Revolution in the mid sixties is powerful, nonstop reading. Fascinating insights into Mao's China during a time when the United States was preoccupied with Vietnam and our own cultural revolution.

Miscellaneous

A Gift from the Sea, Anne Morrow Lindbergh. Lindbergh's reflections on a woman's life and the value of one's inner life in a hectic, pressured world. Timeless. For reading in a quiet space.

House of Light, Mary Oliver. Poetry explores the connectedness of humanity to the elemental forces of nature. Oliver can make us see what she sees and believe what she believes. Deceptively simple. Profoundly true.

Happy to Be Here, Garrison Keillor. Those with adolescent sons will hoot at "Local Family Keeps Son Happy." Witty short stories that will make you happy to be in Keillor's world.

Kaffir Boy, Mark Mathabane. True story of a black youth's coming of age in apartheid South Africa and his triumph over a life of degradation and hopelessness. Powerful.

Nonfiction

The Immense Journey, Loren Eiseley. Nature book intertwines scientific information with Eiseley's vision of life's mysteries. Beautiful.

A Season on the Brink, John Feinstein. If you are going to read only one sports book in your life, read about a year with Bobby Knight and the Indiana Hoosiers. Unique. Discussable.

Nicholas and Alexandra, Robert K. Massie. Brilliant piece of history that reads like a novel. A life drama more interesting than fiction.

Freedom at Midnight, Larry Collins and Dominique LaPierre. Epic portrait of Mahatma Gandhi is a riveting page-turner. Highly recommended.

Confessions of a Medical Heretic, Robert S. Mendelsohn, M.D. Mix the author's premise that annual physicals are a health risk and that hospitals are dangerous places for the sick with two nurses and two physicians' wives and what do you get? One of the most memorable book discussions in the fifteen-year history of our group.

The Disuniting of America, Arthur M. Schlesinger. Examination of the contemporary controversy over multiculturalism and education with the premise that multiculturalism will undermine our republic. Great discussion.

General Fiction

The Dollmaker, Harriette Arnow. This Michigan author tells a powerful story of a courageous Kentucky woman thrust into the ugliness and confusion of wartime Detroit. Arnow is a brilliant storyteller.

Prince of Tides, Pat Conroy. This novel of Tom Wingo and his troubled sister spans forty years. The South Carolina low country is enchanting. Powerful humor, tragedy, and emotions. A favorite.

Run with the Horsemen, Ferrol Sams. Novel of a southern farmboy growing up during the Great Depression. Porter Osborne, Jr., will become a household name because everyone will want to read the book that keeps you laughing out loud. Lots of warmth and humor. First in a delightful trilogy.

The Kitchen God's Wife, Amy Tan. Wonderfully satisfying story of a Chinese woman. Better than Tan's first novel, *The Joy Luck Club*.

Fried Green Tomatoes at the Whistle Stop Café, Fannie Flagg. The negative critiques of this novel were dead wrong. One of the most entertaining narratives that has arrived in the last ten years. "Dot Weems's Weekly" is a jewel. Funny and wise.

Ishmael, Daniel Quinn. Unusual dialogue between a gorilla and a man. Will change your thinking about the role of humans as a species on this planet.

Their Eyes Were Watching God, Zora Neale Hurston. This classic of black literature has had a recent revival. As a black woman in the late thirties, Hurston was given little recognition as a writer. Rich text is written in the dialect of its time and culture. A must-read for book groups.

To Dance with the White Dog, Terry Kay. An unusual and unforgettable story about elderly Sam Peek, who recently lost his wife, and a mysterious white dog who is invisible to everyone but Sam.

Follow the River, James Thom. History lives in this adventure novel of twenty-three-year-old Mary Ingles, who was kidnapped by Indians in

1755. This is the story of a courageous pioneer woman who walked through one thousand miles of wilderness to return to her own people.

Crossing to Safety, Wallace Stegner. Sensitive story of two couples and their long-term give-and-take friendship.

The Education of Little Tree, Forrest Carter. Tears and laughter intertwine while reading this tender story of a Cherokee boy in Tennessee in the thirties. Delightful for children, adolescents, and adults.

The Bean Trees, Barbara Kingsolver. Story of a young woman who finds herself the unlikely mother of an abandoned Native American child. Funny and heartwarming. We want to read more Kingsolver.

The Ginger Tree, Oswald Wynd. Compelling story of a young Scotswoman in Peking in 1903 and her bittersweet romance with a young Japanese nobleman. A favorite.

The Handmaid's Tale, Margaret Atwood. Powerful story about the world of the near future and the question of who controls women's bodies. Chilling. A must-read for book groups.

The Bridges of Madison County, Robert James Waller. Record-setting, bestselling sleeper guarantees a lively evening. Heated discussion between those who get swept away by Harlequin romances and those who oppose "bodice ripper" rip-offs.

My Name Is Asher Lev, Chaim Potok. Another winning story from Potok about the choice of a young man torn between his compelling drive to create art and his Jewish tradition and heritage.

Black Rain, Masuji Ibuse. Story of a Japanese man in the days immediately following the bombing of Hiroshima. Powerful.

A Prayer for Owen Meany, John Irving. Storytelling genius Irving gives us a most unusual hero in Owen Meany. Disturbing and wonderful. Had to read more Irving.

Hot Flashes, Barbara Raskin. Reunion of four extraordinary modern women. Portrays cultural changes from the forties to the eighties with humor. Perfect for the premenopausal group.

The Beans of Egypt, Maine, Carolyn Chute. Quirky, fascinating story of America's rural underclass. Beans are all over America living in mobile homes on the wrong side of the tracks. Comic and tragic.

Noble Road Book Discussion Titles

KATHY EWING   CLEVELAND HEIGHTS, OHIO

The Fever, Wallace Shawn

Road Song, Natalie Kucz

Savage Inequalities, Jonathan Kozol

The People Who Led to My Plays and *Funnyhouse of a Negro*, Adrienne Kennedy

Aururo VII, Thomas Mallon

Disturbances in the Field, Lynne Sharon Schwartz

Testing the Current, William McPherson

A Prayer for Owen Meany, John Irving

Patrimony, Philip Roth

The Drowned and the Saved, Primo Levi

Borrowed Time: An AIDS Memoir, Paul Monette

Race, Studs Terkel

A Home at the End of the World, Michael Cunningham

St. Maybe, Anne Tyler

The Man Who Loved Children, Christina Stead

Ten Seconds, Louis Edwards

The Shawl, Cynthia Ozick

Shadow Play, Charles Baxter

Another Marvelous Thing, Laurie Colwin

The Handmaid's Tale, Margaret Atwood

Father Melancholy's Daughter, Gail Godwin

Babette's Feast, Isak Dinesen

The Hidden Life of Dogs, Elizabeth Marshall Thomas

Child, House, World, Grace Butcher

A Death in the Family, James Agee

White People, Allan Gurganus

Dead Man Walking, Helen Prejean

Modern Baptists, James Wilcox

Den of Lions: Memoirs of Seven Years, Terry Anderson and
  Madeleine Bassil

Spence + Lila, Bobbie Ann Mason

Little Women, Louisa May Alcott

The Loop, Joe Coomer

A Map of the World, Jane Hamilton

Having Our Say: The Delany Sisters' First 100 Years, Sarah and
  A. Elizabeth Delany with Amy Hill Hearth

Ladder of Years, Anne Tyler

To the Lighthouse, Virginia Woolf

Pilgrim at Tinker Creek, Annie Dillard

Housekeeping, Marilynne Robinson

The Good Negress, A. J. Verdelle

Dreaming, Carolyn See

All Hallow's Eve, Charles Williams

Ceremony, Leslie Marmon Silko

An Anthropologist on Mars, Oliver Sacks

Sula, Toni Morrison

Three Farmers on the Way to a Dance, Richard Powers
Private Altars, Katherine Mosby
A Country Year: Living the Questions, Sue Hubbell
The Brothers Karamazov, Fyodor Dostoyevsky
Stones from the River, Ursula Hegi
My Home Is Far Away, Dawn Powell
American Requiem, James Carroll
Autobiography of a Face, Lucy Grealy
Still Life, A. S. Byatt
Dakota: A Spiritual Geography, Kathleen Norris
Song of Solomon, Toni Morrison
The Favourite, Meredith Daneman
In the Time of the Butterflies, Julia Alvarez
The Adventures of Huckleberry Finn, Mark Twain
Every Secret Thing, Gillian Slovo
Fools of Fortune, William Trevor
The Family Markowitz, Allegra Goodman
The Sparrow, Mary Doria Russell
Comfort Woman, Nora Okja Keller
The Cliff Walk, Don Snyder
Middle Passage, Charles R. Johnson
Imaging Robert, Jay Neugeboren
Atticus, Ron Hansen
The God of Small Things, Arundhati Roy
The Dollmaker, Harriette Arnow
Children of God, Mary Doria Russell
Angela's Ashes, Frank McCourt
Miriam's Kitchen, Elizabeth Ehrlich
Leaving Brooklyn, Lynne Sharon Schwartz
Travels with Lizbeth, Lars Eighner

Cold Mountain, Charles Frazier
Affliction, Russell Banks
The Kiss, Kathryn Harrison
The Liars' Club, Mary Karr
The Rector's Wife, Joanna Trollope
On the Outside Looking In, Cristina Rathbone

Finnegans Wake
Reading List

MURRAY J. GROSS   NEW YORK, NEW YORK

THE FOLLOWING FOUR books serve as our core reference material.

Campbell, Joseph, and Robinson, Henry Morton, *A Skeleton Key to Finnegans Wake*, Penguin Books 1986. Pay no attention to the critics who dismiss this as an old-fashioned and awkward approach to the *Wake*. They are wrong; this is one of the most useful books for anyone exploring the *Wake*. By giving an abridged and usually plain language version it is, at least, a starting point; you are not absolutely lost. The critics' quibble is principally with the introductory statements and the footnotes, which tend to interpret the *Wake* in terms of myth. It's not that such interpretation is wrong, it's just that it's only one of many valid ones. I suspect that those advanced Wakeans who denigrate this book keep it under plain covers and surreptitiously dip into it. This is one of the four books you must have.

McHugh, Roland, *Annotations to Finnegans Wake*, Johns Hopkins University Press 1991. Geared to the *Wake* page by page, McHugh gives some of the literary and historical allusions, meanings of strange words, and some cross references gleaned from a variety of sources. It takes a little effort to learn how to use this book with ease, but it's worth the trouble. Although there are some mistakes and many omissions, the book remains absolutely vital to a study of the *Wake*.

Tindall, William York, *A Reader's Guide to Finnegans Wake*, Farrar Straus and Giroux 1969. This is almost a paragraph by paragraph study pointing out allusions, themes, and relevant biographical information. Although written in a breezy, idiosyncratic way, it is packed with useful information.

Atherton, James S., *The Books at the Wake*, Arcturus 1974. A much more detailed examination of the literary sources Joyce used in the *Wake* than the previously listed books, this book augments their terse explanations.

As we study the *Wake*, we need and want more and more help. The next group of books gives that extra assistance.

McHugh, Roland, *The Finnegans Wake Experience*, University of California Press 1981. Interesting for its coverage of ultra-*Wake* material such as Joyce's notebooks, various scholarly works, and the reading group experience. Should be read principally for the detailed analyses of two sections of the *Wake*.

Glasheen, Adaline, *Third Census of Finnegans Wake*, University of California Press 1977. An exhaustive list of the characters and real persons with short descriptions and cross references.

Fargnoli, A. Nicholas, and Gillespie, Michael P., *James Joyce A to Z*, Facts on File 1995. Although it covers all of Joyce, there is a great deal of useful *Wake* material both for the tyro and advanced Wakean. Both this and Glasheen have valuable summaries of each of the chapters of the *Wake*.

Adams, Robert M., *James Joyce: Common Sense and Beyond*, Random House 1966. The sections on the *Wake* give an excellent overview.

Bernstock, Bernard, *Joyce-Again's Wake*, University of Washington Press 1965; Hart, Clive, *Structure and Motif in Finnegans Wake*, Faber and Faber 1962. These two books give sane and cogent interpretations of the whole *Wake* with some detailed analyses. I use the words "sane" and "cogent" to distinguish them from much of the current scholarship on the *Wake*.

Readers of the *Wake* also find themselves consulting the following: The Bible; the OED (Oxford Dictionary of the English Language); the Koran; the Egyptian Book of the Dead; The Book of Kells; the writings of Giordano Bruno of Nola (burned as a heretic in 1600); the plays of Henrik Ibsen; the 11th edition of the Encyclopedia Britannica (which Joyce used), and similar cultural, historical, and literary sources.

Marion Study-Group Book List

ELEANOR HARTSTONE   📖   MARION, MASSACHUSETTS

THE TOWN OF Marion was built on a peninsula that juts out into Buzzards Bay. There are several miles of deep water and the harbor is lined with wharves and docks. Since colonial times, it was a popular place for sailing vessels, many of which were engaged in whaling or China trade. In the 1800s, Marion became known as an artistic center, a popular place for summer visiting. Among those who visited were Henry James, Ethel Barrymore, and Ralph Waldo Emerson. They'd meet to discuss books, plays, and poetry. The building where they met, the Studio, still stands. President Grover Cleveland visited and remarked that "Marion was the most beautiful little town in the United States."

Organizing a book study club in Marion had long been a dream of mine, but it wasn't until a chance meeting with a neighbor and her enthusiastic response that I was inspired to act on it. In October 1985, I invited similarly interested persons to my home to discuss forming a book club. After a few meetings, certain agreements evolved. In the beginning, we concentrated on reading the classics. It was rewarding to read them again, to discover new meaning. We also read Greek plays, with each member taking a turn reading. We read poetry too.

In the past years other book clubs have formed in Marion and we all meet at Christmas time for tea. Each person brings a child's book and we donate them to the Family Crisis Group. This is the only time that all the book club members get together. There are now seven book clubs in this small town of about 5,000 people.

We take pride in the fact that our book club, the first in Marion, inspired other people in our town to discover the joys and rewards of reading. The number of book clubs in Marion is testimony to our belief that reading creates a bond between people that transcends our daily lives. Participating in a book club has been an important and rewarding part of my life. I hope it has been for the other members as well.

1985
The Great Gatsby, F. Scott Fitzgerald
Madame Bovary, Gustave Flaubert
Main Street, Sinclair Lewis
The Sea Wolf, Jack London
The Age of Innocence, Edith Wharton
Sister Carrie, Theodore Dreiser
The Heart Is a Lonely Hunter, Carson McCullers
The Loved One, Evelyn Waugh
Portrait of a Lady, Henry James

1986
The Rector of Justin, Louis Auchincloss
West with the Night, Beryl Markham
Cry, the Beloved Country, Alan Paton
Heart of Darkness, Joseph Conrad
The Good Soldier, Ford Madox Ford
My Antonia, Willa Cather
Lonesome Dove, Larry McMurtry
Moll Flanders, Daniel Defoe
Huckleberry Finn, Mark Twain
Grapes of Wrath, John Steinbeck

1987

Jane Eyre, Charlotte Brontë

The Good Earth, Pearl S. Buck

Nana, Emile Zola

Passage to India, E. M. Forster

Frankenstein, Mary Shelley

Sula and *Beloved*, Toni Morrison

Fathers and Sons, Ivan Turgenev

Mrs. Dalloway, Virginia Woolf

1988

The Scarlet Letter, Nathaniel Hawthorne

A Child's Christmas in Wales, Dylan Thomas

A Christmas Memory, Truman Capote

The Awakening, Kate Chopin

Effi Briest, Theodor Fontane

Manon Lescaut, Abbe Prevost

More Die of Heartbreak, Saul Bellow

Jude the Obscure, Thomas Hardy

The Picture of Dorian Gray, Oscar Wilde

Short Stories, Edgar Allen Poe

Green Mansions, W. H. Hudson

Alice's Adventures in Wonderland, Lewis Carroll

Waterland, Graham Swift

1989

Candide, Voltaire

The Other Wise Man, Henry van Dyke

The Outermost House, Henry Beston

Beautiful Swimmers, William W. Warner

The Hunchback of Notre Dame, Victor Hugo

The Fifth Child, Doris Lessing

Of Human Bondage, Somerset Maugham

Dead Souls, Nikolai Gogol

Heart of a Dog, Mikhail Bulgakov

The Death of Ivan Ilych, Leo Tolstoy

Selected Short Stories, Honoré de Balzac

1990

Eugenie Grandet, Honoré de Balzac

The All of It, Jeanette Haien

The Snow Goose, Paul Gallico

The Red Badge of Courage, Stephen Crane

All Quiet on the Western Front, Erich Maria Remarque

The Ugly American, William Lederer

Barchester Towers and *The Way We Live Now*, Anthony Trollope

Paradise Postponed, John Mortimer

House of the Spirits, Isabel Allende

Life and Death in Shanghai, Nien Cheng

1991

A Room of One's Own, Virginia Woolf

The Bible: The Nativity, Matthew, Mark, Luke, and John

The Importance of Being Earnest, Oscar Wilde

The School for Scandal, R. B. Sheridan

The Thurber Carnival, James Thurber

Three Men in a Boat, Jerome K. Jerome

The Unbearable Lightness of Being, Milan Kundera

Cheri, Colette

Lolita, Vladimir Nabokov

Light in August, William Faulkner

A Connecticut Yankee in King Arthur's Court, Mark Twain

The Optimist's Daughter, Eudora Welty

1992

The Golden Ass, Apuleius

A Christmas Memory, Truman Capote
A Small Miracle, Paul Gallico
Faust (two meetings), Johann von Goethe
Howard's End, E. M. Forster

1993
Anna Karenina, Leo Tolstoy
Tess of the D'Urbervilles, Thomas Hardy
Middlemarch, George Eliot
Walden, Henry David Thoreau
Silent Spring, Rachel Carson
The Gift of the Magi, O. Henry
A Child's Christmas in Wales, Dylan Thomas
A Christmas Memory, Truman Capote

1994
Parallel Lives, Phyllis Rose
Hedda Gabler, Henrik Ibsen
Pygmalion, George Bernard Shaw
The Birds and Lysistrata, Aristophanes
Much Ado about Nothing, William Shakespeare
Pride and Prejudice, Jane Austen
Lie Down in Darkness, William Styron
A Death in the Family, James Agee
Crossing to Safety, Wallace Stegner

1995
Orlando, Virginia Woolf
The Leopard, Giuseppe di Lampedusa
The Red and the Black, Stendhal
Democracy in America, Alexis de Tocqueville
First You Have to Row a Little Boat, Richard Bode
The Stone Diaries, Carol Shields

The Shipping News, E. Annie Proulx
The Buccaneers, Edith Wharton

1996
Small Is Beautiful, E. F. Schumacher
At this point the group disbanded for a year.

1997
The English Patient, Michael Ondaatje
Stones from the River, Ursula Hegi
A River Sutra, Gita Mehta
The God of Small Things, Arundhati Roy

1998
The Architect of Desire, Suzannah Lessare
Under the Tuscan Sun, Frances Mayes
An American Requiem, James Carroll
The Bird Artist, Howard Norman
Mr. Ives' Christmas, Oscar Hijuelos

1999
Death of a Heart, Elizabeth Bowen
The Reader, Bernhard Schlink
The Weight of Water, Anita Shreve

A Chorus for Four Voices Reading List

BECKY HEMPERLY   MEDFORD, MASSACHUSETTS

Backlash, Susan Faludi

Soul of a New Machine, Tracy Kidder

Wouldn't Take Nothing for My Journey Now, Maya Angelou

New York in the 50s, Dan Wakefield

What Is Found There, Adrienne Rich

Dakota, Kathleen Norris

The White Album, Joan Didion

PrairyErth, William Least Heat-Moon

Surprised by Joy, C. S. Lewis

Skin: Talking About Sex, Class, and Literature, Dorothy Allison

The Woman Warrior, Maxine Hong Kingston

A Room of One's Own, Virginia Woolf

A History of God, Karen Armstrong

Dreams of Trespass: Tales of a Harem Girlhood, Fatima Mernissi

Between Friends: Women Writers Celebrate Friendship, Mickey Pearlman, ed.

Two or Three Things I Know for Sure, Dorothy Allison

Vamps and Tramps, Camille Paglia

Operating Instructions, Anne Lamott

Out of Africa, Isak Dinesen

The Road from Coorain, Jill Ker Conway

Midnight in the Garden of Good and Evil, John Berendt

A Leg to Stand On, Oliver Sacks

Pentimento, Lillian Hellman

No Ordinary Time, Doris Kearns Goodwin

Peripheral Visions, Mary Catherine Bateson

Bone Black, bell hooks

High Tide in Tucson, Barbara Kingsolver

Life and Death in Shanghai, Nien Cheng

Emerson: The Mind on Fire, Robert D. Richardson

Boys Like Us: Gay Writers Tell Their Coming Out Stories,
   Patrick Merla, ed.

Naked, David Sedaris

Honor Thy Children, Molly Fumia

A Civil Action, Jonathan Harr

Angela's Ashes, Frank McCourt

Wait Till Next Year, Doris Kearns Goodwin

The Perfect Storm, Sebastian Junger

True Love Waits, Wendy Kaminer

Straight, No Chaser, Jill Nelson

The Color of Water, James McBride

I Know Some Things, Lorrie Moore, ed.

The Liars' Club, Mary Karr

When Memory Speaks: Reflections on Autobiography,
   Jill Ker Conway

The Magician's Assistant, Anne Patchett

The Soul's Code: In Search of Character and Calling, James Hillman

Bettendorf Public Library: Three Different Book Groups, Three Different Lists

HEDY N. R. HUSTEDDE   DAVENPORT, IOWA

SINCE I WROTE my essay for the previous edition of this book, the Contemporary Books Discussion Group grew too large and we split ourselves into two groups, one meeting in the afternoon and one in the morning of the same day. There are usually around fifteen participants in each group so we can all sit around one large oval table. The two groups reads the same titles, but in different months, so the library-purchased books are used twice. You'll find the groups' list below.

I grew to love discussing books so much in this group that I started an informal librarians' discussion group for librarians in the area. We usually meet every six weeks in one of our homes, discuss a book, and have refreshments afterwards. Typically, we will continue discussing the book even when our mouths are full. The titles we've read so far are in List 2 below.

Ever on the lookout for new discussion possibilities, I also started a Mystery Book Discussion Group at the library. It meets on Saturday mornings once a month from September through May. At this time, I lead the discussions and choose the books using some sort of theme. So far the books have all been purchased by the Friends of the Bettendorf Public Library. I hadn't been much of a mystery reader before, but now I guess I can say I am. You'll find the mysteries we've read in List 3 below.

List 1: Contemporary Books Discussion Book List
1988–89
Mortal Choices: Ethical Dilemmas in Modern Medicine, Ruth Macklin. An ethicist at Albert Einstein College of Medicine uses medical case histories to show how philosophers can help doctors make difficult moral decisions. This book motivated me to draw up a living will, copies of which now reside with my doctor, lawyer, parents, and husband.

What's Bred in the Bone, Robertson Davies. "What's bred in the bone will come out in the flesh" is the proverb at the base of this richly textured novel about a famous art expert. A complex and inventive work by an esteemed Canadian author.

Against All Hope, Armando Valladares. A Cuban political prisoner for twenty-five years, the author maintained a relentless resistance to his tormentors despite excruciating conditions and increasing physical paralysis. His poetry, smuggled out of Cuba, led to his cause being taken up by groups such as Amnesty International.

Roughing It, Mark Twain. A record of several years of travel to, in, and around Nevada by one of America's foremost humorists.

The Modern Tradition, collected by Daniel Howard. A short story anthology.

The Closing of the American Mind, Allan Bloom. Bloom decries the state of higher education in the United States. Though his case concerning humanities deserves serious consideration, many critics decry Bloom. This made for a lively discussion.

Slaughterhouse Five, Kurt Vonnegut. The author's black humor on the subject of human stupidity is evident in this novel about the bombing of Dresden.

The Haunted Mesa, Louis L'Amour. A combination of western and occult adventure, with the former given a decided edge. The hero, investigating the mystery of a race of vanished cliff dwellers, "crosses over" into a fourth dimension, which turns out to be another frontier.

The Discoverers, Daniel Boorstin. Humankind's endless adventure in unraveling the mysteries of the universe and the many "discoverers" who have added to our cumulative wisdom are the subjects of this work.

1989–90

The Power of Myth, Joseph Campbell with Bill Moyers. The ways in which mythology illuminates the stages of life. Most of us found our individual faiths strengthened by reading this book, even though it challenged and questioned them.

Manufacturing Consent: The Political Economy of the Mass Media, Edward S. Herman and Noam Chomsky. Argues that America's government and its corporate giants exercise control over what we read, see, and hear. A disturbing picture of a news system that panders to the interests of America's privileged and neglects its duties when the concerns of minority groups and the underclass are at stake.

Foreign Affairs, Alison Lurie. What makes this novel such a delight is the author's feel for the comedy of the human situation in which growing up and learning to love defeats our most cherished preconceptions about ourselves.

The Book and the Brotherhood, Iris Murdoch. Murdoch's twenty-third novel begins at a midsummer ball at Oxford where a group of friends have gathered. Years ago, these friends had financed a political and philosophical book by David Crimond, a monomaniacal Marxist genius. Crimond's actions touch off a crisis and, by night's end, the vindictive ghosts of the past have invaded the present.

Man of the House: The Life and Political Memoirs of Speaker Tip O'Neill, Tip O'Neill with William Novak. For its evocation of the early Boston days alone, this book deserves to be a hit. The politically hooked reader will hear, in the background, the voice of derby-hatted John Kelly calling, "Up, up the Speaker!"

The Flight of the Iguana, David Quammen. Naturalist Quammen's essays are compiled into a lively book. How many of us have stud-

ied the face of a spider or spent an hour thinking about earthworms?
Quammen has and shares his observations with us.

The Trial of Socrates, I. F. Stone. Stone's portrait of Socrates sharply
contrasts with popular hagiographies and will interest a wide range
of readers, although Socratic experts will find much to argue with.
Categorized as fiction, but smacks of fact. It was the first and only
time I've seen a member of the group get so riled that he slammed
the book flat on the table and exclaimed, "I don't like it!!!"

1990–91

Life and Death in Shanghai, Nien Cheng. A woman of wealth and
privilege, Cheng was imprisoned in 1966 at the onset of the Cultural
Revolution. She spent more than six years in solitary confinement,
refusing to confess to false charges against her. Her intelligence, independent spirit, and determination shine through this revealing memoir.

A Yellow Raft in Blue Water, Michael Dorris. In consecutive narratives, three generations of Native American women offer varying
perspectives of their lives on a Montana reservation.

Warrior Queens, Antonia Fraser. Lively, readable history with new
insights into some familiar figures and provocative introductions to
national heroines little known in the West.

The Thrill of the Grass, W. P. Kinsella. Best known for his novel
Shoeless Joe, on which the film *A Field of Dreams* was based, the
author visited our area for a series of lectures, readings, and workshops. The short stories in this volume are all related to baseball.

Wordstruck, Robert MacNeil. In this fond memory of his Nova
Scotia boyhood, the cohost of the MacNeil/Lehrer News Hour
recalls the beginnings of a lifelong love affair with language.

Singular Rebellion, Saiichi Maruya, translated by Dennis Keene.
When a middle-aged, electronics executive marries a beautiful,
young model, he finds out that her grandmother, a convicted mur-
derer just out of jail, is part of the deal. The novel's humor revolves
around being modern and being Japanese.

The Man Who Mistook His Wife for a Hat and Other Clinical Tales,
Oliver Sacks. The author, a neurologist who describes himself as

equally interested in people and in diseases, as scientist and as romantic, has written twenty-four case histories of patients he has treated. Intriguing reading for those who are interested in various permutations of neurological disease.

Angle of Repose, Wallace Stegner. A young married couple goes west at the turn of the century so that the husband can pursue his engineering career. He experiences a series of failures, some because of his own weaknesses and some because of his overzealous sense of integrity. The tale is told by his grandson, a noted historian who has lost a leg and a wife.

The Joy Luck Club, Amy Tan. Common threads of chance and fate woven intricately through stories of four Chinese mothers and their American daughters reveal their struggle for assimilation. A real tearjerker.

1991–92

The Remains of the Day, Kazuo Ishiguro. The story takes place in the summer of 1956 and concerns the insular, fading world of the perfect English butler. A winner of Britain's highest literary award, the Booker Prize.

Jefferson and Monticello: The Biography of a Builder, Jack McLaughlin. A National Book Award nominee in nonfiction, this book is scholarly and immensely readable. Reveals new insights into Jefferson's personality through a detailed examination of his home.

Panther in the Sky, James Alexander Thom. A vigorous and imaginative recreation of the life of the Shawnee Chief Tecumseh (1768–1813).

From Beirut to Jerusalem, Thomas Friedman. A winner of the National Book Award for nonfiction, this book is tough on both the PLO and the Israelis. We agreed that more than anything any of us had read, it clarified and helped us understand the situation between the Israelis and Palestinians in the Middle East.

A Feeling for the Organism: The Life and Work of Barbara McClintock, Evelyn Keller. A clear and exciting picture of one of the most remarkable scientists who ever practiced genetic biology.

You Just Don't Understand: Women and Men in Conversation, Deborah Tannen, Ph.D. Even in the closest relationships, women and men live in different worlds made of different words. This discussion was filled with much laughter as personal anecdote after anecdote was related—all categorically supporting Tannen's ideas.

East is East, T. Coraghessan Boyle. A Japanese sailor jumps overboard off the coast of Georgia, encountering, among other things, a writers' colony and much culture shock. Well, the shock goes both ways.

This Boy's Life: A Memoir, Tobias Wolff. Brings to life the stuff of boyhood and captures fifties America as well. Parts of the story seemed so fantastic that some of us questioned the author's veracity.

The Oldest Living Confederate Widow Tells All, Allan Gurganus. A ninety-nine-year-old widow tells her husband's war stories and more from her bed in a charity rest home in Falls, North Carolina, to a visitor with a tape recorder. Some participants didn't finish this long book. Others were so taken by it, they read it twice! The nonfinishers were persuaded to keep reading post discussion. It was worth it.

1992–93
Father Melancholy's Daughter, Gail Godwin. The world of Margaret Gower, daughter of the rector of St. Cuthbert's Church in Romulus, Virginia, changes forever when Margaret is six. On that day, her mother walks away from her life as a rector's wife, never to return. A moving and spiritual novel.

How to Make an American Quilt, Whitney Otto. Set in a small, central California town, the novel chronicles the local quilting circle and its eight members. This book held special meaning for our group members who quilt. We bind ourselves together in many ways, by quilting and discussing books together.

Amusing Ourselves to Death, Neil Postman. The author contends that today's public media is designed to do little more than entertain. He laments the decline of print intelligence and people's ability to read reflectively and judge the quality of arguments. He examines how Aldous Huxley's *Brave New World* prediction that people can be controlled by inflicting pleasure may be true.

Without Feathers, Woody Allen. This is Jewish, big city, East Coast humor—something we small town, primarily Christian, midwesterners find worth delving into. The title comes from Emily Dickinson's observation that, "Hope is the thing with feathers."

A Natural History of the Senses, Diane Ackerman. A grand tour of the realm of the senses in prose that is sensual in and of itself. One can tell that Ackerman is a poet at heart. Two years later, I am still quoting from this book and giving it as a present to deserving friends.

Honest Effort, Michael Carey. Carey is a farmer who lives near Farragut, Iowa, but was raised on the East Coast. His poems are very accessible to people not familiar with or even interested in poetry. His poetry delighted us so much, I arranged for him to give a reading at our library.

Braided Lives, Marge Piercy. This novel concerns the lives of two women who grew up in the fifties and the major theme is abortion. As in most of Piercy's work, politics and feminism loom large.

Savage Inequalities, Jonathan Kozol. Kozol takes us into schools across the country to describe what is happening to children from poor families in the inner cities and less affluent suburbs and, justifiably so, we are made to feel ashamed. He doesn't just shame us though, he also galvanizes us to change the educational system and its gross and consistent inequalities.

Second Nature: A Gardener's Education, Michael Pollan. Allen Lacy, author of many gardening books, says this book is about gardening, but only in the same way that Dante's Divine Comedy is about getting lost in the woods. Pollan has a lot to say about the overlapping—and sometimes conflicting—moral and political borders of nature and culture.

1993–94

Getting Even and *Side Effects*, Woody Allen. A continuation of last year's readings from *The Complete Prose of Woody Allen*. One group member was reading in bed late into the night, and while he managed not to wake his wife by laughing out loud, he laughed so hard he shook the bed and woke her up anyway.

The Living, Annie Dillard. Set in Bellingham, Washington, from 1855 through 1897, with a large cast of vivid characters, this novel gave us prairie dwellers a different view of trees. Dillard did a lot of primary source research—reading letters and diaries—to be as authentic as possible with language, dress, food, and attitudes.

The Last Word and Other Stories, Graham Greene. This volume gathers previously uncollected stories from the entire range of Greene's career, from 1923 until 1989. One, "A Branch of the Service," had never been printed before. Greene's religious and moral conundrums are always thought provoking.

The Way Things Ought to Be, Rush Limbaugh. *The New York Times Book Review* proclaimed that, "However concocted, this is a work for its time . . . right-wing populism, an American perennial, is in bloom, and at the moment Mr. Limbaugh is its gaudiest flower." We had our largest attendance of the year at this discussion. Many of us voted to read this book because we knew we never would read it on our own.

A River Runs Through It, Norman Maclean. Vivid images of the Big Blackfoot River in Montana; convincing evidence of the parallels between fly-fishing and life; painstaking and painful semiautobiographical analysis of family relationships; writing so subtle and beautiful that the reader laughs and cries almost without knowing why. The last sentence is ultimately memorable, "I am haunted by water."

The Middleman and Other Stories, Bharati Mukherjee. The author sees immigrants to America from Asia, the Middle East, and Latin America as a wave of pioneers who will change their new homeland just as inexorably as the Europeans changed America in the nineteenth and early twentieth centuries. These stories evoke the longing and confusion of both the newest immigrants and the longtime residents. Mukherjee makes us see things through completely different eyes.

Tuva or Bust! Richard Feynman's Last Journey, Ralph Leighton. Tuva is Tuvinskaya, a notch in northwest Mongolia. What Ralph and Richard go through to try to get to Tuva is incredible. Leighton gives the reader ideas for where to get answers from libraries to corresponding with government officials, movie stars, and musicians, to examining maps everywhere, even on shower curtains and piggy banks at K-Mart. We learned a little about Feynman, who won a Nobel Prize in physics, and a lot about Tuva and Tuvans, a place and a people most of us well-read individuals had never heard of before.

Midaq Alley, Naguib Mahfouz. This Egyptian author is the winner of a Nobel Prize in literature. This story concerns the inhabitants of an alley in Cairo in the forties—their comings and goings, births and deaths, timelessness.

My Antonia, Willa Cather. A classic of pioneer America. A Bohemian immigrant girl copes with all the hardships of her life on the Nebraska prairie of the late nineteenth century.

1994–95

Jump and Other Stories, Nadine Gordimer. This South African author is one of the few women to win a Nobel Prize in literature. This collection of stories was cited by the committee awarding the prize. It gives us access to many lands, from suburban London to the veldt in South Africa.

The De-Valuing of America, William Bennett. The author is a patriot and an individualist. Rush Limbaugh thinks he's great (he's quoted on the cover of the paperback edition). They both value America. Bound to be plenty of heated discussion on this one.

The Shipping News, E. Annie Proulx. Darkly humorous and very moving, this novel won both the Pulitzer Prize and the National Book Award. After a series of tragedies in Brooklyn, homely and hesitant Quoyle moves with his two young daughters to Newfoundland, his ancestral family home. He gets a job reporting the shipping news for a local newspaper and meets a bevy of eccentric, lovable (and not so lovable) characters.

Balkan Ghosts: A Journey Through History, Robert Kaplan. A timely study of the countries in the Balkan peninsula, written in travelogue style, insightful and informative. A must for those who would like to understand the plights of these emerging countries in Eastern Europe.

Breaking Barriers: A Memoir, Carl T. Rowan. The author grew up in severe poverty in McMinnville, Tennessee, but through luck and hard work managed to obtain a position at the cutting edge of power

and social change. Rowan's blatant opinions and scathing denuncia-
tions make this memoir both controversial and fascinating.

*The Cavalry Maiden: Journals of a Russian Officer in the Napoleonic
Wars*, Nadezhda Durova, translated by Mary Fleming Zirin. This book
was one of the first autobiographies printed in Russia (1836) and explores a man's world as seen through the eyes of a woman who mas-
queraded as a man for ten years so she could be a soldier in the
Russian Army. (We chose to read it because Ralph Leighton had recommended it in *Tuva or Bust!*, a book we read last year.)

The Great Gatsby, F. Scott Fitzgerald. The leader of this discussion
had done extensive research on Fitzgerald and believes that this is
Fitzgerald's most complete and quintessentially American novel
because of its portrayal of the promise and pathos of wealthy society, specifically in New York City and Long Island.

Jesus: A Life, A. N. Wilson. The author claims that the Jesus of history and the one of faith are really two separate beings with two separate stories. He tells the historical story in an incisive, insightful
way, leaving faith to the spiritual realm.

The English Patient, Michael Ondaatje. Winner of a Booker Prize. In
this novel, four people come together in a deserted Italian villa during the final moments of World War II: a young nurse whose energy
is focused on her last dying patient; the patient who is an unknown
Englishman and survivor of a plane crash; a thief whose skills made
him both a hero and a casualty of war; and an Indian soldier in the
British army who is an expert at bomb disposal.

1995–96

Looking Backward, 2000–1887, Edward Bellamy. Julian West, a
wealthy Bostonian, is hypnotized so he can fall asleep. He awakens
113 years later in 2000 A.D., retaining the vigor and appearance of
his youth, and discovers a different and, he thinks, better world. This
book was published in 1888, and there is an Edward Bellamy
Association located in Chicoppee Falls, Massachusetts.

Smilla's Sense of Snow, Peter Hoeg. Smilla Qaavigaaq Jasperson is
caught between the native Greenland culture of her hunter-tracker

mother and the modern Danish world of her physician-scientist father. When a six-year-old Inuit boy dies mysteriously in a fall from a roof, Smilla feels compelled to investigate. Our book group people called her a female James Bond.

Going After Cacciato, Tim O'Brien. Winner of the National Book Award, this is the dreamlike journey of Paul Berlin, an infantryman during the Vietnamese conflict. One of his platoon members, named Cacciato (which means "the pursued" in Italian), decides to quit fighting in Vietnam and walk to Paris. Berlin and his buddies follow him in order to bring him back.

The Soloist, Mark Salzman. Musical prodigy Renne Sundheimer inexplicably lost his gift at the age of eighteen and for fifteen subsequent years has been a cello teacher at a large university. Two events radically alter his life: he becomes a juror in a trial for the brutal murder of a Buddhist monk and he becomes the teacher of another cello prodigy, a nine-year-old Korean boy who reminds him of himself.

Sand County Almanac, Aldo Leopold. A classic of the conservation movement by one of the world's great naturalists.

Speak, Memory: An Autobiography, Vladimir Nabokov. A memoir of this brilliant author's childhood and youth in the vanished world of prerevolutionary Russia. Puns, allusions, and wordplay bristle throughout his ultimately poetic prose. Nabokov has a great sense of humor and a profound feeling for the details in the life around him. He was a serious lepidopterist (butterfly enthusiast) and wordsmith; you may need access to a dictionary.

A Thousand Acres, Jane Smiley. A King Lear–like novel of fathers, daughters, and the land. We loved the evocations of Iowa (most of us being Iowans): the farmland and the cooking. The plot is complex and the writing is of high quality in the minute, revealing way objects, people, events, and relationships are described. Smiley's way with words is beautiful even when she writes of ugly things like disease, death, depression, and misunderstandings.

A Midwife's Tale: The Life of Martha Ballard, Based on Her Diary, 1785–1812, Laurel Thatcher Ulrich. This simple, matter-of-fact diary was personal—not meant for public eyes—so deciphering it took a keen and persistent mind. It had been ignored for years by more traditional historians as being tedious and unimportant. It took the scholarly and unique perception of Ulrich to fill in the gaps and make the diary flow as a fascinating tour de force of social history.

1996–97

Ishmael, Daniel Quinn. Turned down by the group the year before, two members subsequently read it and both offered to lead a discussion this year. The narrator of this book answers an ad in the newspaper: "Teacher seeks student. Must have earnest desire to save the world. Apply in person." Imagine his surprise when this teacher turns out to be a gorilla who asks him to consider whether it is humankind's ultimate destiny to rule the world. It seems to be the kind of book you either delight in or detest.

Fahrenheit 451, Ray Bradbury. This classic on censorship is named for the temperature at which paper burns. It tells of a world where a fireman's job is to start fires, not put them out. We all explained which book we would memorize for posterity if it came to that.

Snow Falling on Cedars, David Guterson. Winner of the PEN/Faulkner Award, this novel takes place in the Pacific Northwest's San Piedro islands. There are many levels and themes but the basic story is a murder-mystery concerning the death of a German gill-netter and the courtroom trial of the Japanese childhood friend suspected of killing him. It is a long, deep look into the eastern soul and the western heart.

The Stone Diaries, Carol Shields. Winner of both the Pulitzer Prize and National Book Critics Circle Award, this is a novel shaped like a diary that traces one woman's life from her birth in Manitoba in 1905 throughout her years as wife, mother, and widow. Shields experiments with a fictional concept of biography and memoir, including a family tree in the front and a section of photographs in the middle of the book. The different meanings of stone were fun to look for as well.

Outerbridge Reach, Robert Stone. A middle-aged boat salesman enters a solo sailing race around the world, wherein he challenges both his nautical skills and his fundamental beliefs. It is reminiscent of Moby Dick with its abundant symbolism; rethinking of the meaning of life; and the purpose of countries, religion, war, and individuals. The race becomes a sort of spirit quest and a search for truth, be it relative or absolute.

A Ruth Suckow Omnibus, Ruth Suckow. An Iowa author (read in honor of Iowa's sesquicentennial), Suckow attended Grinnell College in the early 1900s and traveled and lived throughout the United States thereafter. However, her stories have always centered on small-town midwestern life.

Assembling California, John McPhee. Presented in a very readable form, this book is about California's human and geologic history centered on the theory of plate tectonics. This is probably the first time we read a geology book.

Sleeping at the Starlite Motel and Other Adventures on the Way Back Home, Bailey White. The author shares the essence of her native south Georgia through a series of unforgettable, amusing, and touching incidents and characters. She teaches elementary school and is a guest contributor on National Public Radio. Listening to a tape of her reading these stories adds much to their enjoyment.

Sastun: My Apprenticeship with a Maya Healer, Rosita Arvigo with Nadine Epstein. The author attempts to preserve the knowledge of a rainforest shaman (Don Elijio Panti in Belize, South America) and also study and sustain rainforest plants.

1997–98

The Messiah Stones, Irving Benig. The Messiah Stones were first discovered in the Middle East after World War II by American intelligence forces working undercover as anthropologists. Over fifty years later, college professor John McGowen discovers that his long-missing father has bequeathed him a secret that will utterly change the lives of anyone who knows it. The Messiah Stones become a beacon to announce the coming of the world's savior at the end of the millennium. This book had potential but most participants thought it didn't live up to it.

Cold Comfort Farm, Stella Gibbons. First published in England in 1932, this remains a comic class of rural life. The author explores the theme of one sane character amidst a group of violent, eccentric types. Viewing the video is fun, too.

A Map of the World, Jane Hamilton. This book is not an easy or light read as it explores the themes of motherhood, death, love, and child abuse. When we think it can't get much worse for the main character, it does. But we are left with a better understanding of the strength of the human heart and the power to rise above calamity.

Mr. Ives' Christmas, Oscar Hijuelos. A spare, modern Christmas fable (with references to Dickens's *A Christmas Carol*), Mr. Ives struggles to reconcile himself to his son's senseless murder. It is very hard and takes a long time. This is the story of his boundless love for his family and for all people, but especially of his religious faith, that most mysterious and private of emotions.

Train Go Sorry: Inside a Deaf World, Leah Hager Cohen. The title is the American Sign Language expression for "missing the boat." Deaf culture is explored powerfully and poignantly as a chronicle of the students of the Lexington School for the Deaf.

The Woman Who Fell from the Sky, Joy Harjo. Harjo is the daughter of a Creek father and a Cherokee-French mother and her Native American heritage is an important part of her writing. These poems are accessible but are best read aloud. Fortunately, we were able to attend a series of readings by Harjo which added immensely to our enjoyment and understanding of her words. She also plays saxophone with a group called Poetic Justice.

The Liars' Club, Mary Karr. Karr's God-awful East Texas childhood has a calamitous appeal. The reader is catapulted between misery and laughter on an arc of beautiful and precise language.

Makes Me Wanna Holler, Nathan McCall. An account of the author's uneasy journey from the segregated black world to the token-integrated fringe of the white world. The title comes from a Marvin Gaye song.

Cloister Walk, Kathleen Norris. Norris relates her experiences as a protestant lay oblate at St. John's Abbey, a Benedictine monastery in Collegeville, Minnesota. The narrative is arranged chronologically according to the rhythm of the Catholic liturgical calendar and includes personal reflections on language and family, as well as academic explorations of the issues of celibacy, liturgy, hospitality, and the virgin martyrs.

1998–99

The Killer Angels, Michael Shaara. Winner of the Pulitzer Prize, the three bloody days of the Battle of Gettysburg are worked into one of the most moving novels about war, with unforgettable portraits of Lee, Longstreet, Chamberlain, and other leaders on both sides of this deadly struggle. The PBS movie *Gettysburg* was based on this novel.

All the Pretty Horses, Cormac McCarthy. Winner of the National Book Award and the National Book Critics Circle Award, this is the first of a trilogy. A young boy heads south to Mexico like Americans used to head west for new frontiers and he travels on a horse like Huck Finn "lit out for the territory" on a raft. It is his story of adventure and discovery. McCarthy is regularly compared to Faulkner and Melville.

How the Irish Saved Civilization: The Untold Story of Ireland's Heroic Role from the Fall of Rome to the Rise of Medieval Europe, Thomas Cahill. Written in an extremely accessible way and full of extraordinary information about the ancient Celtic and early Irish ways of life (so full of nature, sex, and human sacrifice to fearsome gods).

No Ordinary Time: Franklin and Eleanor Roosevelt, by Doris Kearns Goodwin. There are several story lines: Eleanor and Franklin's marriage, Eleanor's life as first lady, and FDR's White House and its impact on America and a world at war. The title comes from Eleanor's speech before the Democratic National Convention in 1940. Goodwin includes wonderful anecdotes about the Roosevelt family as well as absorbing information about controversial topics such as the right of African Americans to fight, the United States turning away Jewish refugees, and putting Japanese-Americans in concentration camps.

Five Equations That Changed the World: The Power and Poetry of Mathematics, Michael Guillen. A Harvard mathematician-physicist profiles five pioneers whose mathematical equations had far-reaching impact: Isaac Newton, Daniel Bernoulli, Michael Faraday,

Rudolf Clausius, and Albert Einstein. It was an easy-to-read blend of dramatic biography with mathematical documentary.

The Family: Opposing Viewpoints. Part of a series used as tools for critical thinking, these are not middle-of-the-road viewpoints; they are definitely *opposing*.

Oscar and Lucinda, Peter Carey. A newly ordained Anglican minister and a young heiress with a lot of passions (among them gambling, religion, and glass) live their lives the best they can being square pegs attempting to fit into the of round holes of England and Australia in the 1860s. Carey is a master of characterization; even his minor characters are vivid and memorable.

Cold Mountain, Charles Frazier. Winner of the National Book Award, this novel details two journeys becoming one. A Confederate soldier grievously wounded in body and soul outside Petersburg decides to desert and head back to his home and the woman he loves in the mountains of North Carolina. For her part, this woman's father has died suddenly and she knows little about how to survive on her own. But, she must learn. The chapters alternate between them.

Housekeeping, Marilynne Robinson. Ruth and her younger sister Lucille grow up haphazardly after their mother commits suicide. At first they are under the care of their relatively competent grandmother. When she dies, their comically bumbling great aunts take over, but just for a short time. Finally, their mother's sister Sylvie shows up. She has been a transient and her effect on the girls and their growing up is unusual, at times troubling, and at other times exhilarating.

List 2: Librarians' Book Discussion Book List
Moon Tiger, Penelope Lively
The Awakening, Kate Chopin
The Left Hand of Darkness, Ursula K. LeGuin
Things Fall Apart, Chinua Achebe
Northanger Abbey, Jane Austen
The Butcher Boy, Patrick McCabe
How the Irish Saved Civilization, Thomas Cahill
Outlander, Diana Gabaldon

Walking Across Egypt, Clyde Edgerton

The Killer Angels, Michael Shaara

In the Time of the Butterflies, Julia Alvarez

Whoredom in Kimmage, Rosemary Mahoney

Out of This World, Mary Swander

Paula, Isabel Allende

Women's Work: The First 20,000 Years: Women, Cloth, and Society in Early Times, Elizabeth Wayland Barber

Woman Hollering Creek, Sandra Cisneros

Personal History, Katharine Graham

The God of Small Things, Arundhati Roy

Among the White Moon Faces, Shirley Geok-Lin Lim

Charming Billy, Alice McDermott

Pigs in Heaven, Barbara Kingsolver

Book of Famous Iowans, Douglas Bauer

List 3: Mystery Book Discussion Book List
1997–98, Prizewinners

Dead Man's Island, Carolyn G. Hart (Agatha Award)

Under the Beetle's Cellar, Mary Willis Walker (Anthony Award)

Past Reason Hated, Peter Robinson (Arthur Ellis Award)

Booked to Die, John Dunning (Dilys Award)

A Dark-Adapted Eye, Barbara Vine (Edgar Award)

Until the Twelfth of Never, Bella Stumbo (Edgar Award)

The Way through the Woods, Colin Dexter (Gold Dagger Award)

A Thief of Time, Tony Hillerman (Macavity Award)

Concourse, S. J. Rozan (Shamus Award)

1998–99, Chicago

I got the titles listed below from *Mystery Reader's Walking Guide: Chicago* by Alzina Stone Dale. It was hard finding books still in print, so I pounced upon whatever title was available, sometimes not knowing much about the book. Some of the Chicago connections are rather tenuous, but the saving grace is that we traveled to Chicago where

Alzina Stone Dale led us on a walking tour after we had lunch together at Miller's Pub.

Edgar A. Poe: Mournful and Never-Ending Remembrance, Kenneth Silverman. This book was leftover as a nonfiction Edgar winner. It was long and scholarly, so we read it over the summer.

Grave Designs, Michael Kahn

Guardian Angel, Sara Paretsky

Sorry Now?, Mark Richard Zubro

Chicago Stories, John Miller and Genevieve Anderson, eds.

When the Dark Man Calls, Stuart Kaminsky

The Wrong Murder, Craig Rice

The Thin Man, Dashiell Hammett

Bum Steer, Nancy Pickard

1999–2000, Multicultural Detectives

We were inspired to do this theme because we became interested in one of Stuart Kaminsky's characters, Inspector Rostnikov.

A Cold Red Sunrise, Stuart Kaminsky (Soviet Union/Russia)

Elephants' Graveyard, Karin McQuillan (Kenya)

Murder in the Place of Anubis, Lynda S. Robinson (Ancient Egypt)

Poets and Murder: A Judge Dee Mystery, Robert Hans Van Gulik (eighth century China). A good read for April, which is National Poetry Month.

Ratking, Michael Dibdin (Italy)

Death of a Blue Lantern, Christopher West (twentieth century China)

A Dying Light in Corduba, by Lindsey Davis (Ancient Rome)

The Salaryman's Wife, Sujata Massey (Japan)

Eleven Days, Donald Harstad. This book doesn't feature a multi-cultural detective but we read it because the author—a retired policeman from Elkader, Iowa—read at the library.

And Then I Read . . .
Reading Across the Groups

JADE14BOOK AS TOLD TO F. R. LEWIS 📖 ALBANY, NEW YORK

FACT IS THAT I'm a book-chat cyber-slut loyal to no group (except the one I co-lead at the moment). I'm liable to show up at any chat that interests me (as in, I've read the book and have opinions), or for which the book nests on my to-be-read pile, or that includes an appearance by an author for whom I have a burning question. And, oh yes, pretty much the latest a group can meet is 10:00 P.M. eastern, and then only if I'm really hot to chat and no one expects intelligent commentary. I've stopped in at all the groups listed here and they are all represented on the list of books that follow.

Groups I've Chatted In
Currents and Classics; Literary Adventures; Short Story Group; Banned Books; Oprah and More; Book Bunch; New England Reads; Pulitzer Reading Group; Book Mavens (Jewish Writers); Southern Writers; and Biographically Speaking.

First-Time Reads 1997–99
Ladder of Years, Anne Tyler
Rose, Martin Cruz Smith

American Tabloid, James Ellroy
Le Divorce, Diane Johnson
Wings of the Dove, Henry James
Paradise, Toni Morrison
The Fixer, Bernard Malamud
Here on Earth, Alice Hoffman
Patti Jane's House of Curl, Lorna Landvik
The Salt Dancers, Ursula Hegi
"Master and the Man," Leo Tolstoy
Great Expectations, Charles Dickens
H, Elizabeth Shepard
Alias Grace, Margaret Atwood
Mr. Sammler's Planet, Saul Bellow
Woman of the Inner Sea, Thomas Keneally
The Romance Reader, Pearl Abraham
"No Taste for Accounting," Cynthia Ozick (*New Yorker* essay)
The Weight of Water, Anita Shreve
Jane Eyre, Charlotte Brontë
The Odyssey by Homer, Robert Fagles, trans.
Mao II, Don DeLillo
Babel Tower, A. S. Byatt
The Family Markowitz, Allegra Goodman
The Color of Water, James McBride
What Looks Like Crazy on an Ordinary Day, Pearl Cleage
God of Small Things, Arundhati Roy
Things Fall Apart, Chinua Achebe
Miramar, Naguib Mahfouz
Jitterbug Perfume, Tom Robbins
Midwives, Chris Bohjalian
Atticus, Ron Hansen
Selected Poems, Langston Hughes

Their Eyes Were Watching God, Zora Neale Hurston

The Djinn in the Nightingale's Eye, A. S. Byatt

Patchwork Planet, Anne Tyler

King Lear, Shakespeare

Short History of a Prince, Jane Hamilton

Nosferatu and *Batting Against Castro*, Jim Shepard

Cold Mountain, Charles Frazier

Corelli's Mandolin, Louis De Bernieres

Fraud, Anita Brookner

Cloud Mountain, Aimee Liu

Body and Soul, Frank Conroy

The Mistress of Spices, Chitra Banerjee Divakaruni

Jewel, Bret Lott

Mission Child, Maureen McHugh

To Kill a Mockingbird, Harper Lee

Antigone by Sophocles, Robert Fagles, trans.

The Sixteen Pleasures, Robert Hellenga

Snow in August, Pete Hamill

The Reader, Bernhard Schlink

Summons to Memphis, Peter Taylor

"Goodbye, My Brother," John Cheever

Cosmicomics, Italo Calvino

The Stone Diaries, Carol Shields

Wait Till Next Year, Doris Kearns Goodwin

The Sparrow and *Children of God*, Mary Doria Russell

The Lone Ranger and Tonto Fistfight in Heaven, Sherman Alexie

West with the Sun, Beryl Markham

The Liars' Club, Mary Karr

Texaco, Patrick Chamoiseau

Saints and Villains, Denise Giardina

The Bone People, Keri Hulme
Best American Short Stories of 1997, E. Annie Proulx, ed.
Best American Short Stories of 1998, Garrison Keillor, ed.
Selected Stories, Katherine Mansfield
Becoming a Man: Half a Life Story, Paul Monette

Books I Read Again
Pride and Prejudice, Jane Austen
Wuthering Heights, Emily Brontë
Breathing Lessons, Anne Tyler
Anna Karenina, Leo Tolstoy
Selected Stories, Grace Paley
The Sound and the Fury, William Faulkner
Beloved, Toni Morrison
The Book of Laughter and Forgetting, Milan Kundera
Great Expectations, Charles Dickens
Love in a Time of Cholera, Gabriel García Márquez
The Woman Warrior, Maxine Hong Kingston
Ulysses, James Joyce
The Color Purple, Alice Walker
Rabbit at Rest, John Updike
One Flew over the Cuckoo's Nest, Ken Kesey
Charming Billy, Alice McDermott
Ruined by Reading, Lynne Sharon Schwartz
"The Open Window," Saki (H. H. Monro)
Medea, Euripides

The Best of the Best Book List

NATALIE KEMMITT   LAFAYETTE, INDIANA

THIS IS A LIST of titles (mainly fiction, with a few memoirs) that have either elicited really memorable discussions or have been unanimously enjoyed by several different book groups that I lead. Of them all, *Corelli's Mandolin* by Louis De Bernieres is the book we all still talk about. Two others at the top of the "Best of the Best" list are Mary Shelley's *Frankenstein* and Mary Doria Russell's *The Sparrow*.

The Accidental Tourist, Anne Tyler. Straightforward story crammed with fascinating characters and interesting situations. A story with no villains, just a lot of endearing people groping about while trying to do the best they can.

Alias Grace, Margaret Atwood. So much to talk about! Consider how the motif of quilting is used in connection with the piecing together of Grace Mark's remarkable story. Consider all the different opinions of Grace that are expressed in the novel. Consider Grace's relationship with her questioner. How far does he ever understand Grace? How far do we?

Atticus, Ron Hansen. When venerable Atticus Cody travels from Colorado to Mexico to claim the body of his son who has killed himself, things about the case just don't add up. Unconvinced that Scott killed himself, Cody becomes embroiled in a murder mystery that tests all his reserves of endurance, love, and forgiveness.

Audrey Hepburn's Neck, Alan Brown. An interesting coming-of-age novel. This is a sometimes saucy, profoundly poignant story of Toshi's attempts to find his place in the world. Fascinated by foreigners, Americans in particular, Toshi struggles to fit into his frenetic and ultramodern Tokyo life.

The Awakening, Kate Chopin. A wonderful and easy read that satisfies readers who want to read things written over a hundred years ago. It is interesting in the case of this book to compare early reviews (harsh) with modern responses to the author and her heroine's dilemma.

Bastard out of Carolina, Dorothy Allison. A memorable tale of one girl's fight to survive despite her clannish, poor family and her step-daddy's attentions. A brutal story that won't suit everybody, but there are real flashes of beauty amidst the ugliness.

Beloved, Toni Morrison. This harrowing and beautiful tale of Sethe, an escaped slave in post–Civil War Ohio, was hard going for some, but the difficulties brought about a lively discussion. Consider ideas of motherhood, the nature of stories, the fusing of past and present, the divide between reality and memory, and the power of unconditional love.

Behind the Scenes at the Museum, Kate Atkinson. The title refers to all the little mundane things that the dead leave behind—buttons, photographs, boots, spoons, lucky charms—and how these things can never tell the full stories of people's lives. A wonderful, sparkling book about the lives of the women in several generations of a family in Yorkshire, England, and how they struggle to retain independence through marriage and motherhood.

The Birthday Boys, Beryl Bainbridge. Fictionalized account of Captain Scott's ill-fated trek to the South Pole told from the points of view of the five very different men who set off walking to the South Pole but didn't make it back.

The Book of Ruth, Jane Hamilton. A disturbing book about one woman and her simple hopes. The end is shattering, but could it have been prevented or predicted? Consider the idea of language, Ruth's love of stories, her aim to tell her story, and her inability to express herself to her mother.

The Bridge on the Drina, Ivo Andric. Nobel Prize–winning novel about a Bosnian community ravaged by history and about the bridge across the river Drina that is the one constant as the cycles of history move along from the sixteenth century to the outbreak of World War I.

Cat's Eye, Margaret Atwood. All of Atwood's books are great for discussion, but this title elicited the best debate. We would still be talking about Elaine's life being blighted by her memories of childhood bullying had the library not closed.

Corelli's Mandolin, Louis De Bernieres. The very best of the best. We talked about this one for two sessions and are talking about it still. It has everything a discussion group needs in a book: a cast of fascinating characters, epic scope, humor, tragedy, history, romance, and a grand setting—the invasion of Cephalonia in World War II. Realism meets magic in an intoxicating blend. But oh, that ending!

The Color of Water, James McBride. Two fascinating stories in one. This compelling memoir was written by a black man as a tribute to his Jewish mother. Consider whether McBride and his many siblings do well in life *because* of their mother's efforts or in spite of her. Consider their mother's idea that God is colorless and that dwelling on issues of race is pointless when a good education is all that matters.

Ellen Foster, Kaye Gibbons. We had a good discussion of Ellen Foster as a group (widely available thanks to Oprah) and everybody also read another novel of their choice by Gibbons. We shared summaries of these and talked about the similarities and differences we detected. It worked well and could be done with many other authors, including Isabel Allende, Tim O'Brien, and Joyce Carol Oates.

The English Patient, Michael Ondaatje. A haunting love story, this is complex novel about the fragmentation caused by war. Sometime *after* we read the novel, it became all the rage because the movie was made. We wanted to get T-shirts printed declaring "We read *The English Patient* before the film." Then of course we wanted T-shirts with "We read *Stones from the River* before Oprah did." When will it all end?

Ethan Frome, Edith Wharton. There is far more to this short tale of frozen lives and thwarted hopes than first meets the eye. This grim and ironic tale of unrequited passion on an isolated New England farm was just the right book for my first ever discussion as a leader. Consider the narrative structure and the function of the storyteller.

The Fifth Child, Doris Lessing, and *The Yellow Wallpaper*, Charlotte Perkins Gilman. Two short reads connected by themes of parenting. Doris Lessing should be on every group's syllabus, and this dark little tale about a child whose birth destroys his parents' dreams of an idyllic family life will give rise to lots of speculation. *The Yellow Wallpaper* is as disturbing as it is interesting, and it could also very fruitfully be compared to Mary Shelley's *Frankenstein*.

Frankenstein, Mary Shelley. This book is possibly more relevant now than when it was published. Consider where your sympathies lie, and which character is guilty of the greatest crimes. The novel is considered to be a gothic and romantic masterpiece as well as one of the first science-fiction novels. What do you understand the elements of these genres to be?

Heat and Dust, Ruth Prawer Jhabvala. This was the first of a series of books we read that dealt with women hemmed in by society's expectations. A double story comparing the potent effect India has on two women from different time periods.

The House of the Spirits, Isabel Allende. How far does the house represent the country of Chile in this sweeping saga? This is a story of a family's fortunes set against a backdrop of political turmoil that threatens to crush all that is lovely and magical in the lives of the novel's women. Also, read Allende's hauntingly beautiful memoir, *Paula*. Writing at the bedside of her desperately sick daughter, Allende delves deep into her family's history and tells a marvelous tale of the personalities and passions that inspired her fiction.

In the Lake of the Woods and *The Things They Carried*, Tim O' Brien. This author's work inspired great arguments. We talked about war, Vietnam in particular, about My Lai, about marriage, and about our expectations of elected politicians. In regard to *In the Lake of the Woods*, we discussed the idea of a split self and the issue of enabling, and we also talked about the unusual structure of the novel, O'Brien's symbolism, and his use of allusions. This novel divided the room like no other book before or since. Great!

In the Time of the Butterflies, Julia Alvarez. Lovingly fictionalized story of the Mirabal sisters who had the courage to stand up to Dominican dictator Trujillo. The structure and narrative method of this novel provoked discussion and the different personalities of the sisters had us talking about how ordinary people suddenly become heroes.

Jane Eyre, Charlotte Bronte. A novel written as a memoir that has many autobiographical elements. Most had read it before, so with the basics of plot and character clear, we were able to consider Jane's feminist message, the gothic elements of the novel, and to ask the questions, why has this novel remained so popular for so long? and what makes a classic?

The Liars' Club, Mary Karr. Poetic, honest, and witty memoir by a published poet. It stands out among other memoirs because its tone is neither self-pitying nor accusing. Karr celebrates her parents' eccentricities in a compelling and lively tale that will have you laughing, cringing, and gasping. Consider the function of stories in the author's childhood.

Lonesome Dove, Larry McMurtry. None of us had ever read a western before; we started with a good one. This novel won the Pulitzer Prize for fiction in 1986, and as we discussed it we debated why. More than a great adventure story of a cattle drive, it is an examination of the pioneer spirit, the personalities involved, and the relationships that were important to the cowboys.

The Magus, John Fowles. I stayed up all night to finish this, and afterwards I wasn't at all sure what I had just experienced! It's best described as a challenging, enigmatic tale with plot twists galore and enough symbolism to keep you busy for a very long time. Two other novels that were real mind stretchers were Iris Murdoch's *The Green Knight* and A. S. Byatt's *Possession*—both academic romps in which eccentric characters find themselves in bizarre situations. These aren't to everyone's taste. They can be totally infuriating, but I admit I love all this English repression and symbolism. The more allusions the better.

Obasan, Joy Kogawa. You can't help but be awed by the dignity of Kogawa's Japanese-Canadian characters in the face of the prejudiced treatment meted out to them during World War II. Consider the damage that secrets kept between generations cause in this poignant novel. Compare it to Brown's *Audrey Hepburn's Neck* and Gail Tsukiyama's lovely *The Samurai's Garden*.

On the Black Hill, Bruce Chatwin. Wonderful novel about a farmhouse straddling the border between England and Wales and how because of this unique position the Jones twins grow up experiencing the best and worst of English and Welsh life.

Perfume, Patrick Süskind. A highly original story of a character with a preternatural sense of smell and a fascinating look at the whole realm of smell and the French perfume industry in particular. Also a study in evil and obsession. Compare it to John Fowles's *The Collector* or Bram Stoker's *Dracula*.

The Remains of the Day, Kazuo Ishiguro. A calm book after some harrowing choices. But describing the book makes it sound as dull as ditch water. A butler journeys from his place of employment across the English countryside to visit a friend from the past, and as he travels we glimpse the years gone by at Darlington Hall when it was a typical bustling English estate. Is it a love story? Is Darlington Hall a microcosm for what was happening all over Europe? Compare it to Bainbridge's *The Birthday Boys* or *Every Man for Himself* in a discussion of how these novels treat the idea of the end of an era.

The Road from Coorain, Jill Ker Conway. Popular with groups, this tale of Conway's escape from the Australian outback life and a dominating mother will give you lots of topics to talk about.

A Room with a View, E. M. Forster. Picaresque qualities in this amusing and satirical study of the English abroad. Some found the novel slow and hard going, but everyone enjoyed its flashes of quiet comedy and the romance between Lucy Honeychurch and George Emerson.

The Sparrow, Mary Doria Russell. How my group groaned when I proposed that we read a science-fiction novel about Jesuits in outer space, and afterward how they all agreed that it is an amazing book to read and discuss. Consider how far it is necessary to suspend your disbelief before you can lose yourself in this moving story. What do we expect from science fiction?

The Stone Diaries, Carol Shields. A great story about an ordinary and yet extraordinary life. Consider the effect of the family tree and the photos in the book. What happens when you mix techniques of novels with those of biographies? Is this mix effective? Compare with Atkinson's *Behind the Scenes at the Museum*.

Stones for Ibarra, Harriet Doerr. A short and gentle read about the adjustments an expatriate couple face when they retire to follow their dreams in Mexico and about the quiet tragedies that occur in ordinary lives. We read passages aloud that illustrated Doerr's wonderful style. And you could spend an hour just talking about the first few paragraphs.

Stones from the River, Ursula Hegi. Such a vast book that we dedicated two meetings to it. Consider what is gained by Hegi's use of Trudi Montag as her main character and consider what the river represents in this wonderfully rich novel. A novel about stories and their importance in our lives, and a novel about the cycles of history.

Things Fall Apart, Chinua Achebe. This novel has a quiet power and dignity as it tells the story of Okwonko and the tragedy of his life and community at the turn of the century. When the internal weaknesses of traditional Ibo society cannot withstand the tide of western colonization, he tries to stand strong as things around him fall apart. Compare with Thomas Hardy's *The Mayor of Casterbridge*.

A Thousand Acres, Jane Smiley. We all went to see the film shortly after we read this harrowing novel. Luckily, we had the cinema to

ourselves since we had a long and heated discussion about what the
movie version had dared to leave out. Read *King Lear*, talk about the
poisoned relationships in the story, and consider the parallels
between the treatment of women in this novel and the mistreatment
of the land from years of overfarming.

Wuthering Heights, Emily Brontë. An unintended inclusion one year,
but we had such a great time with *Jane Eyre* that it seemed like a
good idea to compare Charlotte's greatest book with Emily's only
one. We nearly came to fisticuffs over our opinions of Heathcliff and
whether he is more sinned against or the sinner himself, never mind
our attempt to decide which sister was more talented.

Bookends and Friends Book List

LESLIE KRIEBEL   TELFORD, PENNSYLVANIA

OUR GROUP CELEBRATED its fifth anniversary in September. Most of us work together or are neighbors and have known each other for years. Men have asked to join our book group, but ours is strictly for women. Oprah has definitely influenced us. We often pick a book on Oprah's book club list, although we don't usually read it at the same time that her book club is reading it. The best thing about being in a book group is that we get to share the books we love with other women who share that same love. We have had more fun than anyone can imagine. In just five short years, we have built good memories of great conversations and good times. We have widened our circle of friends and expanded our minds.

1994

The Awakening, Kate Chopin

A Yellow Raft in Blue Water, Michael Dorris

Johnny Got His Gun, Dalton Trumbo

The Cat Who Came for Christmas, Cleveland Amory

1995

Cold Sassy Tree, Olive Ann Burns

The Mother, Pearl S. Buck

The Bean Trees, Barbara Kingsolver

While My Pretty One Sleeps, Mary Higgins Clark

For Love, Sue Miller

Mutant Message Down Under, Marlo Morgan

The Novel, James A. Michener

Celestine Prophecy, James Redfield

The Life and Loves of a She-Devil, Fay Weldon

1996

How to Make an American Quilt, Whitney Otto

The Horse Whisperer, Nicholas Evans

Keeping Secrets, Suzanne Somers

Franny and Zooey, J. D. Salinger

I Know Why the Caged Bird Sings, Maya Angelou

Summer, Edith Wharton

Prince of Tides, Pat Conroy

Cry of the Kalahari, Mark and Delia Owens

The Fountainhead, Ayn Rand

In the Absence of Angels, Elizabeth Glasser

1997

A Doll's House, Henrik Ibsen

Fault Lines, Anne Rivers Siddons

You Learn by Living, Eleanor Roosevelt

She's Come Undone, Wally Lamb

Patty Jane's House of Curl, Lorna Landvik

The Red Badge of Courage, Stephen Crane

Lonesome Dove, Larry McMurtry

The Deep End of the Ocean, Jacquelyn Mitchard

1998

The Color of Water, James McBride

Ladder of Years, Anne Tyler

The Notebook, Nicholas Sparks

Angela's Ashes, Frank McCourt

A Day on Earth, Alice Hoffman

Beach Music, Pat Conroy

Practical Magic, Alice Hoffman

The Christmas Box, Richard Paul Evans

1999

The Perfect Storm, Sebastian Junger

Jewel, Bret Lott

Midwives, Chris Bohjalian

Cold Mountain, Charles Frazier

What Looks Like Crazy on an Ordinary Day, Pearl Cleage

Then She Found Me, Elinor Lipman

White Oleander, Janet Fitch

A Partial List of Books Discussed in Connie's Living Room

KATHRYN J. LORD   GRANBY, CONNECTICUT

*Indicates lots of discussion on the book.

The House of the Spirits, Isabel Allende

The Heart of a Woman, Maya Angelou*

I Know Why the Caged Bird Sings, Maya Angelou*

Cat's Eye, Margaret Atwood* (evoked stories of childhood)

Robber Bride, Margaret Atwood*

Pride and Prejudice, Jane Austen

They Used to Call Me Snow White . . . , Regina Barreca (this book on women's humor fell flat, but we liked the jokes)

Ship Fever, Andrea Barrett (a collection of stories, this connected better with some people more than with others)

Warriors Don't Cry, Melba Pattillo Beals*

My Life, Starring Dara Falcon, Ann Beattie (most didn't like style of writing)

The Prime of Life, Simone de Beauvoir* (only one of us finished it, but we all loved the time period)

Talk Before Sleep, Elizabeth Berg*

Circle of Friends, Maeve Binchy (lightweight)

Come to Me, Amy Bloom* (this collection of stories connected)

Jane Eyre, Charlotte Brontë

Three Daughters of Madame Liang, Pearl S. Buck*

Death Comes for the Archbishop, Willa Cather (either loved or hated)

My Antonia, Willa Cather*

Life and Death in Shanghai, Nien Cheng* (amazing courage)

The Prosperine Papers, Jan Clausen (more interesting to writers than to anyone else)

The Road from Coorain, Jill Ker Conway*

An American Childhood, Annie Dillard*

Arranged Marriage, Chitra Banerjee Divakaruni*

Stones for Ibarra, Harriet Doerr*

The Beet Queen, Louise Erdrich*

Like Water for Chocolate, Laura Esquivel*

Postcards from the Edge, Carrie Fisher (lightweight)

Daisy Fay and the Miracle Man, Fannie Flagg*

Fried Green Tomatoes at the Whistle Stop Cafe, Fannie Flagg*

Dreaming in Cuban, Cristina Garcia*

A Virtuous Woman, Kaye Gibbons*

No Ordinary Time, Doris Kearns Goodwin* (a lot of reading, but provocative; heard her speak)

Fierce Attachments, Vivian Gornick* (the kind of book that turns us into a therapy session)

Autobiography of a Face, Lucy Grealey*

The Kiss, Kathryn Harrison* (roundly disliked; discussion centered on why someone would write about these things)

Owning Jolene, Shelby Hearon

Stones from the River, Ursula Hegi*

Little Foxes, Lillian Hellman (many disliked all of the characters)

The Islanders, Helen Hull* (a treasure—look for it)

Their Eyes Were Watching God, Zora Neale Hurston*

The Mottled Lizard, Elspeth Huxley*

An Unsuitable Job for a Woman, P. D. James

The Autobiography of My Mother, Jamaica Kincaid* (another field trip to hear her speak)

When Sisterhood Was in Flower, Florence King*

Animal Dreams, Barbara Kingsolver (not as successful for us as her first novel)

The Bean Trees, Barbara Kingsolver*

Enduring Women, Diana Koos-Gentry*

The Left Hand of Darkness, Ursula K. LeGuin*

The Dance of Intimacy, Harriet Goldhor Lerner* (one person read a different book by the author, but had no problem following the discussion)

Spring Moon, Bette Bao Lord*

West with the Night, Beryl Markham*

I Am Becoming the Woman I Wanted to Be, Sandra Haldeman Martz, ed. (pleasant, but lightweight)

The Member of the Wedding, Carson McCullers

At Weddings and Wakes, Alice McDermott*

Charming Billy, Alice McDermott*

Bullwhip Days, edited by James Mellon* (contains many oral histories of women)

Beloved, Toni Morrison* (all-time most impact on us)

Bluest Eye, Toni Morrison*

Open Secrets, Alice Munro* (mixed feelings on this collection; takes more than one reading)

Bailey's Cafe, Gloria Naylor* (so depressing we canceled plans to see a stage production of it)

Linden Hills, Gloria Naylor*

Patron Saint of Liars, Ann Patchett (little sympathy for protagonist, more for male characters)

The Street, Ann Petry*

Ship of Fools, Katherine Anne Porter (suffered from style of writing)

The Grass Dancer, Susan Power

The Shipping News, E. Annie Proulx*

Parallel Lives, Phyllis Rose*

The God of Small Things, Arundhati Roy (sharply divided)

When I Was Puerto Rican, Esmeralda Santiago*

Journal of a Solitude, May Sarton (not enough loners in the group to identify with her)

The Stone Diaries, Carol Shields (one member got into imagery, others lukewarm on it)

Outer Banks, Anne Rivers Siddons (lightweight, but one member knew her)

A Thousand Acres, Jane Smiley* (one of our best evenings)

Marilyn, Gloria Steinem (lightweight)

You Just Don't Understand: Women and Men in Conversation, Deborah Tannen.*

Delta Wedding, Eudora Welty*

The Age of Innocence, Edith Wharton*

To the Lighthouse, Virginia Woolf* (difficult)

Book List

SHIRLEY L. LUHRSEN   BOZEMAN, MONTANA

OUR BOOK CLUB, a group of American Association of University Women (AAUW) members, has become a tight, elite cadre of individualistic, dynamic souls. Occasionally, but seldom, weather affects our meeting date. We have come to accept that May and September are not our months. Each member has or has had a career and family. We have all touched distance. One taught in Alaska, another on the border of northern Minnesota, and another in the open spaces of Montana. One has known the winters of Yellowstone, and another the wilderness of the Madison Range. Peggy came from Canada. Suzanne has jet-hopped all over the world during one career. Perhaps our common interest is the exchange of information and ideas about ourselves and others. We all love family, wilderness, and books, and are as certain of God as we are that it will snow in winter in Montana.

Our reading ranges from books by local Montana authors like Swain Wolfe's *The Woman Who Lived in the Earth* to George Eliot's *Middlemarch*. We could not pass up Jill Ker Conway, Barbara Tuchman, Helen Gurley Brown, Wallace Stegner, Beryl Markham, Amy Tan, or Bette Bao Lord. The list below contains other books we've read, or meant to—I must confess that we never did get through *The Second Sex*, though most of us valiantly tried to do so.

Testament of Youth, Vera Brittain

Mrs. Wheeler Goes to Washington, Elizabeth Wheeler Colman
A Thousand Acres, Jane Smiley
The House of the Spirits, Isabel Allende
An American Childhood, Annie Dillard
The Road from Coorain, Jill Ker Conway
The Bridges of Madison County, Robert James Waller
The Second Sex, Simone de Beauvoir
Rising Sun, Michael Crichton
A Place for Us and *Eleni*, Nicholas Gage
Soviet Women: Walking the Tightrope, Francine du Plessix Gray
A Lady's Life in the Rocky Mountains, Isabella Bird
The Sound of Wings: The Life of Amelia Earhart, Mary S. Lovell
My Son's Story, Nadine Gordimer
The Worst Years of Our Lives, Barbara Ehrenreich
Love in a Cold Climate, Nancy Mitford
Heart Earth, Ivan Doig
Buster Midnight's Cafe, Stella Dallas
The Bloody Bozeman, Dorothy Johnson
Jane Eyre, Charlotte Brontë
The Woman Who Lived in the Earth, Swain Wolfe
Middlemarch, George Eliot
A Bright and Shining Lie, Neil Sheehan

More recent reads
The Greatest Generation, Tom Brokaw
Cold Mountain, Charles Frazier
Bucking the Sun, Ivan Doig
Bozeman and the Gallatin Valley, Phyllis Smith
Stones from the River, Ursula Hegi
Monsieur Beaucaire, Booth Tarkington
Land of the Hearts Desire, W. B. Yeats
The Apollo of Bellac, Jean Giraudoux

Selected Poems, James Merrill
A Personal History, Katharine Graham
Memoirs of a Geisha, Arthur Golden
Mankiller: A Chief and Her People, Wilma Mankiller
A Gathering of Finches, Jane Kirkpatrick
Ruth: The Story of Ruth Bell Graham, Patricia Cornwell
Wild Swans, Jung Chang
Montana Sky, Nora Roberts
Montana Women, Tony Volk
My American Journey, Colin Powell
The Mistress of Spices, Chitra Banerjee Divakaruni

The Friends of Mount Prospect Public Library Reading List

LAURA LUTERI AND
JUDY BENNETT

MOUNT PROSPECT,
ILLINOIS

1990

All I Really Need to Know I Learned in Kindergarten, Robert Fulghum

Bonfire of the Vanities, Tom Wolfe

Cold Sassy Tree, Olive Ann Burns

I Know Why the Caged Bird Sings, Maya Angelou

Spring Moon, Bette Bao Lord

The Good War, Studs Terkel

Katherine, Anya Seton

Daughter of Destiny, Benazir Bhutto

The Last Convertible, Anton Myrer

Absent in the Spring, Mary Westmacott

The Joy Luck Club, Amy Tan

In God We Trust, All Others Pay Cash, Jean Shepherd

1991

The Widows' Adventure, Charles Dickinson
Thomas Jefferson: An Intimate History, Fawn M. Brodie
Hollywood, Gore Vidal
Eleanor and Franklin, Joseph Lash
A Prayer for Owen Meany, John Irving
Fried Green Tomatoes at the Whistle Stop Cafe, Fanny Flagg
Eden Close, Anita Shreve
A Woman of Substance, Barbara Taylor Bradford
Saturday Night, Susan Orlean
You Just Don't Understand, Deborah Tannen
Gift from the Sea, Anne Morrow Lindbergh
Jurassic Park, Michael Crichton

1992

The Two Mrs. Grenvilles, Dominick Dunne
The Catcher in the Rye, J. D. Salinger
Lonesome Dove, Larry McMurtry
Broken Chord, Michael Dorris
The Good Earth, Pearl S. Buck
Jumping the Que, Mary Wesley
Thief of Time, Tony Hillerman
Pentimento, Lillian Hellman
Murther and the Walking Spirits, Robertson Davies
Seventh Heaven, Alice Hoffman
How to Make an American Quilt, Whitney Otto
Homecoming, Cynthia Voigt

1993

Life and Death in Shanghai, Nien Cheng
North of Hope, Jon Hassler
The Book of Ruth, Jane Hamilton

A Yellow Raft in Blue Water, Michael Dorris

The End of the Road, Tom Bodett

Rebecca, Daphne du Maurier

Cat's Eye, Margaret Atwood

The Bean Trees, Barbara Kingsolver

The Maltese Falcon, Dashiel Hammett

The Bone People, Keri Hulme

The Book of Common Prayer, Joan Didion

The Bridges of Madison County, Robert James Waller

1994

The Education of Little Tree, Forrest Carter

A Thousand Acres, Jane Smiley

Rising Sun, Michael Crichton

The Hangman's Beautiful Daughter, Sharyn McCrumb

Growing Up, Russell Baker

Mr. Bridge and *Mrs. Bridge*, Evan S. Connell

Cider House Rules, John Irving

The Oldest Living Confederate Widow Tells All, Allan Gurganus

Beloved, Toni Morrison

Duel of Eagles, Jeff Lee

How We Survived Communism and Even Laughed, Slavenka
   Drakulic

Einstein's Dreams, Alan Lightman

1995

Lizzie, Evan Hunter

Picture of Dorian Gray, Oscar Wilde

The Kitchen God's Wife, Amy Tan

A Tale of Two Cities, Charles Dickens

Buffalo Girls, Larry McMurtry

The Road from Coorain, Jill Ker Conway

Sahara, Clive Cussler
Mrs. DeWinter, Susan Hill
Princess, Jeane P. Sasson
In the Electric Mists with the Confederate Dead, James Lee Burke
To Dance with the White Dog, Terry Kay
Walking Across Egypt, Clyde Edgerton

1996
The Eight, Katherine Neville
Bimbos of the Death Sun and *Zombies of the Gene Pool*, Sharyn
   McCrumb
East of Eden, John Steinbeck
The Road to Wellville, T. Coraghessan Boyle
Turtle Moon, Alice Hoffman
The House on the Strand, Daphne du Maurier
The English Patient, Michael Ondaatje
The Glass Lake, Maeve Binchy
Remains of the Day, Kazuo Ishiguro
Stones from the River, Ursula Hegi
The Stone Diaries, Carol Shields
And Ladies of the Club, Helen Hooven Santmyer

1997
Dinosaurs in the Attic, Lincoln Child
The Sixteen Pleasures, Robert Hellenga
Black Water, Joyce Carol Oates
The Wedding, Dorothy West
The Alienist, Caleb Carr
Moo, Jane Smiley
Staggerford, Jon Hassler
Having Our Say: The Delany Sisters' First 100 Years, Sarah and
   A. Elizabeth Delany with Amy Hill Hearth

Snow Falling on Cedars, David Guterson
Practical Magic, Alice Hoffman
If These Walls Had Ears, James Morgan
To Kill a Mockingbird, Harper Lee

1998
The Horse Whisperer, Nicholas Evans
Corelli's Mandolin, Louis De Bernieres
Prince of Tides, Pat Conroy
Mary Todd Lincoln, Jean H. Baker
Midnight in the Garden of Good and Evil, John Berendt
Anatomy of a Murder, Robert Traver
Houses of Stone, Barbara Michaels
The Persian Pickle Club, Sarah Dallas
The Sparrow, Mary Doria Russell
Peregrine's Rest, Jennifer Gostin
Montana 1948, Larry Watson
Watching TV with the Red Chinese, Luke Whisnant

1999
Snow in August, Pete Hamill
Cold Mountain, Charles Frazier
Memoirs of a Geisha, Arthur Golden
Midwives, Chris Bohjalian
I Was Amelia Earhart, Jane Mendelsohn
Lost Lady, Willa Cather
Alias Grace, Margaret Atwood
The Keeper of the House, Rebecca Godwin
Contrary Blues, John Billheimer
The Bird Artist, Howard Norman
The Blue Flower, Penelope Fitzgerald
Where the Heart Is, Betty Lett

Book List

SARA MANEWITH   CHICAGO, ILLINOIS

OUR BOOK CLUB has been meeting (almost) every month since about 1987. While our membership has changed in ten years, our goals remain constant: to analyze, interpret, think, and learn through the discussion of compelling fiction and nonfiction; to share thoughts and ideas; and to socialize with literature as our vehicle.

There's never a shortage of potential reading material and our diversity brings varied suggestions and selections. We have, however, been challenged in selecting material that all members find interesting, and we are often tested in the art of compromise. Clearly, the benefit is that each of us, in turn, is likely to read something she would not have otherwise.

We have focused primarily on women writers; you'll find only a handful of male authors on our list. The first time a male author was suggested, we had considerable discussion. Nonetheless, we were pleased with that early reading of Ralph Ellison. While our group tends toward the female author, men are now easily included. We've returned to some authors again and again—Margaret Atwood, Barbara Kingsolver, and Toni Morrison. We try to stick to paperback books, but we make the occasional exception for something we just can't wait for. We've taken field trips, too: a poetry reading, a play. And we never miss our annual summer retreat to one member's home where we while away the hours on a sun-filled deck eating potluck treats.

Some of the points that have helped keep our meetings lively and our club ongoing follow.

1. We have tried periodically to create themes that will carry us over several meetings: international women writers, women's lives, definitions of community, perspectives on a culture or a continent.

2. After reading several pieces of fiction, we choose a nonfiction selection. Fiction is always a treat; nonfiction seems more difficult, both to agree on and to read.

3. When reading dense books (history, biography), we sometimes divide and assign chapters. Each member is responsible for summarizing her chapter, presenting it to the group, and leading a brief discussion, if appropriate.

4. We all take responsibility for reading book reviews and scouring libraries and bookstores for recommendations.

5. We strongly encourage regular participation. We want a cohesive and reliable group—the right number of members is about seven—to create critical mass and a familiarity with one another that makes for rich discussion.

Over the years, a strong connection has developed among members as we've seen each other through travel and other adventures, career and relationship changes, births, adoptions, and deaths. The readings bring us together, challenge us, and allow us to learn; the friendships sustain us as a group.

Fiction
Alias Grace, Margaret Atwood
Animal Dreams, Barbara Kingsolver
August, Judith Rossner
Bastard out of Carolina, Dorothy Allison
The Beet Queen, Louise Erdrich
Beloved, Toni Morrison
Black Water, Joyce Carol Oates
Breathing Lessons, Anne Tyler

The Bone People, Keri Hulme

The Burger's Daughter, Nadine Gordimer

Cat's Eye, Margaret Atwood

Coffee Will Make You Black, April Sinclair

Disturbances in the Field, Lynne Sharon Schwartz

The Fifth Child, Doris Lessing

God of Small Things, Arundhati Roy

Gone to Soldiers, Marge Piercy

The Good Mother, Sue Miller

The Handmaid's Tale, Margaret Atwood

House of Splendid Isolation, Edna O'Brien

The House of the Spirits, Isabel Allende

House on the Lagoon, Rosario Ferre

How the Garcia Girls Lost Their Accents, Julia Alvarez

The Invisible Man, Ralph Ellison

Jazz, Toni Morrison

The Joy Luck Club, Amy Tan

Lolita, Vladimir Nabokov

The Lost Language of Cranes, David Leavitt

Lucy, Jamaica Kincaid

The Mambo Kings Play Songs of Love, Oscar Hijuelos

Memoirs of a Geisha, Arthur Golden

Memory Mambo, Achy Obejas

Middlemarch, George Eliot

The Moor's Last Sigh, Salman Rushdie

Oldest Living Confederate Widow Tells All, Allan Gurganus

One True Thing, Anna Quindlen

Pigs in Heaven, Barbara Kingsolver

The Poisonwood Bible, Barbara Kingsolver

Practical Magic, Alice Hoffman

Red Azalea, Anchee Min

Regeneration, Pat Barker

Romance Reader, Pearl Abraham

The Screwtape Letters, C. S. Lewis

The Shipping News, E. Annie Proulx

Silent Duchess, Dacia Maraini

Snow Falling on Cedars, David Guterson

The Stone Diaries, Carol Shields

Stones from the River, Ursula Hegi

Things Fall Apart, Chinua Achebe

A Thousand Acres, Jane Smiley

Uncle Tom's Cabin, Harriet Beecher Stowe

Waiting to Exhale, Terry McMillan

The Wedding, Dorothy West

Woman on the Edge of Time, Marge Piercy

A Yellow Raft in Blue Water, Michael Dorris

Short Stories

Ripening, Meridel LeSueur

Woman Hollering Creek, Sandra Cisneros

Collected Short Stories, Eudora Welty

Nonfiction

Among Schoolchildren, Tracy Kidder

A Civil Action, Jonathan Harr

From Beirut to Jerusalem, Thomas Friedman

How We Die, Sherwin Nuland

In Our Defense: The Bill of Rights in Action, Ellen Alderman and
   Caroline Kennedy

Invisible Drama: Women and Change, Carol Becker

Listening to Prozac, Peter Kramer

Parting the Waters: America During the King Years, Taylor Branch

Revelations: Diaries of Women, Mary Moffat

Reviving Ophelia, Mary Pipher

There Are No Children Here, Alex Kotlowitz

Wherever You Go, There You Are, Jon Kabat-Zinn
Women Who Run with the Wolves, Clarissa Pinkola Estes
You Just Don't Understand, Deborah Tannen

Essays
Backlash, Susan Faludi
Beauty Secrets, Wendy Chapkis
Deals with the Devil, Pearl Cleage
Good Girls, Bad Girls, Laurie Bell, ed.
Race Matters, Cornell West
A Room of One's Own, Virginia Woolf

Memoir
An American Childhood, Annie Dillard
Angela's Ashes, Frank McCourt
The Color of Water, James McBride
Darkness Visible, William Styron
Farewell Symphony, Edmund White
Girl, Interrupted, Susanna Kaysen
Having Our Say: The Delany Sisters' First 100 Years, Sarah and
    A. Elizabeth Delany with Amy Hill Hearth
Of Woman Born, Adrienne Rich
Plain and Simple, Sue Bender

Biography and Autobiography
Autobiography of Malcolm X, Alex Haley
Eleanor Roosevelt, Blanche Wiesen Cook
Frida: A Biography of Frida Kahlo, Hayden Herrera
Life and Death in Shanghai, Nien Cheng
Marilyn, Gloria Steinem
Nora, Brenda Maddox
The Road from Coorain, Jill Ker Conway
West with the Night, Beryl Markham
When Heaven and Earth Changed Places, Le Ly Hayslip

Fulton Book Club
Book List

BARBARA MASK   FULTON, ILLINOIS

THE FULTON BOOK Club began meeting in 1973. As founder of the club, I was looking to share an intellectual interaction similar to graduate school. With an original membership of ten, the group has consistently stayed at that size. A new member is invited when someone moves out of town. Each year a member selects a book and researches its background. Some members plan a year in advance and notify members of their selection while others choose a month or two ahead of time and are influenced by what other members want to read. Each member reads the book (well, most do) and while everyone isn't expected to like each book, everyone is expected to have an opinion and to express it. Members have a variety of reasons for why they enjoy our book club. One stated, "because we read everything from class to trash," while another said it makes her a disciplined reader and exposes her to literature she would not have chosen herself. The longevity of our group exemplifies how books connect us to everyday incidents and experiences and how relevant books are to our lives.

Things Fall Apart, Chinua Achebe

A Death in the Family, James Agee

Little Women, Louisa May Alcott

Bastard out of Carolina, Dorothy Allison

The Cat Who Came for Christmas, Cleveland Amory

Bridge on the Drina, Ivo Andric

When I Am an Old Woman, I Shall Wear Purple, Sandra Martz, ed.

The Handmaid's Tale, Margaret Atwood

Pride and Prejudice, Jane Austen

Jonathan Livingston Seagull, Richard Bach

Père Goriot, Honoré de Balzac

The Woman Destroyed, Simone de Beauvoir

Humboldt's Gift, Saul Bellow

The Book of Virtues, William Bennett

Midnight in the Garden of Good and Evil, John Berendt

Diary of a Country Priest, Georges Bernanos

All the President's Men, Carl Bernstein and Bob Woodward

The Closing of the American Mind, Allan Bloom

Brazzaville Beach, William Boyd

Dandelion Wine, Ray Bradbury

Jane Eyre, Charlotte Brontë

The Good Earth, Pearl S. Buck

Captains and Kings, Taylor Caldwell

The Stranger, Albert Camus

All My Patients Are Under the Bed, Louis Camuti

Chicken Soup for the Soul, Jack Canfield and Mark Hansen

Exit 36, Robert Capon

Other Voices, Other Rooms, Truman Capote

How to Stop Worrying and Start Living, Dale Carnegie

Alice's Adventures in Wonderland, Lewis Carroll

Education of Little Tree, Forrest Carter

Death Comes for the Archbishop, Willa Cather

Three Sisters, Anton Chekhov

The Awakening, Kate Chopin

The House on Mango Street, Sandra Cisneros

Mr. Bridge and *Mrs. Bridge*, Evan Connell

Lord Jim, Joseph Conrad

Hardball: A Season in the Projects, Daniel Coyle

Keys of the Kingdom, A. J. Cronin

Inferno, Dante Alighieri

The Peaceable Kingdom, Jan de Hartog

The Blood of the Lamb, Peter De Vries

The Wheel on the School, Meindert DeJong

Having Our Say: The Delany Sisters' First 100 Years, Sarah and
    A. Elizabeth Delany with Amy Hill Hearth

A Book of Common Prayer, Joan Didion

An American Childhood, Annie Dillard

Stones for Ibarra, Harriet Doerr

Realms of Gold, Margaret Drabble

Sister Carrie, Theodore Dreiser

Come Nineveh, Come Tyre, Allen Drury

Rebecca, Daphne du Maurier

The Man Who Loved Cat Dancing, Marilyn Durham

Middlemarch, George Eliot

A Lucky American Childhood, Paul Engle

Love Medicine, Louise Erdrich

That Man Cartwright, Ann Fairbairn

The Sound and the Fury, William Faulkner

The Search for Anna Fisher, Florence Fisher

The Great Gatsby, F. Scott Fitzgerald

Madame Bovary, Gustave Flaubert

A Passage to India, E. M. Forster

The French Lieutenant's Woman, John Fowles

The Women's Room, Marilyn French

Grendel, John Gardner

The Annunciation, Ellen Gilchrist

The Yellow Wallpaper, Charlotte Perkins Gilman

July's People, Nadine Gordimer

Final Payments, Mary Gordon

Without a Guide: Contemporary Women's Travel Adventures,
   Katherine Govier, ed.

The Power and the Glory, Graham Greene

Ordinary People, Judith Guest

Oldest Living Confederate Widow Tells All, Allan Gurganus

Snow Falling on Cedars, David Guterson

Far from the Madding Crowd and *Return of the Native*,
   Thomas Hardy

Games Your Mother Never Taught You, Betty Harragan

I'm OK, You're OK, Thomas Harris

The Scarlet Letter, Nathaniel Hawthorne

Julia, Lillian Hellman

For Whom the Bell Tolls, Ernest Hemingway

My Petition for More Space, John Hersey

Mrs. DeWinter, Susan Hill

A Thief of Time, Tony Hillerman

The Witch's Hammer, Jane Stanton Hitchcock

Smilla's Sense of Snow, Peter Hoeg

A Different Woman and *Families*, Jane Howard

The Death of Common Sense: How Law Is Suffocating America,
   Philip K. Howard

Brave New World, Aldous Huxley

A Doll's House, Henrik Ibsen

A Captive of Time, Olga Ivinskaya

Born to Win, Muriel James and Dorothy Jongeward

The Country of the Pointed Firs, Sarah Orne Jewett

Lake Wobegon Days, Garrison Keillor

Ironweed, William Kennedy

One Flew over the Cuckoo's Nest, Ken Kesey

Animal Dreams, Barbara Kingsolver

Kim, Rudyard Kipling

When Bad Things Happen to Good People, Harold Kushner

The Summer of the Great Grandmother, Madeleine L'Engle

Sarah, Plain and Tall, Patricia MacLachlan

The City of Joy, Dominique Lapierre

Eleanor: The Years Alone, Joseph P. Lash

Lady Chatterley's Lover, D. H. Lawrence

The Birth Order Book, Dr. Kevin Leman

A Sand County Almanac, Aldo Leopold

The Phantom of the Opera, Gaston Leroux

Stepford Wives, Ira Levin

Compulsion, M. Levin

Chronicles of Narnia, C. S. Lewis

Main Street, Sinclair Lewis

Hour of Gold, Hour of Lead, Anne Morrow Lindbergh

West with the Night, Beryl Markham

Chronicle of a Death Foretold, Gabriel García Márquez

Christy, Catherine Marshall

The Goat, the Wolf, and the Crab, Gillian Martin

The Viper's Tangle, Francois Mauriac

So Long, See You Tomorrow, William Maxwell

Angela's Ashes, Frank McCourt

Member of the Wedding, Carson McCullers

Centennial, James Michener

The Crucible, Arthur Miller

Patience and Sarah, Isabel Miller

Please Love Me, Keith Miller

Family Pictures, Sue Miller

Anne of Green Gables, Lucy Maud Montgomery

Life After Life, Raymond Moody

Beloved and *Jazz*, Toni Morrison

The Pursuit of Happiness, David Myers

Megatrends, John Naisbitt

Under the Eye of the Clock, Christopher Nolan

Octopus, Frank Norris

A Good Man Is Hard to Find and *Good Country People*,
   Flannery O'Connor

The English Patient, Michael Ondaatje

You Might as Well Live, Dorothy Parker

Cry, the Beloved Country, Alan Paton

The Road Less Traveled, M. Scott Peck

In Search of Excellence, Tom Peters and Robert Waterman

The Bell Jar, Sylvia Plath

The Shipping News, E. Annie Proulx

Jane and Prudence, Barbara Pym

Atlas Shrugged, Ayn Rand

Where the Red Fern Grows, Wilson Rawls

Trilogy: The Trees, the Field, the Town, Conrad Richter

Even Cowgirls Get the Blues, Tom Robbins

Wicked Loving Lies, Rosemary Rogers

As We Are Now, May Sarton

The Killer Angels, Michael Shaara

Passages and *The Silent Passage*, Gail Sheehy

In His Steps, Charles Sheldon

Frankenstein, Mary Shelley

Sybil, Flora Shreiber

The Penitent, Isaac Bashevis Singer

A Thousand Acres, Jane Smiley

One Day in the Life of Ivan Denisovich, Alexander Solzhenitsyn

Keeping Secrets, Suzanne Somers

Gertrude and Alice, Diana Souhami

The Little Prince, Antoine de Saint-Exupery

Crossing to Safety, Wallace Stegner

The Magician, Sol Stein

Grapes of Wrath, John Steinbeck

Uncle Tom's Cabin, Harriet Beecher Stowe

Pioneer Women: Voices from the Kansas Frontier, Joanna L. Stratton

Gulliver's Travels, Jonathan Swift

The Joy Luck Club, Amy Tan

My Life in the Mafia, Vincent Charles Teresa

Walden, Henry David Thoreau

Lord of the Rings, J. R. Tolkien

Huckleberry Finn, Mark Twain

Kristin Lavransdatter, Sigrid Undset

The Witches of Eastwick, John Updike

Mila 18, Leon Uris

Burr, Gore Vidal

Slaughterhouse Five, Kurt Vonnegut

Jubilee, Margaret Walker

The Bridges of Madison County, Robert James Waller

Montana 1948, Larry Watson

Lives and Loves of a She-Devil, Fay Weldon

Massacre at Fall Creek, Jessamyn West

Ethan Frome, Edith Wharton

The Once and Future King, T. H. White

Brothers and Keepers, John Wideman

Night, Elie Wiesel

The Bridge at San Luis Rey, Thornton Wilder

The Velveteen Rabbit, Margery Williams

Look Homeward Angel, Thomas Wolfe

Winds of War, Herman Wouk

The Word of Yesterday, Stefan Zweig

Book Pairings

JOHN MCFARLAND   SEATTLE, WASHINGTON

The Big Sleep, Raymond Chandler, and *Stick*, Elmore Leonard. The original hard-boiled detective and one of his contemporary equivalents. Guess who won hands down?

Cold Sassy Tree, Olive Ann Burns, and *Stones for Ibarra*, Harriet Doerr. Two wise, loving, and warm novels by contemporary American women of a certain age.

The Handmaid's Tale, Margaret Atwood, and *1984*, George Orwell. Future societies imagined as warnings from artists who worry about the trends they observe.

Venice Observed, Mary McCarthy, and *The Aspern Papers*, Henry James. Nonfiction contemporary classic on Venice and a nineteenth-century novella that describes life in Venice at that time. The surprise is what a page-turner the James novella is, and how vividly he paints the unique experience of living in the city of canals.

Out of Africa, Isak Dinesen, and *White Mischief*, James Fox. Kenya in the early days of coffee plantations and Brits sent away from the country estates because of bad behavior. Dinesen's memoir is in a class with Tolstoy's *Anna Karenina*; Fox's is an indirect indictment of British colonies anywhere.

Old Glory, Jonathan Raban, and *Huckleberry Finn*, Mark Twain. The Mississippi keeps on rolling for contemporary travel writer Raban as he follows the route plotted in Twain's still-exhilarating novel of Huck and his adventures in the messy, untamed America of the nineteenth century.

An American Childhood, Annie Dillard, and *Loitering with Intent*, Muriel Spark. The practice of autobiography, one in a memoir, and one in a riotous novel that could only have emerged from the loopy vision of Muriel Spark.

A Country Year, Sue Hubbell, and *Lives of the Cell*, Lewis Thomas. A naturalist writing about a year on a farm and a scientist's eye view of the universe—precise observation and placing human beings in relation to our cohabitors on the planet.

One Writer's Beginnings, Eudora Welty, and *Summer*, Edith Wharton. Two American women writers, one discussing how she came to be a writer, the other, though her career was winding down, uncompromising in her portrayal of the quality of women's lives under patriarchy.

July's People, Nadine Gordimer, and *A Steam Pig*, James McClure. Literary fiction and detective fiction, both addressing the implications of apartheid for South Africa and Rhodesia.

Berlin Stories, Christopher Isherwood, and *Berlin Diary: 1940–1945*, Marie Vassiltchikov. The city of Berlin in fiction and diary—vivid and scary. Both make you glad not to be living in such a time and place.

Flaubert's Parrot, Julian Barnes, and anything by Gustave Flaubert (*Madame Bovary*, "Temptation of St. Anthony," "Letters from Egypt"). Flaubert in all his guises. A contemplation in novel form by Barnes and Flaubert himself without anyone getting in the way.

Murder in the Cathedral, T. S. Eliot, and any of his poetry ("The Love Song of J. Alfred Prufrock," *The Waste Land*). Our attempt to look at a poet, without concentrating (à la a college poetry course) only on one poem or one theme.

The List

SUSAN MESSER   📖   OAK PARK, ILLINOIS

Angels in America (2 volumes), Tony Kushner. The only play we've ever read. Some members had seen it performed, others found it hard to visualize.

The Bird Artist, Howard Norman. A puzzling book and discussion. Some found the book to be very funny, while others found the circumstances pitiful rather than humorous.

Cave Man's Valentine, George Green. Since we have two psychologists and a psychiatrist in our group, at least some of the discussion centered on the authenticity of the main character's schizophrenia. But this was a really good read.

Crown of Columbus, Michael Dorris and Louise Erdrich. Though we had been intrigued at the idea of a joint project, most considered this minor Erdrich/Dorris.

The Dork of Cork, Chet Raymo

The God of Small Things, Arundhati Roy

The Family Markowitz, Allegra Goodman. The characters and family conflicts portrayed in this book were too painfully familiar to some of the Jewish members of the group (ouch).

Fima, Amos Oz

Foreign Affairs, Alison Lurie

Foucault's Pendulum, Umberto Eco. A serious descent into the arcane. One member did an extensive Internet search on Rosicrucians and other obscure esoteric movements.

Full House, Stephen Jay Gould. Veered off into nonfiction for this exploration of evolution, statistics. Challenging but interesting for the literary types, who often resist nonfiction.

Holder of the World, Bharati Mukherjee

Independent People, Halldór Laxness. The 1955 Nobel Prize winner from Iceland. This was a disturbing book (poverty, disease, loss, exploitation) about a world few of us know much about. We had a small group that night and a good discussion. One member did some research on Iceland and brought photos, including one of the sod houses.

Iona Moon, Melanie Rae Thon

The Killer Angels, Michael Shaara. For the Civil War buffs.

A Lesson Before Dying, Ernest Gaines

Like Water for Chocolate, Laura Esquivel

Longitude, Dava Sobel. Another nonfiction foray. We joked about waiting for the sequel. See if you can guess the title.

Memoirs of a Geisha, Arthur Golden

The Moor's Last Sigh, Salman Rushdie

Mysteries of Pittsburgh, Michael Chabon

Open Secrets, Alice Munro. Gorgeous writing, but the group isn't very good at discussing short stories.

A Piece of My Heart, Richard Ford. Most of the group couldn't stand this book or at least found it very hard to read. A couple members even claimed to have lost it shortly after they bought it.

The Reader, Bernhard Schlink

RL's Dream, Walter Mosley

Snow Falling on Cedars, David Guterson

So Far from God, Ana Castillo

Son of the Circus, John Irving. I gave up on this book after about two hundred pages, but we've got some serious John Irving fans in the group.

Stone Diaries, Carol Shields

The Storyteller, Mario Vargas Llosa

Turtle Moon, Alice Hoffman

When I Was Puerto Rican, Esmeralda Santiago

The Wind-Up Bird Chronicle, Haruki Murakami. This book generated an excellent discussion; almost everyone loved it.

Wuthering Heights, Emily Brontë. It's a pleasure to reread the classics.

The Saturday Night Book Group Book List

MAY MOSKOWITZ   SOUTHFIELD, MICHIGAN

LITTLE DID MY husband and I know in 1973 when we invited a group of friends to our home to discuss the possibility of starting a couples' book discussion group that over the years this group would play such an important part in our lives.

Twenty-six years after our formation, we now have three couples from our original eight. People have moved and unfortunately some have died. We have added members over the years. We now have six couples and four widows. Most of our present members have belonged for more than fifteen years. Our newest member married into the group in 1990.

We have people who prefer fiction to nonfiction books and vice versa, so we have settled on the practice of alternating our choices between these two types of books. Over the years, we have had members who haven't read the assigned book, but an occasional group discussion of this general problem has usually remedied it.

Our members truly like and respect each other. We have read many books that we ordinarily would not have read and gained new perspectives on most of them. At each ten-year anniversary of our group, we hold a party at a restaurant. This year, at our twenty-sixth anniversary, we decided not to wait for our thirtieth anniversary to celebrate. We now plan to hold a party every five years.

At our party, we chose our own Pulitzer Prize winners among the books we read in the last six years. Our favorite book was *The Color of Water* by James McBride. We had a three-way tie for our next favorite. *Ishmael* by Daniel Quinn, *Stones from the River* by Ursula Hegi, and *Wild Swans* by Jung Chang were the runners-up.

1973–83

Future Shock, Alvin Toffler

Book of Daniel, E. L. Doctorow

Female Eunuch, Germaine Greer

The Israelis, Amos Elon

Making of a Psychiatrist, David Viscott

Beyond Freedom and Dignity, B. F. Skinner

First Circle, Alexander Solzhenitsyn

Invisible Man, Ralph Ellison

Rhinoceros, Eugene Ionesco

Harvest Home, Thomas Tryon

Pursuit of Loneliness, Philip Slater

The Best and the Brightest, David Halberstam

O' Jerusalem, Larry Collins

Boss, Mike Royko

Kruschev Remembers, Nikita Kruschev

Travels with Charlie, John Steinbeck

Sheila Levine Is Dead and Living in New York, Gail Parent

Fear of Flying, Erica Jong

Ragtime, E. L. Doctorow

Family Moskat, Isaac Bashevis Singer

Catch-22, Joseph Heller

Small Is Beautiful, E. F. Schumacher

Passover Plot, H. Schonfield

Passages, Gail Sheehy

Wheels of Love, Joyce Carol Oates

Drive for Power, Arnold Hutschnecker

Humboldt's Gift, Saul Bellow

Lillian Hellman's Plays, Lillian Hellman

A Man Called Intrepid, William Stevenson

Falconer, John Cheever

Cat's Cradle, Kurt Vonnegut

Burr, Gore Vidal

Big Money, John Dos Passos

The Night Is Dark and We Are Far from Home, Jonathan Kozol

The Future of China, Ross Terrill

Lives of a Cell, Lewis Thomas

1984, George Orwell

Painted Bird, Jerzy Kosinski

Being There, Jerzy Kosinski

The Russians, Hedrick Smith

Good As Gold, Joseph Heller

Bend in the River, V. S. Naipaul

Number Our Days, Barbara Myerhoff

Song of Solomon, Toni Morrison

The Brethren, Bob Woodward

Dragons of Eden, Carl Sagan

Triple, Ken Follett

Third Wave, Alvin Toffler

Confederacy of Dunces, John Kennedy Toole

Plainly Speaking, Merle Miller

The Stranger, Albert Camus

The Dollmaker, Harriette Arnow

Death in Venice, Thomas Mann

Double Helix, James Watson

The Price, Arthur Miller
The Slave, Isaac Bashevis Singer

1984–93
Passions of the Mind, Irving Stone
Woman Warrior, Maxine Hong Kingston
My Michael, Amos Oz
Megatrends, John Naisbitt
Meridian, Alice Walker
Letters from the Earth, Mark Twain
Elsewhere Perhaps, Amos Oz
The Little Drummer Girl, John Le Carré
Hard Times, Studs Terkel
The Kennedys, John Davis
Davita's Harp, Chaim Potok
In My Mother's House, Kim Chernin
The Joke, Milan Kundera
Accidental Tourist, Anne Tyler
Medusa and the Snail, Lewis Thomas
Iacocca, Lee Iacocca
Contact, Carl Sagan
Lord of the Flies, William Golding
Lonesome Dove, Larry McMurtry
The Handmaid's Tale, Margaret Atwood
Cold Sassy Tree, Olive Ann Burns
Crossing to Safety, Wallace Stegner
Presumed Innocent, Scott Turow
Veil, Bob Woodward
Summons to Memphis, Peter Taylor
Bonfire of the Vanities, Tom Wolfe
A Yellow Raft in Blue Water, Michael Dorris

Timebends, Arthur Miller

The Closing of the American Mind, Allan Bloom

Bless Me Ultima, Rudolfo Anaya

The March of Folly, Barbara Tuchman

Waiting for the Barbarians, J. M. Coetzee

Paris Trout, Peter Dexter

The Reckoning, David Halberstam

My Name Is Asher Lev, Chaim Potok

The Remains of the Day, Kazuo Ishiguro

Acquainted with the Night, Lynne Sharon Schwartz

Loving Kindness, Anne Roiphe

A Late Divorce, A. B. Yehoshua

Inside Outside, Herman Wouk

Surely You're Joking Mr. Feynman, Richard Feynman

Sleepwalking Through History, Haynes Johnson

To Dance with the White Dog, Terry Kay

Saint Maybe, Anne Tyler

Einstein, Ronald Clark

Arab and Jew, David Shipler

1993–99

Devil's Night, Ze'ev Chafets

Eleanor Roosevelt, Blanche Wiesen Cook

Rising Sun, John Toland

Mr. Mani, A. B. Yehoshua

Lost in Translations, Eva Hoffman

She's Come Undone, Wally Lamb

Clear and Present Danger, Tom Clancy

Staggerford, Jon Hassler

The Secret History, Donna Tartt

Mezuzzah in the Madonna's Foot, Trudi Alexy

Flowers in the Blood, Gay Courter

The Jew in the Lotus, Roger Kamenetz

Montana 1948, Larry Watson

Ishmael, Daniel Quinn

Stones from the River, Ursula Hegi

No Ordinary Time, Doris Kearns Goodwin

Snow Falling on Cedars, David Guterson

The Cunning Man, Robertson Davies

Ben Bradlee: A Good Life, Ben Bradlee

Mother Night, Kurt Vonnegut

The Color of Water, James McBride

Pigs in Heaven, Barbara Kingsolver

Walk to Freedom, Nelson Mandela

Independent People, Halldór Laxness

Wild Swans, Jung Chang

A Civil Action, Jonathan Harr

Angela's Ashes, Frank McCourt

A Reporter's Life, Walter Cronkite

Shadow Man, Mary Gordon

The Reader, Bernhard Schlink

Some American Books

DAVE NARTER   📖   CHICAGO, ILLINOIS

The Young Nation
The Scarlet Letter, Nathaniel Hawthorne
The Awakening, Kate Chopin
Uncle Tom's Cabin, Harriet Beecher Stowe
The Adventures of Tom Sawyer, Mark Twain

Early Twentieth Century
Their Eyes Were Watching God, Zora Neale Hurston
The Call of the Wild, Jack London
The Grapes of Wrath and *East of Eden*, John Steinbeck
The Forty-Second Parallel, John Dos Passos
A Farewell to Arms and *The Sun Also Rises*, Ernest Hemingway
Native Son, Richard Wright

Some Great Southerners
A Light in August and *The Sound and the Fury*, William Faulkner
Wise Blood and *A Good Man Is Hard to Find*, Flannery O'Connor
The Confessions of Nat Turner, William Styron
All the Pretty Horses and *The Crossing*, Cormac McCarthy

The Non-Conformists
Johnny Got His Gun, Dalton Trumbo
One Flew over the Cuckoo's Nest, Ken Kesey
On the Road, Jack Kerouac
Catch-22, Joseph Heller
Slaughterhouse Five, *Cat's Cradle*, *The Sirens of Titan*, *Mother Night*,
    and *Player Piano*, Kurt Vonnegut
A Confederacy of Dunces, John Kennedy Toole

The East Coast
The Catcher in the Rye and *Franny and Zooey*, J. D. Salinger
Goodbye Columbus, Philip Roth
A Prayer for Owen Meany, John Irving

Some Great Plays
Long Day's Journey into Night, Eugene O'Neill
Death of a Salesman, Arthur Miller
Who's Afraid of Virginia Woolf?, Edward Albee

Some of Today's Finest
Ragtime, E. L. Doctorow
Song of Solomon and *Beloved*, Toni Morrison
The Handmaid's Tale, Margaret Atwood (from our 51st state)
Continental Drift, Russell Banks
A Thousand Acres, Jane Smiley
Maus and *Maus II*, Art Speigelman

Nonfiction
There Are No Children Here, Alex Kotlowitz
The Beauty Myth, Naomi Wolf
The Content of Our Character, Shelby Steele
Savage Inequalities, Jonathan Kozol
An American Childhood, Annie Dillard

Selected Discussion Books: Des Plaines Public Library

CHRISTINE POSINGER   DES PLAINES, ILLINOIS

Waiting to Exhale, Terry McMillan. The group thoroughly enjoyed the four women in this novel but objected to the racy language.

The Joy Luck Club, Amy Tan. This book explores the generational differences between four Chinese American women and their mothers. It was a huge success.

Hotel du Lac, Anita Brookner. All of us disliked Brookner's writing style.

The House on Mango Street, Sandra Cisneros. This book was warmly received; the Chicago setting was a factor in that.

The Playboy of the Western World, John Millington Synge. Yes, we did a play! And, while we had a smaller group than usual, it was one of our best and most heated discussions. We even had two men attend.

A Christmas Memory, *One Christmas*, and *The Thanksgiving Visitor*, Truman Capote. Everyone loved this holiday selection, but agreed there wasn't much to discuss.

Paula, Isabel Allende. Allende's memoir telling the story of her family was a difficult book to read.

Cold Sassy Tree, Olive Ann Burns. The group raved about this book.

Snow Falling on Cedars, David Guterson. As good as it gets! Guterson's haunting story provided us with many good discussion topics.

Into the Forest, Jean Hegland. Our group really enjoyed this novel set in the near future. They were able to speculate on how they would cope if placed in similar circumstances.

The God of Small Things, Arundhati Roy. With its exotic locale and lush language, this prize-winning novel was different from any other book we read. A first-rate discussion.

The Magician's Assistant, Ann Patchett. A very popular choice.

Pope Joan, Donna Woolfolk Cross. This historical novel brings the legend of a woman who ascends the papal throne to life. This was our group's favorite book.

A Civil Action, Jonathan Harr. An eye-opening account of how the law works. Good discussion.

Cold Mountain, Charles Frazier. A wounded Confederate soldier heads home to Cold Mountain. The group liked this book.

The Ann Arbor Society of the Written Word Book List

PAUL D. REINGOLD   ANN ARBOR, MICHIGAN

As THE KEEPER of the list, I have added to it (in parentheses) the books that I have read at about the same time, by the same author. So for me, the list includes not just the official monthly selections, but also the books I read in the months shortly before or after our meeting because we had selected that author. The list reflects the order in which we read the titles.

1982–98

The Autobiography of Alice B. Toklas, Gertrude Stein

Burger's Daughter, Nadine Gordimer

Ballad of the Sad Cafe, Stories, and *A Member of the Wedding*, Carson McCullers

Billiards at Half-Past Nine, Heinrich Böll

Enemies, A Love Story, *Seance*, and *The Magician of Lublin*, Isaac Bashevis Singer

The Horse's Mouth, Joyce Cary

Bellefleur, Joyce Carol Oates

War and Peace, Leo Tolstoy

The Return of Eva Peron, Guerrillas, and *(A Bend in the River)*,
  V. S. Naipaul

Life on the Mississippi and *The Mysterious Stranger and Stories*,
  Mark Twain

The Stories and *The Wapshot Chronicle*, John Cheever

The Woman Warrior, Maxine Hong Kingston

Coming up for Air and *Homage to Catalonia*, George Orwell

The Professor's House and *Death Comes for the Archbishop*,
  Willa Cather

Stories, Franz Kafka

The Book of Laughter and Forgetting and *The Unbearable Lightness
  of Being*, Milan Kundera

July's People, Nadine Gordimer

Waiting for the Barbarians, J. M. Coetzee

Cry, the Beloved Country, Alan Paton

You Can't Go Home Again, Thomas Wolfe

Light Years, (A Sport and a Pastime), and *(Solo Faces)*, James Salter

The Human Comedy and *My Name Is Aram*, William Saroyan

Gabriela, and *Clove and Cinnamon*, Jorge Amado

I Know Why the Caged Bird Sings and *Heart of a Woman*,
  Maya Angelou

Fathers and Sons and *On the Eve* [of Revolution], Ivan Turgenev

The Color Purple, Alice Walker

Their Eyes Were Watching God, Zora Neale Hurston

The Complete Stories, Flannery O'Connor

The Complete Stories, Eudora Welty

People of the Abyss, The Sea Wolf, The Call of the Wild, and *White
  Fang and Stories*, Jack London

*The Defense, Invitation to a Beheading, Pale Fire, Lolita, Speak,
  Memory*, and *(Pnin)*, Vladimir Nabokov

Bleak House, Charles Dickens

The Forty-Second Parallel, Nineteen Nineteen, The Big Money, and
  (The U.S.A. Trilogy), John Dos Passos

The Baron in the Trees and *Marcovaldo*, Italo Calvino

The Dollmaker, Harriette Arnow

Shiloh and Other Stories, Bobbie Ann Mason

The Late Bourgeois World, Nadine Gordimer

The Life and Times of Michael K., J. M. Coetzee

Legs, Billy Phelan's Greatest Game, Ironweed, and *(The Albany Trilogy)*, William Kennedy

Under the Volcano, Malcolm Lowry

During the Reign of the Queen of Persia, Joan Chase

Shoeless Joe, W. P. Kinsella

The Conservationist, Nadine Gordimer

A Story Like the Wind, Laurens Van der Post

The Idiot, Fyodor Dostoyevsky

A Passage to India, A Room with a View, and *(Maurice)*, E. M. Forster

The Adventures of Tom Sawyer and *Huckleberry Finn*, Mark Twain

The Lost Honor of Katarina Blum, The Clown, and *(Group Portrait with Lady)*, Heinrich Böll

Love Medicine, Louise Erdrich

The Moccasin Telegraph, W. P. Kinsella

Stones for Ibarra, Harriet Doerr

Things Fall Apart, A Man of the People, and *No Longer at Ease*, Chinua Achebe

The Heart of the Matter and *The Power and the Glory*, Graham Greene

Fifth Business, The Manticore, World of Wonders, (The Deptford Trilogy), and *(The Rebel Angels)*, Robertson Davies

Victory over Japan, In the Land of Dreamy Dreams, and *The Annunciation*, Ellen Gilchrist

Madame Bovary, Gustave Flaubert

Flaubert's Parrot, Julian Barnes

Waterland, (The Sweetshop Owner), (Shuttlecock), Graham Swift

The Periodic Table and *If Not Now, When?*, Primo Levi

Son of the Morning Star, Evan S. Connell

The Transit of Venus, Shirley Hazzard

The Bone People, Keri Hulme

The Good Conscience, The Old Gringo, and *(Distant Relations)*,
  Carlos Fuentes

A Tale of Two Cities, Charles Dickens

Lucky Jim, I Like It Here, (One Fat Englishman), and *(The Anti-
  Death League)*, Kingsley Amis

The Magic Mountain, Thomas Mann

*Cakes and Ale, The Razor's Edge, The Moon and Sixpence, (Of
  Human Bondage)*, Somerset Maugham

What's Bred in the Bone and *(The Salterton Trilogy: Tempest-Tost,
  Leaven of Malice, A Mixture of Frailties)*, Robertson Davies

The Prince of Tides, Pat Conroy

Lady Oracle, Margaret Atwood

The Diviners, Margaret Laurence

A Summons to Memphis, The Old Forest, and *(In the Miro District)*,
  Peter Taylor

Nostromo and *(Victory)*, Joseph Conrad

Jane and Prudence, A Few Green Leaves, and *(Excellent Women)*,
  Barbara Pym

Song of Solomon and *Beloved*, Toni Morrison

The Moonstone and *(The Woman in White)*, Wilkie Collins

Bandits and *(La Brava)*, Elmore Leonard

Famous Last Words and *Not Wanted on the Voyage*, Timothy Findley

Dona Flor and Her Two Husbands and *Captains of the Sands*,
  Jorge Amado

Angle of Repose, Crossing to Safety, and *(The Sound of Mountain
  Water)*, Wallace Stegner

The Bonfire of the Vanities, Tom Wolfe

Out of Africa, Isak Dinesen

West with the Night, Beryl Markham

House of the Spirits and *(Of Love and Shadows)*, Isabel Allende

A Yellow Raft in Blue Water, Michael Dorris

The Master and Margarita, Mikael Bulgakov

Love in the Time of Cholera, Gabriel García Márquez

A Dry White Season, *An Instant in the Wind*, and *(The Ambassador)*, Andre Brink

Skinwalkers, *A Thief of Time*, *(Talking God)*, *(The Ghostway)*, *(The Dark Wind)*, *(People of Darkness)*, *(Listening Woman)*, *(Dance Hall of the Dead)*, *(The Blessing Way)*, and *(The Fly on the Wall)*, Tony Hillerman

Celestial Navigation and *Breathing Lessons*, Anne Tyler

Johnny Got His Gun, Dalton Trumbo

All Quiet on the Western Front, Erich Maria Remarque

The Wars, Timothy Findley

To the Lighthouse, *A Room of One's Own*, *Three Guineas*, and *The Waves*, Virginia Woolf

The Assault, Harry Mulisch

The Fall, Albert Camus

The Joy Luck Club, Amy Tan

The Mambo Kings Sing Songs of Love, Oscar Hijuelos

The Sheltering Sky, Paul Bowles

The Wine of Astonishment, Earl Lovelace

You Alone Are Dancing, Brenda Flanagan

The Mystic Masseuse, V. S. Naipaul

The Bean Trees and *Homeland and Other Stories*, Barbara Kingsolver

Vineland, Thomas Pynchon

Jane Eyre, Charlotte Brontë

The Wide Sargasso Sea, Jean Rhys

The Black Box, Amos Oz

See: Under Love, David Grossman

Imagining Argentina, Lawrence Thornton

The Widows, Ariel Dorfman

Where I'm Calling From, Raymond Carver

An Artist of the Floating World and *The Remains of the Day*, Kazuo
    Ishiguro

Possession, A. S. Byatt

Northanger Abbey, Jane Austen

Frankenstein, Mary Shelley

The Good Soldier, Ford Madox Ford

Portrait of the Artist as a Young Man and *Dubliners*, James Joyce

The Awakening, Kate Chopin

Howards End, E. M. Forster

A Thousand Acres and *Ordinary Love and Good Will*, Jane Smiley

Heat and Dust, Ruth Prawer Jhabvala

The Confessions of Nat Turner, William Styron

The Bridges of Madison County, Robert James Waller

Fried Green Tomatoes at the Whistle Stop Café, Fannie Flagg

The Spectator Bird, *The Collected Stories*, and *Essays: Where the
    Bluebird Sings to the Lemonade Springs*, Wallace Stegner

The Girl on the Swing, Richard Adams

The Saddest Pleasure, Moritz Thomsen

All the Pretty Horses, *(Blood Meridian)*, *(The Crossing)*, and *(Cities
    of the Plain)*, Cormac McCarthy

Sailor's Song, Ken Kesey

Animal Dreams and *Pigs in Heaven*, Barbara Kingsolver

Ethan Frome and *The House of Mirth*, Edith Wharton

Hotel du Lac and *Providence*, Anita Brookner

The Smile of the Lamb, David Grossman

A Good Scent from a Strange Mountain, Robert Olen Butler

The Things They Carried and *(Going After Cacciato)*, Tim O'Brien

The Commitments, *The Snapper*, *The Van*, and *(Paddy Clark Ha Ha
    Ha)*, Roddy Doyle

Babette's Feast and other Anecdotes of Destiny, Isak Dinesen

Like Water for Chocolate, Laura Esquivel

The English Patient, Michael Ondaatje

The Shipping News, E. Annie Proulx

Changing Places and *(Paradise News)*, David Lodge

Ceremony, Leslie Marmon Silko

The Delicacy and Strength of Lace, James Wright

Anna Karenina, Leo Tolstoy

Silence and *(Deep River)*, Shusaku Endo

A Very Long Engagement, Sebastien Japrisot

Black Rain, Masuji Ibuse

A Frolic of One's Own, William Gaddis

Snow Falling on Cedars, David Guterson

Spartina, John Casey

Places in the World a Woman Could Walk and *Obscene Gestures for Women*, Janet Kauffman

Edisto and *Edisto Revisited*, Padgett Powell

House of Splendid Isolation, Edna O'Brien

Moo, Jane Smiley

The Sportswriter, *(Independence Day)*, and *(Rock Springs)*, Richard Ford

Therapy, David Lodge

Stones from the River, Ursula Hegi

The Great Gatsby, *Tender Is the Night*, and *(This Side of Paradise)*, F. Scott Fitzgerald

A Good Man in Africa, *(An Ice Cream War)*, and *(The Blue Afternoon)*, William Boyd

Middlemarch, George Eliot

The Woman Who Walked into Doors, Roddy Doyle

Last Orders, Graham Swift

The Robber Bride, Margaret Atwood

Vanity Fair, William Makepeace Thackery

The Blue Flower, Penelope Fitzgerald

Independent People, Halldór Laxness

The Sleeping Car Murders, One Deadly Summer, Lady in a Car with Glasses and a Gun, and *(Trap for Cinderella)*, Sebastien Japrisot

The God of Small Things, Arundhati Roy

Behind the Scenes at the Museum, Kate Atkinson

Midnight in the Garden of Good and Evil, John Berendt

Light in August, William Faulkner

The Ghost Road, (Regeneration), (The Eye in the Door), (World War I Trilogy), Pat Barker

First Light, Charles Baxter

A Fine Balance, Rohinton Mistry

The Honorary Consul and *Our Man in Havana*, Graham Greene

Tell Me a Riddle, Tillie Olsen

Gorilla, My Love, Toni Cade Bambara

Friend of My Youth and *(Selected Stories)*, Alice Munro

The Poisonwood Bible, Barbara Kingsolver

The Sea, The Sea and *A Severed Head*, Iris Murdoch

Affliction, Russell Banks

Cities of the Plain, Cormac McCarthy

Fugitive Pieces, Anne Michaels

Dreaming in Cuban, Cristina Garcia

How the Garcia Girls Lost Their Accents, Julia Alvarez

Cold Mountain, Charles Frazier

Memoirs of a Geisha, Arthur Golden

Fairview Lake Book Group Reading List, 1995–99

KATHARINE W. RICE   📖   CHAPPAQUA, NEW YORK

Fiction

The Scarlet Letter, Nathaniel Hawthorne. A classic, but worthy of being discussed anew.

A Month of Sundays, John Updike. Another minister's adulterous affair. Lively discussion.

Philadelphia Fire, John Wideman. An impassioned work by one of America's best black writers. Based on a true event.

Of Human Bondage, Somerset Maugham. Classic English novel. We also viewed the movie version.

The Stone Diaries, Carol Shields. Pulitzer Prize winner. Not everyone thought it deserved it.

Madame Bovary, Gustave Flaubert. Another classic. Most thought it worth reading, but disliked Mme. B. herself.

Anna Karenina, Leo Tolstoy. One of the greatest female characters ever created. Fascinating to us all, and oh, those movie versions.

The Awakening, Kate Chopin. Again, a wife who leaves her family. Beautifully written and liked by all. Most had never heard of this book before.

Ladder of Years, Anne Tyler. Our co-leaders disagreed on the virtues of this one, so discussion got lively.

The Giver, Lois Lowery. Written for young adults, but all of us got some insight from it.

The Handmaid's Tale, Margaret Atwood. Chilling it its depiction of the future. Excellent movie version.

Paris Trout, Peter Dexter. Strong stuff and vivid characters. None of us had read it before. Again, a good movie.

The Cunning Man, Robertson Davies. One of Canada's best writers. New to most of us and well liked.

Points of View. An anthology of short stories. For four years we read two or three stories from it for one meeting, all by well-known authors from various eras.

The Cat, Georges Simenon. A change of pace by a mystery writer. Members found it intriguing, quick, and easy to read.

House of Splendid Isolation, Edna O'Brien. Hauntingly beautiful. Ireland during the Troubles. It opened our eyes in many ways.

The Riders, Tim Winton. Strange and challenging. Each of us had a different interpretation of who the Riders were.

The All of It, Jeanette Haien. A gem of a small novel. New to all of us, and well received.

Alice's Adventures in Wonderland, Lewis Carroll. We talked mostly about the author himself and his various hang-ups.

The God of Small Things, Arundhati Roy. One of our co-leaders said, "I hated it but couldn't get it out of my mind." Best discussion ever.

As I Lay Dying, William Faulkner. Not pleasant to read, but easier to manage than most Faulkner novels.

The Giant's House, Elizabeth McCracken. Surely one of the most unusual love stories ever published. Comments ranged from dumb to superb.

Ironweed, William Kennedy. Grim, but good for us to read. Like taking a dose of medicine?

Metamorphosis, Franz Kafka. Suggested by one of our members. Weird and fascinating.

Ceremony, Leslie Marmon Silko. Our first venture into literature about Native Americans.

Nonfiction

Conundrum, Jan Morris. Author undergoes a sex change. Beautiful writing saves it from sensationalism. Good discussion.

Libby, Betty John, ed. Letters and diaries of her grandmother's life on a remote island. Loved by all of us; probably our favorite of all the books read.

The Uses of Enchantment, Bruno Bettelheim. Psychologist writes of the place of fairy tales in our lives. Tough going for most of us, and we read only parts of it.

Darkness Visible, William Styron. The author's triumph over deep depression. Sparked lengthy discussion of mental illness.

Under the Tuscan Sun, Frances Mayes. Charming travel memoir. We thought the author was rather a snob.

Angela's Ashes, Frank McCourt. A bestseller, and deservedly so. Heartbreaking yet humorous. A few found it difficult to deal with.

The Color of Water, James McBride. Touching memoir about the author's mother. All of us found her to be fascinating and admirable. We compared her to Frank McCourt's mother in *Angela's Ashes*.

Red Azalea, Anchee Min. Growing up in China during the Revolution. Another strong woman.

The Undertaking, Thomas Lynch. Essays on life and death and love by an undertaker who is also a published poet. Marvelous meat for discussion.

How Wal-Mart Is Destroying the U.S.A., Bill Quinn. Everyone in America should read this little book.

Tender at the Bone, Ruth Reichl. Charming memoir by a former New York restaurant critic. Lighter fare for our summer reading; easy to digest.

Personal History, Katharine Graham. Her life thus far. Well written, but did it deserve a Pulitzer Prize? Not everyone thought so.

Poetry
Anne Sexton, best discussion
Sylvia Plath
Elizabeth Bishop
Dorothy Parker
Nikki Giovanni
Mary Oliver
Emily Dickinson
Billy Collins (at last, a male poet!)

Almost Complete List—
Firstar Book
Discussion Group

JOAN ROZANSKI   📖   MILWAUKEE, WISCONSIN

Affliction, Russell Banks
The Age of Grief, Jane Smiley
Angle of Repose, Wallace Stegner
Animal Dreams, Barbara Kingsolver
All the Pretty Horses, Cormac McCarthy
Annie John, Jamaica Kincaid
At Weddings and Wakes, Alice McDermott
Bailey's Cafe, Gloria Naylor
Bastard out of Carolina, Dorothy Allison
The Bean Trees, Barbara Kingsolver
Beloved, Toni Morrison
Best Laid Plans, Gail Parent
Betsey Brown, Ntozake Shange
Beyond Deserving, Sandra Scofield

The Book of Ruth, Jane Hamilton

Bridges of Madison County, Robert James Waller

The Broken Cord, Michael Dorris

The Chant of Jimmy Blacksmith, Thomas Keneally

Charms for the Easy Life, Kaye Gibbons

Cloudstreet, Tim Winton

Cold Sassy Tree, Olive Ann Burns

The Color Purple, Alice Walker

Continental Drift, Russell Banks

Creek Mary's Blood, Dee Brown

Crossing to Safety, Wallace Stegner

Daisy Fay and the Miracle Man, Fannie Flagg

Dandelion Wine, Ray Bradbury

Daughters, Paule Marshall

Dinner at the Homesick Restaurant, Anne Tyler

Dreams of Sleep, Josephine Humphreys

East Is East, T. Coraghessan Boyle

The Education of Little Tree, Forrest Carter

Family Dancing, David Leavitt

A Farm Under a Lake, Martha Berglund

Fear and Loathing in Las Vegas, Hunter S. Thompson

Floating in My Mother's Palm, Ursula Hegi

Foster Child, Mary Bauer

Gaston's War, Gaston Vandermeersche

Gather Together in My Name, Maya Angelou

Good Hearts, Reynolds Price

Goodbye Without Leaving, Laurie Colwin

Gorky Park, Martin Cruz Smith

The Handmaid's Tale, Margaret Atwood

Her First American, Lore Segal

Hotel du Lac, Anita Brookner

Housekeeping, Marilynne Robinson
How the García Girls Lost Their Accents, Julia Alvarez
How to Make an American Quilt, Whitney Otto
Hug Dancing, Shelby Hearon
I Been There Before, David Carkeet
I Heard the Owl Call My Name, Margaret Craven
I Know Why the Caged Bird Sings, Maya Angelou
If the River Was Whiskey, T. Coraghessan Boyle
I'm Dancing As Fast As I Can, Barbara Gordon
In Country, Bobbie Ann Mason
Iron and Silk, Mark Salzman
It's Raining in Mango, Thea Astley
Jailbird, Kurt Vonnegut
The Joy Luck Club, Amy Tan
Just Above My Head, James Baldwin
Kaffir Boy, Mark Mathabane
Kate Vaiden, Reynolds Price
Leaving the Land, Douglas Ungar
Legacies, Bette Bao Lord
The Life of Helen Alone, Karen Lawrence
Like Water for Chocolate, Laura Esquivel
Lives of the Poets, E. L. Doctorow
Lonesome Dove, Larry McMurtry
Love in the Time of Cholera, Gabriel García Márquez
The Lover, Marguerite Duras
Lovingkindness, Anne Roiphe
Lying Low, Diane Johnson
Lucy, Jamaica Kincaid
Marvin and Tige, F. Glass
Maus, Art Spiegelman
Middle Passage, Charles Johnson

The Middleman and Other Stories, Bharati Mukherjee
Morgan's Passing, Anne Tyler
Mrs. Peabody's Inheritance, Elizabeth Jolley
The Object of My Affection, Stephan McCauley
The Oldest Living Confederate Widow Tells All, Allan Gurganus
Palomino, Elizabeth Jolley
Paris Trout, Peter Dexter
Pastorale, Susan Engberg
Patrimony, Philip Roth
Pentimento, Lillian Hellman
A Piece of Mine, J. California Cooper
The Progress of Love, Alice Munro
Ragtime, E. L. Doctorow
Raw Silk, Janet Burroway
The Remains of the Day, Kazuo Ishiguro
Rich in Love, Josephine Humphreys
Russian Journal, Andrea Lee
Say Goodbye to Sam, Michael Arlen
Self-Help, Lorrie Moore
Seventh Heaven, Alice Hoffman
Sheila Levine Is Dead and Living in New York, Gail Parent
The Sheltering Sky, Paul Bowles
Sleeping Arrangements, Laura Cunningham
Spartina, John Casey
Spence + Lila, Bobbie Ann Mason
A Story Like the Wind, Laurens Van der Post
Starting in the Middle, Judith Wax
Strange Fits of Passion, Anita Shreve
A Summons to Memphis, Peter Taylor
A Taste for Death, P. D. James
Testing the Current, William McPherson

Their Eyes Were Watching God, Zora Neale Hurston

Then She Found Me, Elinor Lipman

To Dance with the White Dog, Terry Kay

Toots in Solitude, John Yount

Tracks, Louise Erdrich

Two Old Women, Velma Willis

Typical American, Gish Jen

Utz, Bruce Chatwin

Variations in the Night, Emily Listfield

Victory over Japan, Ellen Gilchrist

Waiting to Exhale, Terry McMillan

Waking, Eva Figes

The Way Men Act, Elinor Lipman

White Palace, Glenn Savan

White Swan, Frances Turk

A Woman of Independent Means, Elizabeth Forsythe Hailey

The World Around Midnight, Patricia Browning Griffith

A Yellow Raft in Blue Water, Michael Dorris

More Recent Reads

Bitter Grounds, Sandra Benitez

Carolina Moon, Jill McCorkle

A Chance to See Egypt, Sandra Scofield

Divine Secrets of the Ya-Ya Sisterhood, Rebecca Wells

Into the Forest, Jean Hegland

The Mistress of Spices, Chitra Banerjee Divakaruni

The Road from Coorain, Jill Ker Conway

Sights Unseen, Kaye Gibbons

True North, Jill Ker Conway

Tuesdays with Morrie, Mitch Albom

And Ladies of the Club Book List

DOROTHY A. RUTISHAUSER   AUSTIN, TEXAS

OUR GROUP IS called "And Ladies of the Club" after the first book we read together. We are a group of twenty-five, though only about fifteen make it to any given meeting. We all read the book—usually. A rotating committee chooses the list of books for each year.

1985–86
And Ladies of the Club, Helen Hooven Santmyer
The Discoverers, Daniel Boorstin
Megatrends, John Naisbitt
The Third Wave, Alvin Toffler
Heart of Darkness, Joseph Conrad
The Road Less Traveled, M. Scott Peck
Lake Wobegon Days, Garrison Keillor
Depths of Glory, Irving Stone
Women of the Four Winds, Elizabeth Fagg Olds
Galina, Galina Vishnevskaya
Peter the Great, Robert Massie

Lonesome Dove, Larry McMurtry

1986–87
Kristin Lavransdatter, Sigrid Undset
Portrait of a Marriage, Nigel Nicholson
Emma, Jane Austen
Son of the Revolution, Liang Heng, et al.
Benito Cereno, Herman Melville
Cheri and *The Last of Cheri*, Colette
The King Must Die and *The Bull from the Sea*, Mary Renault
I, Claudius and *Claudius, the God*, Robert Graves
Parallel Lives, Phyllis Rose
The House of Mitford, Jonathan and Catherine Guinness

1987–88
Crime and Punishment, Fyodor Dostoyevsky
West with the Night, Beryl Markham
Wind, Sand, and Stars, Antoine de Saint-Exupery
The Real Thing, Tom Stoppard
The Age of Innocence, Edith Wharton
The Odyssey, Homer
The Greek Way, Edith Hamilton
The Serpent and the Rainbow, E. Wade Davos
The Thanatos Syndrome, Walker Percy
Confederacy of Dunces, John Kennedy Toole
An Academic Question, Barbara Pym

1988–89
Fire and Blood, T. R. Fehrenbach
Love in the Time of Cholera, Gabriel García Márquez
Darwin and the Beagle, Alan Moorehead
Man and Superman, Candida, and *The Devil's Disciple*, George
 Bernard Shaw

Cold Sassy Tree, Olive Ann Burns

Canterbury Tales, Chaucer

Life and Times of Chaucer, John Gardner

All Passions Spent, A Room of One's Own, and *Mrs. Dalloway*,
   Virginia Woolf

Clementine, Mary Sommes

The Last Lion, William Manchester

Montaillou, Emmanuel Le Roy Ladurie

The Fatal Shore, Robert Hughes

The Songlines, Bruce Chatwin

1989–90

Uncle Vanya and *The Cherry Orchard*, Anton Chekhov

Land of the Firebird, Suzann Massie

Anna Karenina, Leo Tolstoy

Lev and Sonya, Louise Smoluchowski

A Tale of Two Cities, Charles Dickens

Happy All the Time and *Family Happiness*, Laurie Colwin

The Republic, Plato

Democracy in America, Alexis de Tocqueville

The Closed Circle, David Pryce-Jones

Midaq Alley, Naguib Mahfouz

Bonfire of the Vanities, Tom Wolfe

Eleanor of Aquitaine, Marian Meade

Eleanor and the Four Kings, Amy Kelly

1990–91

The Quincunx, Charles Palliser

The Making of Modern Austin: Power, Money, and People,
   Anthony Orum

The Storyteller, Mario Vargas Llosa

In Africa with Sweitzer, Edgar Berman

The Killer Angels, Michael Shaara

The Joy Luck Club, Amy Tan
Living Well Is the Best Revenge, Calvin Tomkins
Tender Is the Night, F. Scott Fitzgerald
The Vanderbilt Era, Louis Auchincloss
The Unbearable Lightness of Being, Milan Kundera
My Antonia, Willa Cather

1991–92
A Peace to End All Peace, David Fromkin
From Beirut to Jerusalem, Thomas Friedman
Pavilion of Women, Pearl S. Buck
One Hundred Years of Solitude, Gabriel García Márquez
The Blood of Brothers, Stephen King
Run with the Horsemen, Ferrol Sams
An American Childhood, Annie Dillard
The Summer of the Great Grandmother, Madeleine L'Engle
Angle of Repose, Wallace Stegner
Possession, A. S. Byatt

1992–93
Pillars of the Earth, Ken Follett
Miramar, Naguib Mahfouz
Love Is a Wild Assault, Elithe Hamilton Kirkland
Children of Cain, Tina Rosenberg
Babbitt, Sinclair Lewis
Children of the Arbat, Anatoli Rybakov
The Divine Sarah, Arthur Gold and Robert Fizdale
Five of Hearts, Patricia O'Toole
Daughters and Rebels, Jessica Mitford

1993–94
The Wives of Henry VIII, Antonia Fraser
The Sound and the Fury, William Faulkner

Our Finest Hour, Gregory Fossedal
Delta Wedding, Eudora Welty
Their Eyes Were Watching God, Zora Neale Hurston
God's Trombones, James Weldon Johnson
O'Keefe and Stieglitz, Benita Eisler
In the Absence of the Sacred, Jerry Mander
Mariette in Ecstasy, Ron Hansen
Children of Men, P. D. James
Einstein's Dreams, Alan Lightman
Rising Sun, Michael Crichton

1994–95
Lenin's Tomb: The Last Days of the Soviet Empire, David Remnick
Having Our Say: The Delany Sisters' First 100 Years, Sarah and
    A. Elizabeth Delany with Amy Hill Hearth
A History of God, Karen Armstrong
All the Pretty Horses, Cormac McCarthy
Confessions of a Literary Archeologist, Carlson Lake
Young Men and Fire, Norman Maclean
Life and Death in Shanghai, Nien Cheng
Joseph Banks: A Life, Patrick O'Brien
Beloved, Toni Morrison
Breathing Lessons, Anne Tyler

1995–96
House of Mirth, Edith Wharton
Edith Wharton, Eleanor Dwight
Smilla's Sense of Snow, Peter Hoeg
A Thousand Acres, Jane Smiley
Stories of God, Rainer Maria Rilke
Friday Night Lights, H. M. Bissinger
In the Lake of the Woods, Tim O'Brien

A Natural History of the Senses, Diane Ackerman
The Man Who Loved Children, Christina Stead
Make Way for Lucia, E. F. Benson
The World of Jeeves, P. G. Wodehouse
True Women, Janice Windle

1996–97

Pillars of Hercules, Paul Theroux
Road from Coorain, Jill Ker Conway
The Right to Privacy, Caroline Kennedy and Ellen Alderman
The Matisse Stories, A. S. Byatt
Midnight in the Garden of Good and Evil, John Berendt
The Creators, Daniel Boorstin
Dubliners, James Joyce
A Delicate Balance and *Three Tall Women*, Edward Albee
The Death of Satan, Andrew Delbanco
Père Goriot, Honoré de Balzac

1997–98

The Greek Way, Edith Hamilton
The People's Choice, Jeff Greenfield
What's Bred in the Bone, Robertson Davies
Selected Stories, Alice Munro
The English Patient, Michael Ondaatje
American First Ladies, Lewis L. Gould, ed.
Portrait of a Lady, Henry James
Angela's Ashes, Frank McCourt
Henry and Clara, Thomas Malon
In the Time of the Butterflies, Julia Alvarez

1998–99

The Rape of Europa, Lynn Nicholas
Black Box, Amos Oz

Nine Parts of Desire, Geraldine Brooks
Is Sex Necessary, James Thurber
Booked to Die, John Dunning
Founding Father, Richard Brookhiser
The Fifties, David Halberstam
Romola, George Eliot
Jude, the Obscure, Thomas Hardy
The Art of Eating, M. F. K. Fisher

1999–2000
Death of a Salesman, The Price, and *After the Fall*, Arthur Miller
Titan, the Life of John D. Rockefeller, Ron Chernow
The Sun Also Rises, Ernest Hemingway
How Proust Can Change Your Life, Alain De Botton
Brave New World, Aldous Huxley
1984, George Orwell
The Sea, The Sea, Iris Murdoch
Summer for the Gods, Edward Larson
The God of Small Things, Arundhati Roy
Content of Our Character, Shelby Steele

Book List

LEE STRICKLAND   CHICAGO, ILLINOIS

No ONE IN our book group has ever kept a comprehensive list over the almost twenty-five years we have been meeting. Mostly, we have read contemporary fiction books. Following is our list from 1999 as well as the books we committed to read in 2000.

1999
Alias Grace, Margaret Atwood
Martin Dressler, Stephen Millhauser
The Samurai's Garden, Gail Tsukiyama
Quantum Leaps, Charlotte Shelton
Floating in My Mother's Palm, Ursula Hegi
Poisonwood Bible, Barbara Kingsolver
Going to the Sun, James McManus
The Reader, Bernhard Schlink
Widow for One Year, John Irving
White Oleander, Janet Fitch

2000
Guided Tours of Hell, Francine Prose
Vox, Nicholson Baker

Lolita, Vladimir Nabokov
Hanna's Daughters, Marianne Fredriksson
Writing a Woman's Life, Carolyn Heilbrun
Spending, Mary Gordon
The Hours, Michael Cunningham
Turbulent Souls, Steven Dubner
The Beach, Alex Garland

The Chapter Four Society Book List

CINDY THELEN AND
DAVID VICK

WESTERN SPRINGS,
ILLINOIS

1990

Illusions, Richard Bach
The Deerslayer, James Fenimore Cooper
Pride and Prejudice, Jane Austen
The Importance of Being Earnest, Oscar Wilde

1991

The Accidental Tourist, Anne Tyler
The Great Gatsby, F. Scott Fitzgerald
Dear Dad, Louie Anderson
Dubliners, James Joyce
Frankenstein, Mary Shelley
Don Quixote, Miguel de Cervantes
Pudd'n Head Wilson, Mark Twain
Around the World in Eighty Days, Jules Verne
As You Like It, William Shakespeare

A Brief History of Time, Stephen Hawking

Watership Down, Richard Adams

1992

The Tao of Pooh, Benjamin Hoff

Galapagos, Kurt Vonnegut

Dracula, Bram Stoker

Still Life with Woodpecker, Tom Robbins

Portrait of Jennie, Robert Nathan

Magnetic North, David Halsey

Alice in Wonderland, Lewis Carroll

There Are No Children Here, Alex Kotlowitz

The Summer of Katya, Trevanian

The Hunchback of Notre Dame, Victor Hugo

Zen and the Art of Motorcycle Maintenance, Robert Pirsig

1993

A Tale of Two Cities, Charles Dickens

The Remains of the Day, Kazuo Ishiguro

Like Water for Chocolate, Laura Esquivel

Slim's Table, Mitchell Duneier

On the Road, Jack Kerouac

King Rat, James Clavell

The Mists of Avalon, Marion Zimmer Bradley

Brave New World, Aldous Huxley

The Kitchen God's Wife, Amy Tan

The Stars Shine Down, Sidney Sheldon

1994

The Celestine Prophecy, James Redfield

Interview with the Vampire, Anne Rice

The Handmaid's Tale, Margaret Atwood

Cooler by the Lake, Larry Heinemann

A Thousand Acres, Jane Smiley

How the Garcia Girls Lost Their Accents, Julia Alvarez
Cry, the Beloved Country, Alan Paton
The Harafish, Naguib Mahfouz
Einstein's Dreams, Alan Lightman
The Painted Bird, Jerzy Kosinski
Master and Commander, Patrick O'Brien
A Yellow Raft in Blue Water, Michael Dorris

1995

The Princess Bride, William Goldman
Uncle Tom's Cabin, Harriet Beecher Stowe
Felicia's Journey, William Trevor
Rabbit, Run, John Updike
City of Joy, Dominique Lapierre
A Hundred Years of Solitude, Gabriel García Márquez
Jane Eyre, Charlotte Brontë
How We Die, Sherwin Nuland
Dirty White Boys, Stephen Hunter
A Woman Destroyed, Simone de Beauvoir
Anna Karenina, Leo Tolstoy

1996

Way of the Peaceful Warrior, Dan Millman
Prize Stories 1996: The O. Henry Awards, William Abrahams, ed.
The Count of Monte Cristo, Alexander Dumas
The Catcher in the Rye, J. D. Salinger
The Bean Trees, Barbara Kingsolver
When Elephants Weep, Jeffrey Masson
The Hound of the Baskervilles, Sir Arthur Conan Doyle
Nicholas and Alexandra, Robert Massie
Man and Superman, George Bernard Shaw
The Secret History, Donna Tartt
Possession, A. S. Byatt

1997
Midnight in the Garden of Good and Evil, John Berendt
A Single Shot, Matthew Jones
Montana 1948, Larry Watson
Lolita, Vladimir Nabokov
A Confederacy of Dunces, John Kennedy Toole
Alias Grace, Margaret Atwood
Beloved, Toni Morrison
The Unbearable Lightness of Being, Milan Kundera
Dreaming in Cuban, Cristina Garcia
The Women on the Porch, Caroline Gordon
Woman of the Inner Sea, Thomas Keneally

1998
Ishmael, Daniel Quinn
Cold Mountain, Charles Frazier
Charming Billy, Alice McDermott
Death Comes for the Archbishop, Willa Cather
The Crossing, Cormac McCarthy
I Was Amelia Earhart, Jane Mendelsohn
A Separate Peace, John Knowles
The Beauty of Men, Andrew Halloran
The Education of Little Tree, Forrest Carter
Wicked, Gregory Maguire
Crime and Punishment, Fyodor Dostoyevsky

1999
The Bell Jar, Sylvia Plath
A Civil Action, Jonathan Harr
The Reader, Bernhard Schlink
The Locket, Richard Paul Evans
Pope Joan, Donna Woolfolk Cross

The All-Star Reading List

KAREN L. THOMSON   📖   EVANSTON, ILLINOIS

As A PROFESSIONAL book discussion leader, my method of book selection entails a complicated process of reading reviews, talking to many book lovers both in and out of my groups, and, of course, reading.

The books chosen out of all this must meet certain basic criteria. The language must satisfy my poet's ear—the writing must be beautiful and evocative, with words that are well chosen, sentences that sing, and paragraphs that flow with natural rhythm and meaning. I choose books whose stories appear in my dreams after reading, or that move me to silent contemplation, great intellectual excitement, or genuine laughter in recognition of the human condition—books that reach the heart of the reader.

Finally, there is sometimes an intuitive element involved in my selection process. I try to construct a group of books for six months or a year that flow together in a path toward learning. I look for a variety of voices, styles, and genres that complement each other and protect readers from sameness, so that interest builds as we progress. Sometimes a theme emerges, but it's not always what I had initially planned. That is, an almost subconscious scheming goes on as the readings unfold themselves to us. I plan and plot, but a richer process actually emerges. This is a joy to me.

*All of the novels by this author are good for discussion, but I chose my favorite for the All-Star List.

**I recommend virtually all of the writer's work for discussion choices.

The Accidental Tourist, Anne Tyler.* A wonderfully funny story full of quirky characters who have to make their various kinds of peace with being on life's journey.

The Age of Iron, J. M. Coetzee.* A most moving study of apartheid and its demands on all citizens to realize their political positions in regard to the downtrodden.

An American Childhood, Annie Dillard. A poignant memoir of growing up in Pittsburgh during the fifties.

The Awakening, Kate Chopin. This feminist classic shows women's position and personal power in New Orleans society in the late nineteenth century. A lovely book that won the author social ostracism for writing "sex fiction."

Bastard out of Carolina, Dorothy Allison. A devastating novel about poor whites in the South. It clearly shows how feelings of powerlessness and shame contribute to sexual abuse and child neglect.

Because It Is Bitter and Because It Is My Heart, Joyce Carol Oates. The story of an unusual friendship and a tragic murder that affects the heroine. Oates is superb at showing family breakdowns throughout various classes. Engrossing, intelligent book.

Beloved, Toni Morrison.* In my opinion, one of the greatest novels of the century. In poetic language, it tells the story of slavery in this country from an inside, deeply affecting perspective. The ghost Beloved and what she represents are equally unforgettable.

Cat's Eye, Margaret Atwood.* An excellent novel about girls growing up and how they exercise their power on each other. This is a must for women to discuss in terms of their own experiences as well.

Ceremony, Leslie Marmon Silko. The story of a Native American World War II veteran who has to make sense of war and its connections to the destruction of his people. The ceremony is one of finding a path for spiritual, as well as actual, survival.

Copper Crown, Lane von Herzen. An almost-perfect first novel about an unusual biracial friendship in early twentieth-century Texas. A magical tale of visible spirits, wise women, and the redemptive power of love.

The English Patient, Michael Ondaatje. An intellectually stimulating tale about four characters brought together in a villa in Italy during World War II. Its antiwar message is filled with carefully crafted images of western civilization in literature, technology, art, and religion. Two readings before discussion are helpful.

Family Pictures, Sue Miller.* A well-written novel about family relationships as affected by the presence of an autistic child.

The Fifth Child, Doris Lessing.* A fable about a family in England whose fifth child is antisocial, a "throwback." Haunting, unforgettable tale.

The Girl, Meridel LeSueur. A wonderful study of the language and life of the poor young women who found themselves in the big cities in the Midwest during the thirties. A proletarian novel with vision.

God's Snake, Irini Spanidou. An unusual book about a little girl growing up in Greece with a strict, military father. Quite evocative and powerful.

A Good Scent from a Strange Mountain, Robert Olen Butler. A collection of stories about refugees from Vietnam who have settled in Louisiana. Wonderful characterizations and much wisdom about human needs for meaning and connection.

The House on Mango Street, Sandra Cisneros. A series of short stories-almost-poems about the lives of Chicana girls growing up in Chicago. Read aloud as much as possible before discussing.

Jane Eyre, Charlotte Brontë. The classic that never quits teaching. A deeply symbolic story of a girl's struggle for independence in Victorian England.

A Lesson Before Dying, Ernest J. Gaines. A story of a Louisiana execution in the forties that is really a lesson on how to live with dignity in the face of discrimination and death in the pre–Civil Rights South. Moving and excellent for discussion of values.

Middlemarch, George Eliot.* The great classic of middle-class life in mid-nineteenth-century England. Eliot's characters are unforgettable and engaging, embodying human foibles and greatness alike.

My Antonia, Willa Cather.* A beautiful story within a story about people who were early settlers of the prairie lands. Full of fairy tales and moving in its portrayal of the beauty of lifelong friendship.

My Son's Story, Nadine Gordimer.* An excellent story about apartheid and infidelity and their various destructions. Set in South Africa.

The Passion, Jeanette Winterson. Antiwar novel that explores the nature of passion and possession in unusual storytelling about Venice, Napoleon, and various lovers. Fabulous in more than one way.

The Shipping News, E. Annie Proulx. A great big novel about a loser named Quoyle who finds himself in his work and family and becomes a contributing member of his community in Newfoundland. Excellent writing—good use of symbols for discussion. A redemptive novel about possibilities for change.

Storming Heaven, Denise Giardina. Story of the 1921 coal miners strike in West Virginia and the beginnings of unions for coal miners. Enlightening historical novel with some wonderful characters.

Their Eyes Were Watching God, Zora Neale Hurston. A beautifully written tale of a woman in the South in the early twentieth century who dares to keep holding her dreams in her heart through a series of disappointing relationships until she finds true love. Sometimes called a Harlem Renaissance classic—a must read.

A Thousand Acres, Jane Smiley.* Epic novel of the demise of a patriarchal farm family in the United States. Related to destruction of the land under patriarchal abuses. Great for discussion.

To the Lighthouse, Virginia Woolf.* Woolf's study of becoming an artist to form a self apart from her beloved but busy mother and demanding, patriarchal father.

Tracks, Louise Erdrich.* A wonderful story of Native Americans trying to preserve their spirits as they lose valuable land and mythic helpers. Poetic and lovely writing with great characters.

The Yellow Wallpaper, Charlotte Perkins Gilman. Another classic of the late nineteenth century, this one about a woman locked in a room for a rest cure for her restless, creative nature. Short; excellent for discussion of women and mental health.

Biographies

Eleanor Roosevelt, Volume I, 1884–1933, Blanche Wiesen Cook. Fascinating portrait of the real person behind the heroine—a look at her private passions as well as her personal heroism. Inspiring and informative.

Frida: A Biography of Frida Kahlo, Hayden Herrera. Stimulating story of the great artist who painted her emotional and physical pain in exquisite, unforgettable self-portraits.

Isak Dinesen: The Life of a Storyteller, Judith Thurman. A Pulitzer Prize–winning book about the making of Isak Dinesen as a writer of such works as *Out of Africa* and "Babette's Feast." One of the best biographies I've read.

Portrait of an Artist: A Biography of Georgia O'Keeffe, Laurie Lisle. An inspiring story of a strong, gifted woman who knew what she wanted to be, and how she became one of the great artists of this century.

Virginia Woolf: A Biography, Quentin Bell. The definitive biography of the great writer, written with all attention to the intricacies of the Bloomsbury group and the early twentieth-century artistic flowering in England. Supplement with Louise DeSalvo's biography of Woolf detailing her experience of sexual abuse and its effect.

More recent reads include

Wuthering Heights, Emily Brontë, and *Here on Earth*, Alice Hoffman.** These two books make up a two-month set which is really fun to discuss. Brontë's classic revisited brings up new issues on the meanings of love and the idea of soul mates, while Hoffman's modern version gives us a way to look at the story from a domestic abuse standpoint. Hoffman's translation is fun to trace: family relationships, the moors, the dogs, the names, etc.

Comfort Woman, Nora Okja Keller. This is a beautifully lyric book about Korean "comfort women," and it's a mother-daughter story as well.

Wild Swans, Jung Chang. Nonfiction story of three generations of Chinese women. It takes the reader from concubinage to the Cultural

Revolution and beyond. Excellent picture of women through much of the century.

God of Small Things, Arundhati Roy. One of the best books for discussion in the past few years. Winner of England's Booker Prize for its unusual voice and beautiful writing about a family in southern India in the sixties.

Crossing to Safety, Wallace Stegner.** This book continues to delight readers for its use of language and issues of friendship and marriage explored so lovingly.

The Distance from the Heart of Things, Ashley Warlick. A first novel by a young woman from the South. It is wise beyond its years for its commentary on family dynamics. Kudzu abounds, metaphorically and literally.

In the Lake of the Woods, Tim O'Brien.** This is a must-read for discussion on the politics of U.S. involvement in the Vietnam War and how it affects us. It is compelling and sad, one of the best-written books I've found recently.

Paradise, Toni Morrison.** Another masterpiece by one of our great writers, this book needs several readings and much discussion, and it deserves every bit of time you give it. It is a story of women, values, race.

Open Secrets, Alice Munro.** A wonderful collection of stories. Each takes the reader into a labyrinth of involvement with small-town Canada and its people (brilliant on women). Each is not about what it first appears to be.

Sweetbitter, Reginald Gibbons. This is a beautiful love story set in early 1900s southern Texas with all its racism and social rules. Read it and weep for its phrases.

American Pastoral, Philip Roth. A Pulitzer Prize went to this outstanding dark novel about, well, you decide. It is a story of Nathan Zuckerman's idol, the "Swede," and his radical daughter. It is a story about the fifties and Jewish assimilation. It is a story about the sixties and the alienation of our children and the American dream.

While You Were Gone, Sue Miller.** This is a good book to read next to *American Pastoral* for contrast and comparison. It, too, deals with some of the results of the sixties, although from a different perspective, that of a married couple who live an idyllic life in the East.

Animal Dreams, Barbara Kingsolver. This book is a good read and it includes dreams and symbols that carry the reader along the path to discovery and growth with the characters. Good feeling for the Southwest.

The Reader, Bernhard Schlink. Excellent book to discuss the effects of the Nazi regime on successive generations of Germans. Moral literacy is the big question.

Breath, Eyes, Memory, Edwidge Danticat. This is a beautiful peek into a little-understood country, Haiti. The language is gorgeous and the story is a heartbreaking mother-daughter study.

Spending, Mary Gordon.** This is a wonderfully intelligent book on desire, art, sex, and power, in which the woman artist finds a male muse in a funny role reversal study of relationships.

The Samurai's Garden, Gail Tsukiyama. Set in 1937, this book tells the story of a young man's moral development during the Chinese war with Japan. It is full of love and wisdom and a great book to discuss with a group.

The Magician's Assistant, Ann Patchett. This is a quirky, lovely story of a magician's assistant who goes on a journey from Los Angeles to Nebraska to find her way home.

A Farewell to Arms, Ernest Hemingway.** In this centennial season of Hemingway's birth, a group would do well to go back to some of his classics. This is a beautiful story of disenchantment and courage. He is one of the best.

A study of Isak Dinesen. Try reading *The Life of a Storyteller*, Judith Thurman, an engaging biography of the great Danish writer. Follow this with *Babette's Feast*, a novella (and watch the movie afterwards). Follow that with *Gothic Tales*, especially "The Monkey."

The Top Nineteen Books of Nineteen Years Reading

JANET TRIPP   MINNEAPOLIS, MINNESOTA

I<small>N THE NINETEEN</small> years of my book group's monthly meetings, we have read 228 books and we're not done yet. That's the best part. We're ongoing and all-consuming, self-perpetuating, and cost efficient. We're the perfect activity for the new millennium.

Our selection is biased because we read with a feminist eye. Each six months our selections are required to include one poet, one book from an earlier time, and at least one writer of color. We are an all-women group of fifteen that reads only female authors. After twenty and forty and eighty years of shaping by men's words, we seek to establish a balance. By learning of other women's lives, we discover who we are.

The Top Two
Possession: A Romance, A. S. Byatt. One of the two most frequently listed favorite books is this engrossing and cleverly disguised story that explores two love affairs occurring in two different centuries. It is a mystery using several different genres to explore the two relationships, the intricacies of desire, and the process of biographical inquiry.

378

Stones from the River, Ursula Hegi. Our other most favorite book is this story of a small German town during World War II. It is about a child born a dwarf who in the end the reader loves like a sister, wanting only her happiness. A chronicle about being different and the power held by the one who tells the stories.

Seventeen Others

The Shipping News, E. Annie Proulx. Pulitzer Prize in 1994. A comic, gothic tale where the country of Newfoundland is as alive as any character, and whose hero, Quoyle, would do justice to Flannery O'Connor.

Refuge: An Unnatural History of Family and Place, Terry Tempest Williams. Creative nonfiction. Eloquent stories of her native Utah. Exploring family, loss, and community within the grand design of nature. Williams says this book "really asks the question: How do you find refuge in change?"

The Stone Diaries, Carol Shields. Pulitzer Prize in 1995. Fiction disguised as biography wherein the heroine claims her own life. "Dreaming her way backward in time," she tells sad stories of words not said, and we are beguiled by the characters.

The God of Small Things, Arundhati Roy. Winner of the Booker Prize in England. A tale of passion. A tragedy that reads like a puzzle. In the end when you finally "know," you want to start at the beginning and read it through again. Rich, colorful images of India that live in your mind.

Divine Secrets of the Ya-Ya Sisterhood, Rebecca Wells. The solidarity of four Southern women, best friends from childhood, who struggle to build families as close as their friendship. Wells captures family, friendships, mother-daughter struggles, and sends you out to buy a copy for your best friend.

War Baby Express, Roseann Lloyd. Nonintimidating, accessible, felt poems of family, childhood, loss, and body. "Symptoms are a way to have feelings: / the body keeps on living / after annihilation"

Daniel Deronda, George Eliot. A classic. Eliot turned to contemporary (1876) English life to express her own idealism. An investigation into psychology. Excellent introduction by University of London professor of English, Graham Handley.

Kristin Lavransdatter, Sigrid Undset. This absorbing trilogy of epic pageantry is the story of a woman's life in medieval Norway. It was startling to learn that Undset was the first woman to receive a Nobel Prize for literature, yet her work was unknown to us all.

Middlemarch, George Eliot. A masterpiece. English provincial life in the early nineteenth century. Virginia Woolf called it, "One of the few English novels written for grown-up people."

The Waves, Virginia Woolf. Novel without a narrator. The interior monologue of a group of six friends. They speak in rotation with interludes of nature: seasons, waves, sun. Challenging and heady.

The Dollmaker, Harriette Arnow. A Kentucky family is dislocated to Detroit. In a life of cyclic tragedy, the mother's strength and her wood carving is the hope for her family.

Their Eyes Were Watching God, Zora Neale Hurston. This novel, from 1937, is about a strong black woman. Wonderful characters, vivid speech and images.

Beloved, Toni Morrison. Myth and art. Sethe, an escaped slave in post-Civil War Ohio, struggles to bury the past.

Bastard out of Carolina, Dorothy Allison. A moving account of a poor southern child growing up among love and abuse.

Parallel Lives, Phyllis Rose. The marriages of five prominent Victorian writers. The women's heroic survival within the institution.

Mean Spirit, Linda Hogan. North American magical realism. Despite oil, greed, and murder, the spirit of the Oklahoma Osage Indians survives.

The Color Purple, Alice Walker. Masterful language. Celie's letters to God and to her sister Nettie, living in Africa, tell Celie's story of abuse by her father and her husband. She leaves her husband and the farm, moving with her lover to a new life in Memphis.

The League Legacy Book Group Book List

LEE VOEGTLEN   INGLEWOOD, CALIFORNIA

IN MY ESSAY, I mentioned many of the books and authors our group has read and discussed. Here are more covering our whole span of years (we began in 1967). In most cases, I have mentioned only one book by each author, in order to give a representative sample of our reading. Of course, in many cases, such as Jane Austen, Toni Morrison, Robertson Davies, and Henry James, we read many more books by the author. I notice that we were more likely to do classics, plays, and concepts (such as the Richard III books) in our earlier years. Now, as we get older, our books get younger.

The Red Badge of Courage, Stephen Crane

The Plague, Albert Camus

The Crucible and *After the Fall*, Arthur Miller

Topic: Queen Elizabeth I

Electra, Euripedes, and *Mourning Becomes Electra*, Eugene O'Neill

Portrait of the Artist As a Young Man, James Joyce

Topic: Charles I of England, Cromwell, and the Puritan Revolution

The Immense Journey, Loren Eiseley

The Screwtape Letters, C. S. Lewis, and *A Free Man's Worship*, Bertrand Russell

The Metamorphosis, Franz Kafka

Steppenwolf, Hermann Hesse

The Invisible Man, Ralph Ellison

The Bell Jar, Sylvia Plath

"The Figure in the Carpet" and "The Lesson of the Master," Henry James

Topic: Arthurian Legends

Waiting for Godot, Samuel Beckett and *Rhinoceros*, Eugene Ionesco

Topic: Poetry of Edwin Arlington Robinson

Madame Bovary, Gustave Flaubert

One Flew over the Cuckoo's Nest, Ken Kesey

The Nazarene, Sholem Asch

A Clockwork Orange, Anthony Burgess

The Portrait of Mr. W. H., Oscar Wilde and Shakespeare's Sonnets

The Book of Job, Bible and *J.B.*, Archibald MacLeish

Herzog, Saul Bellow

Travesties, Tom Stoppard, and *The Importance of Being Earnest*, Oscar Wilde

Mythology, Edith Hamilton

The Three Sisters, Anton Chekhov

Main Street, Sinclair Lewis

The Song of the Lark, Willa Cather

Eugenie Grandet, Honoré de Balzac

Who's Afraid of Virginia Woolf?, Edward Albee

Beggar in Jerusalem, Elie Wiesel

A Distant Mirror, Barbara Tuchman

The Sound and the Fury, William Faulkner

Shogun, James Clavell. A few of us disliked this mightily and would not finish it, a sin of which we are not often guilty.

The House of Mirth, Edith Wharton

My Mother/Myself, Nancy Friday. Simplistic.

My Name Is Asher Lev, Chaim Potok. As fascinating to our Gentile members as to those who are Jewish.

Short stories of Guy de Maupassant

The Aquarian Conspiracy, Marilyn Ferguson. Our unenthusiastic bow to New Age.

Fathers and Sons, Ivan Turgenev

Nana, Emile Zola

Back to Methuselah, George Bernard Shaw

The Thirteen Clocks, James Thurber

Clan of the Cave Bear, Jean Auel

Topic: Henry II of England, his marriage to Eleanor of Aquitaine, and the founding of the legal system (two months)

Dinner at the Homesick Restaurant, Anne Tyler

Tale of Genji, Murasaki Shikibu

The Daughter of Time, Josephine Tey. A mystery about Richard III for our newer members who had missed the first go-round. Could someone here be a Ricardian?

The Color Purple, Alice Walker

Topic: Poetry of Robinson Jeffers

Anatomy of an Illness and *The Healing Heart*, Norman Cousins

Topic: Leonardo da Vinci

The Warden, or Barchester Towers, Anthony Trollope

Topic: Lillian Hellman

The Name of the Rose, Umberto Eco. We scarcely noticed the length; we loved it.

The Witches of Eastwick, John Updike

The Great Gatsby, F. Scott Fitzgerald

Diaries, Anais Nin. Presented by a member who had actually known Nin.

Sula, Toni Morrison. We later read, and preferred, *Beloved*.

Kim, Rudyard Kipling

Sister Carrie, Theodore Dreiser

Lake Wobegon Days, Garrison Keillor

Memento Mori, Muriel Spark

And Ladies of the Club, Helen Hooven Santmyer. Another case in
which length didn't matter; we could *identify*.

The Barretts of Wimpole Street, Rudolf Besier. Poetry by Elizabeth
Barrett Browning and other material on Elizabeth and Robert Browning.

Hotel du Lac, Anita Brookner

Gulliver's Travels, Jonathan Swift

Love in the Time of Cholera, Gabriel García Márquez. One of the
best if not *the* best modern book we've read.

Fifth Business, Robertson Davies. We became so intrigued with Davies
that we read a number of his books. This was the best, we thought.

Death in Venice, Thomas Mann

A Thief of Time, Tony Hillerman. "A mystery!" I exclaimed, feeling
that it was beneath us. Instead, we were all fascinated, and my family later toured the area Hillerman used as his setting.

Hedda Gabler, Henrik Ibsen, and *Miss Julie*, August Strindberg

Parallel Lives, Phyllis Rose. This proves that the real lives and,
especially, marriages of five Victorian writers and artists are stranger
and more intriguing than most fiction.

Topic: Eugene O'Neill plays; a reassessment.

The Bloody Chamber, Angela Carter. A feminist/modernist retelling
of certain fairy tales. The chamber is, of course, Bluebeard's. Not to
be missed by modern women.

Truman, David McCullough

Changing Places, David Lodge. An academic hoot.

Lincoln, Gore Vidal

The Book Group Book, Ellen Slezak, ed. We used both the first and
second editions and had a great discussion. Several members subsequently used the reading lists both for their own reading and for suggestions for the group.

Offshore, Penelope Fitzgerald. A great new discovery: a Brit who
published her first book at age sixty. All her novels are short, beautifully written, and absorbing.

Looking Backward, Edward Bellamy

No Ordinary Time, Doris Kearns Goodwin

The Remains of the Day, Kazuo Ishiguro

Recapitulation, Wallace Stegner. Later we read *The Spectator Bird*.

The Color of Water, James McBride

The Sin Eater, Alice Thomas Ellis. Another discovery: another Brit who writes short novels, beautifully expressed, with not a wasted word. She does not suffer fools gladly, and sometimes seems to prefer cats to people.

Cakes and Ale, Somerset Maugham

The Hemingway Women, Bernice Kert. Fascinating; a revelation to Hemingway admirers; a justification to the rest of us.

The Woman Warrior, Maxine Hong Kingston

A Death in the Family, James Agee

The Shipping News, E. Annie Proulx

The Arabian Nights, selections

A Gathering of Old Men, Ernest J. Gaines

Rebecca, Daphne du Maurier. A reassessment.

Kenilworth, Walter Scott

Corelli's Mandolin, Louis de Bernicres

The Control of Nature, John McPhee

The Baron in the Trees, Italo Calvino

The Reader, Bernhard Schlink

Sleeping at the Starlight Motel, Bailey White

Mrs. Dalloway, Virginia Woolf

Undaunted Courage, Stephen Ambrose

The Freedom Song, Amit Chaudhuri

The Robber Bride, Margaret Atwood

My Antonia, Willa Cather

Parrot in the Oven, Victor Martinez

Serious Reading Book List

DAVID WELLENBROCK   📖   STOCKTON, CALIFORNIA

The Fall of Public Man, Richard Sennett
The Idea of a Critical Theory, Raymond Geuss
The Zero-Sum Society, Lester Thurow
Theory of Justice, John Rawls
Eichmann in Jerusalem, Hannah Arendt
Democracy in America, Alexis de Tocqueville
Minding America's Business, Ira Magaziner and Robert Reich
Pragmatics of Human Communication, Paul Watzlawick, Janet
   Bavelas, and Don Jackson
Zen and the Art of Motorcycle Maintenance, Robert Pirsig
Secrets, Sissela Bok
Collective Action, Russell Hardin
The World We Have Lost, Peter Laslett
Topic: Post-Mao China
Anarchy, State, and Utopia, Robert Nozick
One Hundred Years of Solitude, Gabriel García Márquez
Topic: Contemporary Central America
Tragic Sense of Life, Miguel de Unamuno

The Neo-Liberals, Randall Rothenberg

Topic: Water in California

Topic: Postcolonial, sub-Saharan Africa

Just and Unjust Wars, Michael Walzer

The Prince, Nicolo Machiavelli

The Spirit of Democratic Capitalism, Michael Novak

The Triumph of Politics, David Stockman

Sovieticus, Stephen F. Cohn

Habits of the Heart, Robert Bellah et al.

Beyond Entitlement, Lawrence Mead

The Federalist Papers, Alexander Hamilton, James Madison, and
   John Jay

Foundations of Jurisprudence, Jerome Hall

The Mathematical Experience, Phillip J. Davis and Reuben Hersh

Topic: Bioethics

Burr, Gore Vidal

Topic: United States Supreme Court

Heroin: The Hardest Drug, John Kaplan

Defense Sense, Ronald Dellums

The Closing of the American Mind, Allan Bloom

The Protestant Ethic and the Spirit of Capitalism, Max Weber

Perestroika, Mikhail Gorbachev

Topic: Nietzsche

National Debt, Lawrence Malkin

Topic: Evolution

Civilization and Its Discontents, Sigmund Freud

Topic: Environmental Ethics

Contact, Carl Sagan

The Rise and Fall of the Great Powers, Paul Kennedy

Anatomy of a Revolution, Crane Brinton

Topic: Islam

Tales of a New America, Robert Reich
Global Warming, Stephen H. Schneider
Topic: Animal Rights/Deep Ecology
On Liberty, John Stuart Mill
Topic: Book by Václav Havel
Setting Limits, Daniel Callahan
The Third Wave, Alvin Toffler, *G-forces*, Frank Feather
And the Band Played On, Randy Shilts
The New Russians, Hedrick Smith
Topic: Affirmative Action
Politics of Rich and Poor, Kevin Phillips
The True and Only Heaven: Progress, Christopher Lasch
Topic: Contemporary Middle East
Wonderful Life, Stephen J. Gould
The Structure of Scientific Revolutions, Theodore Kuhn
Solomonic Judgments, Jon Elster
The Good Society, Robert Bellah et al.
A Street Is Not a Home, Robert C. Coates
Head to Head, Lester Thurow
A Room of One's Own, Virginia Woolf
Who Will Tell the People?, William Greider
Topic: Public Schools, K–12
Shadows of Forgotten Ancestors, Carl Sagan and Ann Druyan
The Tempting of America, Robert Bork
The Moral Dimension, Amitai Etzioni
Preparing for the Twenty-First Century, Paul Kennedy
Re-Inventing Government, David Osborne and Ted Gaebler
Earth in the Balance, Albert Gore
The Enigma of Japanese Power, Karel van Wolferen
Topic: Islam
Kindly Inquisitors, Jonathan Rauch, and *Only Words*, Catharine
  MacKinnon

Topic: Book by Camille Paglia, Susan Faludi, or Naomi Wolf
Makes Me Wanna Holler, Nathan McCall
Topic: Book by F. A. Hayek
The Transformation of War, Martin van Creveld, or *War and Anti-War*, Alvin Toffler
The New Politics of Poverty, Lawrence Mead
How and Why We Age, Leonard Hayflick
The Sixties: Years of Hope, Days of Rage, Todd Gitlin
Topic: Contract with America
The Death of Common Sense, Philip K. Howard
The Least Dangerous Branch, Alexander M. Bickel
The Theory of Moral Sentiment, Adam Smith
The Next American Revolution, Michael Lind
Trust, Francis Fukuyama
Vulnerable But Invincible, Emmy E. Werner and Ruth S. Smith
When Corporations Rule the World, David C. Korten
Reflections on the Revolution in France, Edmund Burke
Reconstruction of Philosophy, or the Quest for Certainty, John Dewey
Evolution of Culture in Animals, John Tyler Bonner
Topic: The Media
Emotional Intelligence, Daniel P. Goleman
The Transcendent Child, Lillian B. Rubin
The Clash of Civilizations, Samuel P. Huntington
They Only Look Dead, E. J. Dionne
Guns, Germs, and Steel, Jared Diamond
Everything for Sale, Robert Kuttner
The End of Science, John Horgan
The Moral Sense, James Q. Wilson
Original Meanings, Jack N. Rakove
Beyond Engineering, Robert Pool
The Scandal of Pleasure, Wendy Steiner
Wall Street, Doug Henwood

Anti-Intellectualism in American Life, Richard Hofstadter

The Heavenly City of the Eighteenth-Century Philosophers, Carl
   Lotus Becker

Shopping for Faith, Richard Cimino and Don Lattin

The Morality of Law, Lon Fuller

The Corrosion of Character, Richard Sennett

The Cost of Rights, Stephen Holmes and Cass R. Sunstein

Four Women Reading Book List

RITA WUEBBELER   ATLANTA, GEORGIA

1988

Going out of Our Minds, Sonia Johnson
AIDS: The Women, Inez Ricder and Patricia Ruppelt
The Politics of Reality, Marilyn Frye

1989

Through Other Eyes, Irene Zahava
Beloved, Toni Morrison
The Dance of Anger, Harriet Lerner
The Bone People, Keri Hulme
The Temple of My Familiar, Alice Walker
Mama Day, Gloria Naylor

1990

The Unbearable Lightness of Being, Milan Kundera
Rough Strife, Lynne Sharon Schwartz
Kalki, Gore Vidal

Breathing Lessons, Anne Tyler

Orlando, Virginia Woolf

West with the Night, Beryl Markham

Bitter Medicine, Sara Paretsky

The Joy Luck Club, Amy Tan

Excellent Women, Barbara Pym

1991

Homeland and Other Stories, Barbara Kingsolver

Housekeeping, Marilynne Robinson

Oranges Are Not the Only Fruit, Jeanette Winterson

Iron John, Robert Bly

Mary Reilly, Valerie Martin

Ghost Dance, Carol Mazo

Floating in My Mother's Palm, Ursula Hegi

Annie John, Jamaica Kincaid

The Remains of the Day, Kazuo Ishiguro

1992

The Ship That Sailed into the Living Room, Sonia Johnson

The Tao of Pooh, Benjamin Hoff

Many Lives, Many Masters, Brian Weiss

Maus, Art Spiegelman

Backlash, Susan Faludi

Revolution from Within, Gloria Steinem

Interview with the Vampire, Ann Rice

Little Women, Louise May Alcott

A Yellow Raft in Blue Water, Michael Dorris

1993

Bastard out of Carolina, Dorothy Allison

Cowboys Are My Weakness, Pam Houston

Shooting the Boh, Tracy Johnston

Mariette in Ecstasy, Ron Hansen

Waiting to Exhale, Terry McMillan

How We Survived Communism and Even Laughed, Slavenka Drakulic

The Bridges of Madison County, Robert James Waller

The Solace of Open Spaces, Gretel Erlich

Jazz, Toni Morrison

1994

To Dance with the White Dog, Terry Kaye

A Thousand Acres, Jane Smiley

Coming Through Slaughter, Michael Ondaatje

How the Garcia Girls Lost Their Accents, Julia Alvarez

Mutant Message down Under, Marlo Morgan

Pigs in Heaven, Barbara Kingsolver

Everyday Acts and Small Subversions, Anndee Hochman

The Shipping News, E. Annie Proulx

The Beans of Egypt, Maine, Carolyn Chute

1995

Midnight in the Garden of Good and Evil, John Berendt

Praying for Sheetrock, Melissa Faye Green

Brazzaville Beach, William Boyd

The Celestine Prophecy, James Redfield

The Robber Bride, Margaret Atwood

The House on Mango Street, Sandra Cisneros

The Singing Creek Where the Willows Grow: The Mystical Nature Diary of Opal Whitely, Benjamin Hoffman, ed.

Walking Across Egypt, Clyde Edgerton

The Book Group Book II, Ellen Slezak, ed.

1996

Smilla's Sense of Snow, Peter Hoeg

The Parable of the Sower, Octavia Butler

Possession, A. S. Byatt

The Pause, Lonnie Barbach

Paula, Isabel Allende

Refuge, Terry Tempest Williams

High Tide in Tucson, Barbara Kingsolver

1997

Snow Falling on Cedars, David Guterson

Ship Fever, Andrea Barrett

Their Eyes Were Watching God, Zora Neale Hurston

The Book of Ruth, Jane Hamilton

The Color of Water, James McBride

Soul Kiss, Shay Youngblood

Jane Eyre, Charlotte Brontë

I Was Amelia Earhart, Jane Mendelsohn

Sula, Toni Morrison

1998

Frankenstein, Mary Shelley

Yo!, Julia Alvarez

Divine Secrets of the Ya-Ya Sisterhood, Rebecca Wells

Sister to Sister, Patricia Foster

Cold Mountain, Charles Frazier

The Riverhouse Stories, Andrea Carlisle

My Antonia, Willa Cather

The Sunflower, Simon Wiesenthal

The God of Small Things, Arundhati Roy

1999

Comfort Woman, Nora Okja Keller

What Looks Like Crazy, Pearl Cleage

Memoirs of a Geisha, Arthur Golden

Aimee and Jaguar, Erika Fischer

And we know we read these books, but we can't remember when.

Women of Brewster Place, Gloria Naylor

Ellen Foster, Kaye Gibbons

Daughters of Copper Woman, Ann Cameron

The Bean Trees, Barbara Kingsolver

Rainbow Roun' Mah Shoulder, Linda Beatrice Brown

An Invitation to Book Group Members

IF YOU ARE a member of a book group and would like to be considered as a contributor to future editions of *The Book Group Book*, please send your name, address, telephone number, and e-mail address, and a brief description of your group (no more than 250 words, please) to:

Editor, *The Book Group Book*
Chicago Review Press
814 N. Franklin Street
Chicago, IL 60610